LEVEL 1 PRACTICE EXAMS – VOLUME 1

CFA® LEVEL 1 PRACTICE EXAMS – VOLUME 1

©2009 Kaplan, Inc. All rights reserved.

Published in 2009 by Kaplan Schweser.

Printed in the United States of America.

ISBN: 1-4277-9473-1

PPN: 4550-0110

USE YOUR SCHWESER ONLINE ACCESS ACCOUNT

All purchasers of the SchweserNotes™ package are sent login information for Online Access in an email. This is your login to view video volumes in the Schweser Library, use the Schweser Study Planner, use Performance Tracker, and (if you purchased the Essential, Premium, or Premium Plus Solutions) join Instructor-led Office Hours. Simply login at www.schweser.com and select "Online Access" to use any of these features. If you need password help, go to www.schweser.com/password or use the "Password Help" link that appears if your login is unsuccessful.

VOLUME 1 ONLINE FEATURES AT A GLANCE

Links to Curriculum

Within the online answer explanations, we have included page references to the relevant text in both the SchweserNotes and the CFA Institute program texts.

Exam Diagnostics

When you enter your answers in our Performance Tracker utility, you can request a breakdown of your overall score on any one-half (120 question) exam. See how you performed by topic area, study session, or reading. You can also get the Learning Outcome Statement references for questions you answered incorrectly to help you focus your review efforts.

Performance Comparison

When you enter your answers on the page for Performance Tracker, you can find out how your score on each half-exam compares to the scores of others who entered their answers.

HOW TO USE THIS BOOK

Volume 1 is a very important part of the Schweser Study Program. **Don't skip over it.**

You shouldn't take the Level 1 CFA® Exam without lots of practice answering questions.

Test yourself with these practice exams only after you have completed all the assigned readings.

The purpose of these questions is to make sure that you know all the concepts and ideas that are in the assigned readings. If you truly know the material you will do well on the actual exam. While our practice questions cover all the material, **they are not actual exam questions.** Our practice exams are not designed to predict your score on the actual CFA exam, although we try to match the level of difficulty on the exam. Use them to practice and identify those areas in which you need additional work.

Remember though, that CFA Institute® tries very hard every year to come up with new and innovative ways to test you. Your only defense against a good exam writer is to actually know the material. Learning the material and how to pace yourself on the exam is what our practice questions are designed to help you do.

The CFA exam is structured so that the morning and afternoon exams are each independent exams covering all topic areas. So, the three 6-hour practice exams here in Volume 1 are really six 3-hour practice exams. This gives you several opportunities to test your progress.

Our recommendations for using this book are:

- After you have finished your first complete review of the assigned reading material, take the morning portion of Practice Exam 1. Take your time on this exam. Enter your answers online. Performance Tracker will identify your weak spots. Go back and restudy everything, giving special emphasis to your weak areas.
- After you have completely reviewed the material, take the afternoon portion of Practice Exam 1. Again, take your time and do a complete review of the material, placing special emphasis on the weak spots pointed out by the exam.
- On the Saturday three weeks before the exam, take the first half of Practice Exam 2. But this time give yourself exactly three hours to complete the exam. If you spend more time than this, you will get a false reading of your performance. Remember that a big portion of the exam is the time pressure that you will be put under. A lot of the questions appear to be easy if you give yourself extra time or take a peek in the study guide for hints. Again, review your weak areas.
- On the Saturday two weeks before the exam, do the second half of Practice Exam 2 in three hours. Use Performance Tracker to identify weak areas and compare your score to those of other candidates.
- On the Saturday before the exam take the entire Practice Exam 3 in six hours. Review again.

Don't plan on passing the exam by memorizing questions and answers. Instead, learn the logic behind each of the questions. CFA Institute® isn't going to ask you our questions, but they will ask you questions that address the same concepts, logic, and definitions necessary to answer the practice exam questions.

EXAM 1
MORNING SESSION

Calculating Your Score

Topic	Maximum Score	Your Score
Ethical and Professional Standards	18	
Quantitative Methods	14	
Economics	12	
Financial Reporting and Analysis	24	
Corporate Finance	10	
Portfolio Management	6	
Equity Investments	12	
Fixed Income	14	
Derivatives	6	
Alternative Investments	4	
Total	120	

The morning and afternoon exams are identically weighted over the topics and readings. You can therefore treat the morning and afternoon exams as independent exams.

If you took more than three hours (180 minutes) to complete this portion of the exam, you should adjust your score downward by one point for each minute you ran over.

Remember: the real exam *will be more difficult* than these practice exams. The main reason for this is the general anxiety and stress that you will be feeling on exam day, coupled with the time pressure you will be under. Many of the questions on this practice exam and the real exam are not individually difficult, so if you take extra time to answer the questions on this practice exam, your score will go up significantly. However, if you want an accurate measure of your potential performance on the exam, adhere to the 3-hour time limit.

After you have finished grading your practice exam, you may find it useful to use the exam questions and recommended solutions for review. Many of these questions were specifically written for your use as study tools. Once again, I feel I should remind you not to rely on memorizing these questions; you are not likely to see them on the actual exam. What you will see on the exam, though, are the concepts, terms, and procedures presented in these questions.

Your actual exam will most likely look different than what you see in this book. Please remember, no study provider knows the content of the actual exam. These practice exams are our best guess as to the structure, content, and difficulty of an actual exam.

Test Answers

1.	(A)	(B)	(C)
2.	(A)	(B)	(C)
3.	(A)	(B)	(C)
4.	(A)	(B)	(C)
5.	(A)	(B)	(C)
6.	(A)	(B)	(C)
7.	(A)	(B)	(C)
8.	(A)	(B)	(C)
9.	(A)	(B)	(C)
10.	(A)	(B)	(C)
11.	(A)	(B)	(C)
12.	(A)	(B)	(C)
13.	(A)	(B)	(C)
14.	(A)	(B)	(C)
15.	(A)	(B)	(C)
16.	(A)	(B)	(C)
17.	(A)	(B)	(C)
18.	(A)	(B)	(C)
19.	(A)	(B)	(C)
20.	(A)	(B)	(C)
21.	(A)	(B)	(C)
22.	(A)	(B)	(C)
23.	(A)	(B)	(C)
24.	(A)	(B)	(C)
25.	(A)	(B)	(C)
26.	(A)	(B)	(C)
27.	(A)	(B)	(C)
28.	(A)	(B)	(C)
29.	(A)	(B)	(C)
30.	(A)	(B)	(C)
31.	(A)	(B)	(C)
32.	(A)	(B)	(C)
33.	(A)	(B)	(C)
34.	(A)	(B)	(C)
35.	(A)	(B)	(C)
36.	(A)	(B)	(C)
37.	(A)	(B)	(C)
38.	(A)	(B)	(C)
39.	(A)	(B)	(C)
40.	(A)	(B)	(C)

41.	(A)	(B)	(C)
42.	(A)	(B)	(C)
43.	(A)	(B)	(C)
44.	(A)	(B)	(C)
45.	(A)	(B)	(C)
46.	(A)	(B)	(C)
47.	(A)	(B)	(C)
48.	(A)	(B)	(C)
49.	(A)	(B)	(C)
50.	(A)	(B)	(C)
51.	(A)	(B)	(C)
52.	(A)	(B)	(C)
53.	(A)	(B)	(C)
54.	(A)	(B)	(C)
55.	(A)	(B)	(C)
56.	(A)	(B)	(C)
57.	(A)	(B)	(C)
58.	(A)	(B)	(C)
59.	(A)	(B)	(C)
60.	(A)	(B)	(C)
61.	(A)	(B)	(C)
62.	(A)	(B)	(C)
63.	(A)	(B)	(C)
64.	(A)	(B)	(C)
65.	(A)	(B)	(C)
66.	(A)	(B)	(C)
67.	(A)	(B)	(C)
68.	(A)	(B)	(C)
69.	(A)	(B)	(C)
70.	(A)	(B)	(C)
71.	(A)	(B)	(C)
72.	(A)	(B)	(C)
73.	(A)	(B)	(C)
74.	(A)	(B)	(C)
75.	(A)	(B)	(C)
76.	(A)	(B)	(C)
77.	(A)	(B)	(C)
78.	(A)	(B)	(C)
79.	(A)	(B)	(C)
80.	(A)	(B)	(C)

81.	(A)	(B)	(C)
82.	(A)	(B)	(C)
83.	(A)	(B)	(C)
84.	(A)	(B)	(C)
85.	(A)	(B)	(C)
86.	(A)	(B)	(C)
87.	(A)	(B)	(C)
88.	(A)	(B)	(C)
89.	(A)	(B)	(C)
90.	(A)	(B)	(C)
91.	(A)	(B)	(C)
92.	(A)	(B)	(C)
93.	(A)	(B)	(C)
94.	(A)	(B)	(C)
95.	(A)	(B)	(C)
96.	(A)	(B)	(C)
97.	(A)	(B)	(C)
98.	(A)	(B)	(C)
99.	(A)	(B)	(C)
100.	(A)	(B)	(C)
101.	(A)	(B)	(C)
102.	(A)	(B)	(C)
103.	(A)	(B)	(C)
104.	(A)	(B)	(C)
105.	(A)	(B)	(C)
106.	(A)	(B)	(C)
107.	(A)	(B)	(C)
108.	(A)	(B)	(C)
109.	(A)	(B)	(C)
110.	(A)	(B)	(C)
111.	(A)	(B)	(C)
112.	(A)	(B)	(C)
113.	(A)	(B)	(C)
114.	(A)	(B)	(C)
115.	(A)	(B)	(C)
116.	(A)	(B)	(C)
117.	(A)	(B)	(C)
118.	(A)	(B)	(C)
119.	(A)	(B)	(C)
120.	(A)	(B)	(C)

Exam 1
Morning Session

The following 18 questions relate to Ethical and Professional Standards.
(27 minutes)

1. An analyst for a foreign branch of HB Investments, which is based in Lagos, has just issued a recommendation on an IPO. Unknown to the analyst, who is a CFA charterholder, members of her team manipulated the valuation model to increase the newly public company's stock price. She and all of the analysts on the team purchased shares of the oversubscribed IPO for their personal accounts and then purchased the remainder of the firm's allocation of shares for appropriate client accounts, a practice which is permitted by local securities laws. The analyst:
    A. did not violate the Standard I(A) Knowledge of the Law.
    B. violated Standard I(A) Knowledge of the Law by purchasing the shares of the IPO but not by allowing the report to be published.
    C. violated Standard I(A) Knowledge of the Law both by allowing the report to be published and by purchasing the shares of the IPO.

2. Green Investments utilizes the CFA Institute Standards of Professional Conduct as their standards for ethical practice. For purposes of compliance, which of the following is *least likely* a violation of Green Investments' policies?
    A. One of Green Investments' marketing brochures states that several of the firm's portfolio managers passed all three levels of the CFA exam on their first attempts.
    B. At a meeting with potential clients, chief investment officer Bill Ray, CFA, states that he is among an "elite group of the most qualified investment professionals who have earned the right to use the CFA designation."
    C. In interviewing a prospective employee, a portfolio manager at the firm says that the position could be financially rewarding because "CFA charterholders are known to achieve superior performance results."

3. Charmaine Townsend, CFA, has been managing a growth portfolio for her clients using a screening process that identifies companies that have high earnings growth rates. Townsend has decided that, because of a volatile economy, she is going to adopt a value strategy using a screening process that identifies companies that have low price-earnings multiples. Townsend will violate the Code and Standards if she makes this change in her investment process without:
    A. promptly notifying her clients of the change.
    B. getting written permission from her clients in advance of the change.
    C. getting prompt written acknowledgment of the change from her clients within a reasonable time after the change was made.

4. Emily Wells, CFA, retail broker for Charthouse Securities, has been asked by a retail client to buy a substantial position in Computo, Inc., a highly speculative company that is working on developing a solar-powered computer. Wells believes that this would be an inappropriate investment for the client. According to Standard III(C) Suitability, Wells should take which of the following actions?
    A. Execute the order if her supervisor approves the trade.
    B. Execute the trade in accordance with the client's request, but mark the ticket "Unsolicited."
    C. Seek an affirmative statement from the client that suitability is not a consideration in this trade and refuse to execute the trade without such a statement.

5. Jim James, CFA, supervises several financial analysts at his firm. James's compensation is tied to the commissions of the brokers in the firm. James tells Sally Jones, an analyst, to use a report prepared by a rival firm as the basis for her report. He tells her that she will need to make minor changes and that she can then put her name on the report before sending it to clients. The report contains a "Buy" recommendation on a stock in which James's supervisor owns a large stake. If Jones complies with James's request:
    A. she has violated Standard I(C) Misrepresentation, but James has not.
    B. both she and James have violated Standard I(C) Misrepresentation.
    C. James has violated Standard I(C) Misrepresentation, but Jones has not.

6. Laura Grayson, CFA, is a partner in a small investment advisory firm that caters to high net worth individuals. Grayson also manages an investment account for her mother. Her mother's accountant has advised Grayson that, for tax purposes, Grayson should sell her mother's position in Safety Airlines, realizing a large gain, and then immediately repurchase the position. Several of Grayson's clients also hold positions in Safety Airlines. According to the CFA Institute Standards of Professional Conduct, if Grayson follows the advice of the accountant, she:
   A. is not in violation of any Standards.
   B. is in violation of Standard III(B) Fair Dealing for not dealing fairly with all clients.
   C. is in violation of Standard II(B) Market Manipulation for engaging in a practice that will artificially inflate the trading volume of a security.

7. Judy Dudley, CFA, is an analyst and plans to visit a company that she is analyzing in order to prepare a research report. Standard I(B) Independence and Objectivity:
   A. requires Dudley to pay for her own transportation costs and not to accept any gifts or compensation for writing the report, but allows her to accept accommodations and meals that are not lavish.
   B. requires Dudley not to accept any compensation for writing a research report, but allows her to accept company paid transportation, lodging, and meals.
   C. allows Dudley to accept transportation, lodging, expenses, and compensation for writing a research report, but requires that she disclose such an arrangement in her report.

8. Campbell Hill, CFA, has recently joined a pension fund management company as its Chief Compliance Officer. One of Hill's first priorities in his new position is to formalize the company's investment policies and procedures. Hill distributes a memo stating that effective immediately, material supporting all company research reports will be kept in the company database in electronic form for ten years, while hard copies of the same material will be maintained for one year only. The memo also states that hard copy records of all material supporting investment-related communications with clients must be kept on file for five years (the period mandated by local regulations). With respect to Standard V(C) Record Retention:
   A. neither of Hill's policies violates Standard V(C).
   B. Hill's policies regarding both research reports and investment-related communications violate Standard V(C).
   C. Hill's policy regarding investment actions does not violate Standard V(C), but the policy regarding investment-related communications does because Standard V(C) requires records be kept for seven years.

9. In calculating total firm assets for a GIPS-compliant performance statement, Allen Bund, CFA, finds that there is a mix of fee-paying and non-fee-paying accounts, some of which are discretionary and some of which are non-discretionary accounts. Should Bund include non-discretionary accounts and non-fee-paying accounts in the calculation of total firm assets?

	Non-discretionary accounts	Non-fee-paying accounts
A.	Yes	Yes
B.	No	Yes
C.	No	No

10. Dawn Shepard, CFA, is a broker for a regional brokerage firm. Her company's research department has recently changed its recommendation on the common stock of Orlando, Inc., from "Buy" to "Sell." Concurring with the report's analysis, Shepard faxed the change to all her current customers who hold Orlando, Inc., in their accounts. The next day, one of her customers, who had never before expressed an interest in Orlando, calls and places a "Buy" order for 500 shares of Orlando. According to Standard III(B) Fair Dealing, Shepard, under these circumstances:
   A. has complied with the Fair Dealing Standard and may accept the order because it is unsolicited.
   B. may accept the order but must advise the customer of the change in recommendation before accepting the order.
   C. may accept the order only if the customer acknowledges in writing that she was notified of the change in the recommendation.

11. Paul James, CFA, is a retail stock broker for a national financial services corporation. James's client base is mainly comprised of small to medium-sized individual accounts. James notices that one client in particular, Chet Young, Ph.D., is particularly adept at picking undervalued stocks. James decides to watch Young's trades and mimic them in his own account. James:
   A. is not in violation of any Standards.
   B. is in violation of Standard VI(B) Priority of Transactions because he is front running the client's account.
   C. is in violation of Standard I(D) Misconduct because he has misappropriated confidential client information.

12. Nicholas Hart, CFA, is a retail broker for a national financial institution and has a client base composed mainly of high net worth individuals. During the past year, Hart's wife was extremely ill and was hospitalized for several months. Hart was financially responsible for her mounting medical bills and tried to pay them as best as he could. Despite his best efforts to meet his obligations, Hart was forced to declare personal bankruptcy but did not disclose this to any of his clients. According to the CFA Institute Standards of Professional Conduct, Hart:
    A. is not in violation of any Standard.
    B. is in violation of Standard V(B) Communication with Clients and Prospective Clients for not disclosing his bankruptcy to his clients.
    C. is in violation of Standard I(D) Misconduct for personal misconduct that reflects adversely on his professional reputation.

13. Marie Marshall, CFA, is a registered representative for Everest Broker-Dealer who maintains a client base of high net worth individuals, trusts, endowments, and foundations. Such clients pay Everest a quarterly fee, as well as commissions on securities transactions. Marshall receives compensation based on the overall success of the firm, along with a recently implemented quarterly bonus based on the trading volume in her clients' accounts. During her annual portfolio reviews with clients, Marshall receives several questions regarding recent increases in portfolio turnover. Marshall truthfully indicates that recent increases in volatility caused the firm to make more tactical investment recommendations in client portfolios but does not mention her potential volume-based bonus. Marshall has violated:
    A. Standard V(B) Communication with Clients and Prospective Clients.
    B. Standard IV(B) Additional Compensation Arrangements.
    C. Standard VI(A) Disclosure of Conflicts.

14. Lunar Investment Management is a subsidiary of a larger company, Galaxy Financial. Lunar's CEO, Travis Howry, would like to have Lunar present GIPS-compliant performance data and has taken the steps necessary to ensure that Lunar's performance presentation is compliant. He asks Galaxy's President, Don Wiggins, about Galaxy's interest in presenting GIPS-compliant performance data. Wiggins informs Howry that Galaxy is not interested. Lunar may:
    A. not claim compliance because compliance must be made on a company-wide basis.
    B. claim compliance as long as Lunar is advertised as a distinct business entity, separate from Galaxy.
    C. claim partial compliance if Lunar's performance presentations are in compliance but disclose that Galaxy's are not and in which ways.

15. Fred Reilly, CFA, is an investment adviser at a regional office of a national financial institution. A long-term client, Rob Harrison, decides to terminate the relationship and move his company's pension plan and his personal account to another firm. Reilly obliges and completes the paperwork to close the account. As Reilly gathers the files on Harrison's personal account to put into storage, he notices some discrepancies which lead him to suspect that Harrison has engaged in illegal activity with regard to company funds. Which of the following actions is *most appropriate* for Reilly to take under the Standards?
    A. Report his suspicions to outside counsel.
    B. Do nothing since he must maintain the confidentiality of client information even after the client has left the firm.
    C. Inform Harrison's business partners of the suspected illegal activities because he is no longer a client, and they may have legal liability as well.

16. Fred Dean, CFA, has just taken a job as trader for LPC, a large insurance company. One of his first duties in his new position is to execute the purchase of a block of East Street Industries, a firm that is a major client of his previous employer. During his prior employment, Dean was informed directly by East Street's CEO that the company's sales have experienced a sudden drop and are 20% below current analyst estimates. This information has not yet been announced. In reviewing the research report supporting the purchase decision, Dean realizes that the buy decision is based on sales forecasts that he knows are wrong. Which of the following actions would be the *most appropriate* for Dean to take according to CFA Institute Standards of Professional Conduct?
    A. Post the information about the drop in sales on an internet bulletin board to achieve public dissemination and inform his supervisor of the posting.
    B. Contact the CEO and urge him to make the information public and make the trade if he refuses.
    C. Request that the firm place East Street's stock on a restricted list and refuse to make any buy or sell trades of the company's stock.

17. When members and candidates report performance data, according to the Standards, it is:
    A. permissible to leave details out in a brief presentation.
    B. recommended that a minimum of five years performance history be included.
    C. a requirement to present composite performance rather than individual account performance.

18.   Bob Sampson is employed by a mid-sized money management firm in Munich. He is the head portfolio manager for a Global Equities fund. The fund has been in existence for eight years. Beginning this year, the firm has decided to present all of its performance information in compliance with the Global Investment Performance Standards (GIPS). To claim GIPS compliance, the firm must present at least:
A. eight years of GIPS-compliant performance information.
B. five years of GIPS-compliant performance information with no additional disclosure required for prior years.
C. five years of GIPS-compliant performance information and non-compliant performance information since inception in the "Disclosures" section.

The following 14 questions relate to Quantitative Methods. (21 minutes)

19.   An investor wants to receive $10,000 annually for ten years with the first payment five years from today. If the investor can earn a 14% annual return, the amount that she will have to invest today is *closest* to:
A. $27,091.
B. $30,884.
C. $52,161.

20.   Which of the following statements about the frequency distribution shown below is *least accurate*?

Return Interval	Frequency
0% to 5%	10
> 5% to 10%	20
> 10% to 15%	30
> 15% to 20%	20

A. The return intervals are mutually exclusive.
B. The cumulative absolute frequency of the fourth interval is 20.
C. The relative frequency of the second return interval is 25%.

21.   A contrarian technical analyst is *most likely* to be bullish when:
A. the mutual fund cash position is low.
B. investors' credit balances in brokerage accounts are rising.
C. over-the-counter volume is increasing relative to NYSE volume.

22. An investor in a mutual fund earns a 25% return the first year, loses 25% in the second year, gains 30% in the third year, and then loses 30% in the fourth year. The average annual compound growth rate of this investment is *closest* to:
    A. −3.9%.
    B. 0.0%.
    C. 5.6%.

23. An analyst obtains the following annual returns for a group of stocks: 10%, 8%, 7%, 9%, 10%, 12%, 11%, 10%, 30%, and 13%. This distribution:
    A. has a median greater than its mode.
    B. is skewed to the right, and the mean is less than the median.
    C. is skewed to the right, and the mean is greater than the mode.

24. An analyst gathers the following data about the mean monthly returns of three securities:

Security	Mean Monthly Return	Standard Deviation
X	0.9	0.7
Y	1.2	4.7
Z	1.5	5.2

    Which security has the highest level of relative risk as measured by the coefficient of variation?
    A. X.
    B. Y.
    C. Z.

25. The median of a distribution is *least likely* equal to the:
    A. second quartile.
    B. third quintile.
    C. fifth decile.

26. Which of the following statements about probability concepts is *most accurate*?
    A. Subjective probability is a probability that is based on personal judgment.
    B. A conditional probability is the probability that two or more events happen concurrently.
    C. An empirical probability is one based on logical analysis rather than on observation or personal judgment.

27. Which of the following is *least likely* an underlying assumption of technical analysis?
    A. Supply and demand are governed solely by rational behavior.
    B. Actual shifts in supply and demand can be observed in market price behavior.
    C. Prices for individual securities and the market tend to move in trends that persist for long periods of time.

28. Alex White, CFA, is examining a portfolio that contains 100 stocks that are either value or growth stocks. Of these 100 stocks, 40% are value stocks. The previous portfolio manager had selected 70% of the value stocks and 80% of the growth stocks. What is the probability of selecting a stock at random that is either a value stock or was selected by the previous portfolio manager?
    A. 28%.
    B. 76%.
    C. 88%.

29. Which of the following statements about the normal distribution is *least accurate*? The normal distribution:
    A. has a mean of zero and a standard deviation of one.
    B. is completely described by its mean and standard deviation.
    C. is bell-shaped, with tails extending without limit to the left and to the right.

30. A manager forecasts a bond portfolio return of 10% and estimates a standard deviation of annual returns of 4%. Assuming a normal returns distribution and that the manager is correct, there is a:
    A. 90% probability that the portfolio return will be between 3.2% and 17.2%.
    B. 95% probability that the portfolio return will be between 2.16% and 17.84%.
    C. 32% probability that the portfolio return will be between 6% and 14%.

31. An investment has an expected return of 10% with a standard deviation of 5%. If the returns are normally distributed, the chance of losing money is *closest* to:
    A. 2.5%.
    B. 5.0%.
    C. 16.0%.

32. Which of the following statements about sampling and estimation is *least accurate*?
    A. Sampling error is the difference between the observed value of a statistic and the value it is intended to estimate.
    B. A simple random sample is a sample obtained in such a way that each element of the population has an equal probability of being selected.
    C. The central limit theorem states that the sample mean for a large sample size will have a distribution that is the same as the distribution of the underlying population.

The following 12 questions relate to Economics. (18 minutes)

33. The crowding-out effect suggests that:
    A. government borrowing will lead to an increase in private savings.
    B. as government spending increases, so will incomes and taxes, and the higher taxes will reduce both aggregate demand and output.
    C. greater government deficits will drive up interest rates, thereby reducing private investment.

34. An economist is developing a model of real GDP as a function of labor input. She needs to select a time series that represents the total amount of labor performed in a year. The *most appropriate* indicator of total labor performed that she can use for this model is:
    A. aggregate hours.
    B. number of employed.
    C. total labor compensation.

35. At the equilibrium levels of output and price in a competitive industry without taxes:
    A. consumer and producer surplus are equal.
    B. both consumer and producer surplus are maximized.
    C. the sum of producer and consumer surplus is maximized.

36. Which of the following does the U.S. central bank *most often* use to change the money supply?
    A. The discount rate.
    B. Open market operations.
    C. The required reserve ratio.

37. An increase in the demand for labor is *most likely* to be caused by a(n):
    A. decrease in labor productivity.
    B. decrease in the price of production machinery.
    C. increase in the demand for the final good or service.

38. In the short run, will an increase in the money supply increase the price
     level and real output?
     A. Both will increase in the short run.
     B. Neither will increase in the short run.
     C. Only one will increase in the short run.

39. The law of diminishing marginal returns explains:
     A. the shape of the long-run average cost curve.
     B. the upward sloping portion of the short-run marginal cost curve.
     C. the upward sloping portion of the long-run marginal cost curve.

40. A firm in a perfectly competitive market will tend to expand its output as
     long as:
     A. its marginal revenue is positive.
     B. the market price is greater than the marginal cost.
     C. its marginal revenue is greater than the market price.

41. Which of the following statements regarding economic costs is *most
     accurate*?
     A. In the long run, expected average marginal cost is the most relevant
        cost to the firm.
     B. Fixed costs are not a consideration in the short-run operating decision
        but must be considered in the long run.
     C. The marginal revenue from selling an additional unit of output must be
        at least as great as the expected average total cost.

42. Which of the following statements regarding economic and technological
     efficiency is *most accurate*?
     A. An economically efficient production process must be technologically
        efficient.
     B. An economically efficient production process need not be
        technologically efficient as well.
     C. A productive process cannot be technologically efficient unless it is
        economically efficient.

43. The Laffer curve indicates that:
     A. increasing tax rates can reduce tax revenues.
     B. tax revenues are a positive function of GDP.
     C. reducing inflation will likely increase unemployment.

44. A natural monopoly is *most likely* to exist when:
     A. economies of scale are great.
     B. ATC increases as output increases.
     C. a single firm owns essentially all of a productive resource.

The following 24 questions relate to Financial Reporting and Analysis. (36 minutes)

45.   Which of the following statements about types of nonrecurring items under U.S. GAAP is *least accurate*?
        A. Unusual or infrequent items are included in income from continuing operations.
        B. Extraordinary items are unusual and infrequent items that are reported net of taxes and included in nonrecurring income from continuing operations.
        C. Discontinued operations are reported net of taxes below income from continuing operations.

46.   A company has the following sequence of events regarding its stock:
        •   The company had 1,000,000 shares outstanding at the beginning of the year.
        •   On June 30, the company declared and issued a 10% stock dividend.
        •   On September 30, the company sold 400,000 shares of common stock at par.

        The number of shares that should be used to compute basic earnings per share at year end is:
        A. 1,000,000.
        B. 1,100,000.
        C. 1,200,000.

47.   An analyst has found that a firm's cash conversion cycle has decreased significantly over the past year and suspects accounting manipulation of cash flows. The *least likely* way for the company to have decreased its cash conversion cycle is by:
        A. financing payables.
        B. stretching out payables.
        C. securitization of receivables.

48.   If a company presents its balance sheet in a format that includes subtotals for current assets, current liabilities, noncurrent assets, and noncurrent liabilities, it is *most likely* presented:
        A. in a report format.
        B. in an account format.
        C. as a classified balance sheet.

49. Which of the following statements about the analysis of cash flows is *least accurate*?
     A. Interest payments on debt are not a financing cash flow under U.S. GAAP.
     B. Both the direct and indirect methods involve adding back noncash items such as depreciation and amortization.
     C. When using the indirect method, an analyst should add any losses on the sales of fixed assets to net income.

50. Assuming stable inventory quantities, in a period of:
     A. rising prices, LIFO results in higher cash flows and higher net income than FIFO.
     B. falling prices, LIFO results in lower working capital, and FIFO results in lower inventory balances.
     C. rising prices, FIFO results in higher taxes, lower cash flows, and higher working capital, while LIFO results in higher COGS and lower inventory balances.

51. An analyst gathered the following data about a company:

	20X6	20X7
EBIT margin (EBIT / revenue)	0.15	0.10
Asset turnover (revenue / assets)	1.5	1.8
Leverage multiplier (assets / equity)	1.5	1.6
Tax burden (net income / EBT)	0.7	0.7
Interest burden (EBT / EBIT)	0.85	0.85

     The company's return on equity:
     A. decreased because the company's profit margin decreased.
     B. increased because the company's asset turnover and leverage increased.
     C. remained constant because the company's decreased profit margin was just offset by increases in asset turnover and leverage.

52. Firms that prepare their financial statements according to International Financial Reporting Standards are *least likely* to:
     A. use last-in, first-out inventory accounting.
     B. use proportionate consolidation for a joint venture.
     C. recognize unrealized losses from held-for-trading securities in net income.

53. Bentlom Company's common-size financial statements show the following information:

    - Earnings after taxes   15%
    - Current liabilities   20%
    - Equity   45%
    - Sales $800
    - Cash   10%
    - Total assets $2,000
    - Accounts receivable   15%
    - Inventory   20%

    Bentlom's long-term debt-to-equity ratio and current ratio are *closest* to:

Long-term debt-to-equity ratio	Current ratio
A. 78%	2.25
B. 88%	2.50
C. 98%	2.75

54. Consider a manufacturing company and a financial services company. Interest expense is *most likely* classified as a non-operating component of income for:
    A. both of these companies.
    B. neither of these companies.
    C. only one of these companies.

55. Jerry Clark, CFA, is considering investing in a company and is concerned that the company is being overly aggressive in its accounting practices. Which of the following company activities would be *least likely* to increase current period net income?
    A. Due to a recent jump in prices, the company has decided to change its inventory valuation method from FIFO to LIFO.
    B. The company amortizes its advertising costs over three years.
    C. The company books the full value of any new contracts it obtains as revenue only when at least 25% of the payment has been received.

56. Compared to an operating lease, a capital lease will have what effects on operating income and net income in the first year?
    A. Both will be lower.
    B. Both will be higher.
    C. One will be lower and one will be higher.

57. An analyst gathered the following data about a company:
    - 1,000 common shares are outstanding (no change during the year).
    - Net income is $5,000.
    - The company paid $500 in preferred dividends.
    - The company paid $600 in common dividends.
    - The average market price of their common stock is $60 for the year.
    - The company had 100 warrants (for one share each) outstanding for the entire year, exercisable at $50.

    The company's diluted earnings per share is *closest* to:
    A. $4.42.
    B. $4.55.
    C. $4.83.

58. Which of the following sources of information should an analyst consider the *least* reliable?
    A. Form 10-Q.
    B. Proxy statement.
    C. Corporate press release.

59. A company takes a $10 million impairment charge on a depreciable asset in 20X3. The *most likely* effect will be to:
    A. increase reported net income in 20X4.
    B. decrease net income and taxes payable in 20X3.
    C. increase return on equity and operating cash flow in 20X4.

60. Xanos Corporation faced a 50% marginal tax rate last year and showed the following financial and tax reporting information:
    - Deferred tax asset of $1,000.
    - Deferred tax liability of $5,000.

    Based only on this information and the news that the tax rate will decline to 40%, Xanos Corporation's:
    A. deferred tax asset will be reduced by $400 and deferred tax liability will be reduced by $2,000.
    B. deferred tax liability will be reduced by $1,000 and income tax expense will be reduced by $800.
    C. deferred tax asset will be reduced by $200 and income tax expense will be reduced by $1,000.

61. East Company incurs $110,000 of costs to establish technological feasibility of a new software application it hopes to sell and $90,000 of costs to develop the application. West Company incurs $110,000 of research costs related to a new product and $90,000 of development costs for the product. If East reports under U.S. GAAP and West reports under IFRS, these projects will:
    A. increase East's total assets more the West's total assets.
    B. increase West's total assets more than East's total assets.
    C. have the same effects on East's and West's total assets.

62. A company that capitalizes costs instead of expensing them will have:
    A. higher income variability and higher cash flows from operations.
    B. lower cash flows from investing and lower income variability.
    C. lower cash flows from operations and higher profitability in early years.

63. If market interest rates change, the change in market value of a U.S. firm's outstanding debt is reported in its financial statements:
    A. in a footnote.
    B. as an adjustment to income.
    C. only if the debt is refinanced or exchanged.

64. Al Pike, CFA, is analyzing Red Company by projecting pro forma financial statements. Pike expects Red to generate sales of $3 billion and a return on equity of 15% in the next year. Pike forecasts that Red's total assets will be $5 billion and that the company will maintain its financial leverage ratio of 2.5. Based on these forecasts, Pike should project Red's net income to be:
    A. $100 million.
    B. $300 million.
    C. $500 million.

65. A company issues $10 million in 8% annual-pay, 5-year bonds, when the market rate is 8.25%. The initial balance sheet liability and liability one year from the date of issue are *closest* to:

	Initial liability	Liability one year later
A.	$9,900,837	$9,917,656
B.	$10,000,000	$9,975,000
C.	$10,099,163	$10,082,344

66. Which of the following items would affect owners' equity and also appear on the income statement?
    A. Dividends paid to shareholders.
    B. Unrealized gains and losses on trading securities.
    C. Unrealized gains and losses on available-for-sale securities.

67. Copper, Inc., had $4 million in bonds outstanding that were convertible into common stock at a conversion rate of 100 shares per $1,000 bond. In 20X1, all of the outstanding bonds were converted into common stock. Copper's average share price for 20X1 was $15. Copper's statement of cash flows for the year ended December 31, 20X1, should *most likely* include:
    A. a footnote describing the conversion of the bonds into common stock.
    B. cash flows from financing of +$4 million from issuance of common stock and –$4 million from retirement of bonds.
    C. cash flows from financing of +$6 million from issuance of common stock and –$4 million from retirement of bonds and cash flows from investing of –$2 million for a loss on retirement of bonds.

68. Which of the following is the *most appropriate* adjustment for an analyst to make to account for off-balance-sheet financing?
    A. Add the present value of capital leases to both liabilities and assets.
    B. Treat the sale of receivables with recourse as borrowing and increase cash flow from operations by the sale amount.
    C. Adjust liabilities upward for debt guarantees for joint ventures.

The following 10 questions relate to Corporate Finance. (15 minutes)

69. An analyst identifies the following cash flows for an average-risk project:
    - Year 0   –$5,000
    - Years 1–2 $1,900
    - Year 3 $2,500
    - Year 4 $2,000

    If the company's cost of capital is 12%, the project's discounted payback period is *closest* to:
    A. 2.5 years.
    B. 3.0 years.
    C. 3.9 years.

70. Mary Miller, CFA, manages the short-term cash position for Young Company. Miller can invest in one of three securities that will mature in 180 days: a Treasury bill priced at 97.5% of par, commercial paper with a bond-equivalent yield of 5.10%, and a 6-month certificate of deposit that will return 2.5% over the 180-day holding period. Miller should purchase the:
    A. Treasury bill.
    B. commercial paper.
    C. certificate of deposit.

71. Which of the following is the *least appropriate* method for estimating a firm's before-tax cost of debt capital?
    A. Use the market yield on bonds with a rating and maturity similar to the firm's existing debt.
    B. Assume the firm's cost of debt capital is equal to the yield to maturity on its publicly traded debt.
    C. Use the coupon rate on the firm's most recently issued debt.

72. Which of the following types of companies are *more likely* to use the payback method to evaluate capital projects?
    A. European companies and private companies.
    B. Asian companies and larger companies.
    C. European companies and larger companies.

73. Sarah Evens has been studying the effects of takeover defenses on shareholder value. Evens is evaluating various uses of golden parachutes, poison pills, and greenmail, all of which can affect share value. Good corporate governance requires a careful review of a firm's takeover defenses. When conducting this review, Evens should *most likely* consider which of the following a negative factor?
    A. In a hostile bidder situation, the board would be willing to pay cash to such a bidder to preserve the company's independence.
    B. Shareholders have voted down an amendment to the bylaws that would have provided a poison pill.
    C. A change of control issue would not trigger the interest of a local government.

74. The following information applies to World Turn Company:
    - 10% rate of interest on newly issued bonds.
    - 7% growth rate in earnings and dividends.
    - The last dividend paid was $0.93.
    - Shares sell for $16.
    - Stock's beta is 1.5.
    - Market risk premium is 6%.
    - Risk-free rate of interest is 5%.
    - The firm is in a 40% marginal tax bracket.

    If the appropriate risk premium relative to the bond yield is 4%, World Turn's equity cost of capital using the dividend discount model is *closest* to:
    A. 12.8%.
    B. 13.2%.
    C. 14.0%.

75. The committee charged with recommending a compensation package for members of a firm's board of directors has recommended that in addition to compensation of $10,000 for each board meeting attended, board members (1) will be able to use one of the firm's corporate jets up to twice each year and (2) will receive a finder's fee of 0.1% if they identify an acquisition target that the firm acquires while the member is still on the board. Are these policies consistent with good corporate governance practices?
    A. Both policies are consistent with good corporate governance.
    B. Neither policy is consistent with good corporate governance.
    C. Only one of these policies is consistent with good corporate governance.

76. Which of the following is *least likely* a problem associated with the internal rate of return (IRR) method of choosing investment projects?
    A. Using IRR to rank mutually exclusive projects assumes reinvestment of cash flows at the IRR.
    B. For independent projects, the IRR and NPV can lead to different investment decisions.
    C. If the project has an unconventional cash flow pattern, the result can be multiple IRRs.

77. Break points in a firm's marginal cost of capital schedule are *best* interpreted as representing the:
    A. maximum amounts of debt, preferred stock, and common stock the firm can issue.
    B. amounts of new securities a firm would need to issue to take advantage of flotation cost discounts.
    C. amounts of capital expenditure at which the company's weighted average cost of capital increases.

78. Which of the following policies regarding shareowner rights for equity investors is *most likely* detrimental to the shareowners' interests?
    A. The company uses a third-party entity to tabulate shareowner votes.
    B. Shareowners are permitted to vote either by paper ballot or a proxy voting service.
    C. Shareowners can approve changes to the corporate structure only with a supermajority vote.

The following 6 questions relate to Portfolio Management. (9 minutes)

79. Which of the following statements about portfolio theory is *least accurate*?
    A. As the correlation between two assets increases, the benefits of diversification also increase.
    B. The efficient frontier represents the set of portfolios that has the highest rate of return for every given level of risk or the lowest risk for every level of return.
    C. The inputs required for Markowitz portfolio optimization are the expected return for each asset available for investment, the standard deviation for each asset, and the correlation between each pair of assets.

80. Which of the following statements about risk is correct?
    A. The capital market line plots expected return against market risk.
    B. The efficient frontier plots expected return against unsystematic risk.
    C. The security market line plots expected return against systematic risk.

81. A portfolio manager is constructing a new equity portfolio consisting of a large number of randomly chosen domestic stocks. As the number of stocks in the portfolio increases, what happens to the expected levels of systematic and unsystematic risk?

	Systematic risk	Unsystematic risk
A.	Increases	Remains the same
B.	Decreases	Increases
C.	Remains the same	Decreases

82. The risk-free rate is 5% and the expected market return is 15%. A portfolio manager is estimating a return of 20% on a stock with a beta of 1.5. Based on the SML and the analyst's estimate, this stock is:
    A. properly valued.
    B. overvalued.
    C. undervalued.

83. Refusing to invest in companies that sell tobacco products, alcohol, or products that are harmful to the environment would constitute a set of investment restrictions that *best* illustrates which of the following investment constraints?
    A. Regulatory factors.
    B. Unique needs and preferences.
    C. Legal restrictions.

84. Which of the following statements regarding portfolio theory is *least likely* correct?
    A. Adding riskier assets to a portfolio can decrease the portfolio's risk.
    B. A security will plot on the CML if it is priced at its equilibrium level.
    C. All securities and portfolios plot on the SML when their prices are in equilibrium.

The following 12 questions relate to Equity Investments. (18 minutes)

85. Which of the following statements about types of orders is *least accurate*?
    A. Market orders are orders to buy or sell at the best price available.
    B. Limit orders are orders to buy or sell at or away from the market price.
    C. A stop buy order is typically used to protect a short position in a security and is placed below the current market price.

86. Which of the following statements about short sales is *least accurate*?
    A. Proceeds from short sales cannot be withdrawn from the account.
    B. The short seller must pay the lender of the stock any dividends paid by the company.
    C. The short seller is required to replace the borrowed securities within six months of a short sale.

87. The required rate of return used in the dividend discount model is *least likely* to be affected by a change in the:
    A. expected rate of inflation.
    B. real risk-free rate of return.
    C. growth rate of earnings and dividends.

88. When estimating the risk premium to include in the required rate of return on a foreign security, an analyst would *least appropriately* consider:
    A. uncertainty about exchange rates.
    B. potential unexpected economic and political events in the country.
    C. transactions costs and brokerage fees that investors must pay in the foreign country.

89. With regard to the implications of stock market efficiency for technical analysis and fundamental analysis, if market prices are:
    A. weak-form efficient, technical analysis that depends only on past trading data should be of limited or no value.
    B. semistrong-form efficient, fundamental analysis using the top-down approach should yield consistently superior returns.
    C. semistrong-form efficient, fundamental analysis using only publicly available market information should generate abnormal returns after considering risk and transaction costs.

90. The following data pertains to a firm's common stock:
     - The stock will pay no dividends for two years.
     - The dividend three years from now is expected to be $1.
     - Dividends are expected to grow at a 7% rate from that point onward.

     If an investor requires a 17% return on this investment, how much will the investor be willing to pay for this stock now?
     A. $6.24.
     B. $7.31.
     C. $8.26.

91. An analyst forecasts the following for a stock:
     - The normalized trailing price earnings (P/E) ratio will be 12X.
     - The stock's price currently is $100.
     - The stock is expected to pay a $5 dividend this coming year on projected earnings of $10.

     If the analyst were to buy and hold the stock for the year, the projected rate of return based on these forecasts is *closest* to:
     A. 15%.
     B. 20%.
     C. 25%.

92. A stock has the following data associated with it:
     - A required rate of return of 14%.
     - A return on equity of 15%.
     - An earnings retention rate of 40%.

     The stock's price-to-earnings ratio should be:
     A. 5.0.
     B. 6.7.
     C. 7.5.

93. Fred Kohlmeier, CFA, is reviewing academic studies that show low positive correlations between global stock indexes and the U.S. S&P 500 Index and between global and U.S. government bond indexes. Kohlmeier states that (1) a portfolio that matches a U.S. government bond index would benefit from diversifying into global bonds, but (2) a portfolio that matches the S&P 500 Index is already well-diversified and, therefore, would not benefit from diversifying into global stocks. Are Kohlmeier's statements correct?
     A. Both statements are correct.
     B. Neither statement is correct.
     C. Only one of the statements is correct.

94. The top-down approach to security valuation begins with the analysis of:
    A. an industry.
    B. the economy.
    C. portfolio risk and return.

95. Which of the following statements about the application of the constant growth dividend discount model to the valuation of an equity security is *least likely* correct? Other things being equal, the:
    A. price is positively related to the growth rate and negatively related to the dividend.
    B. required rate of return is negatively related to the price and positively related to the growth rate.
    C. growth rate is positively related to the return on equity and negatively related to the dividend payout ratio.

96. Stephen Kroller, CFA, an analyst at J.P. Brothers LLC, analyzes international equity funds. Kroller constructs a sample of funds that have 10-year performance histories at a minimum. Based on the returns of the funds in his sample, Kroller concludes that international equity funds outperformed their comparable U.S. stock indexes over the 10-year period. Kroller's sample and test results are *most likely* subject to:
    A. survivorship bias.
    B. sample selection bias.
    C. nonsynchronous trading bias.

The following 14 questions relate to Fixed Income. (21 minutes)

97. Other things equal, for option-free bonds:
    A. a bond's value is more sensitive to yield increases than to yield decreases.
    B. the value of a long-term bond is more sensitive to interest rate changes than the value of a short-term bond.
    C. the value of a low-coupon bond is less sensitive to interest rate changes than the value of a high-coupon bond.

98. An investor is considering floating-rate debt and other investments to protect against unexpected increases in inflation. Her friend suggests Treasury Inflation Protected Securities (TIPS) because the coupon rate is adjusted for inflation semiannually. The friend also states on-the-run Treasury issues have narrower bid-ask spreads than other Treasury issues. Are the friend's statements correct?
    A. Both of these statements are correct.
    B. Neither of these statements is correct.
    C. Only one of these statements is correct.

99.   An investor in the 28% tax bracket is considering buying one of the following securities:
- A fully taxable Treasury security offering a 6.0% yield.
- A municipal bond priced at par offering a 4.0% yield.

The taxable-equivalent yield on the municipal bond is *closest* to:
A. 2.9%.
B. 4.3%.
C. 5.6%.

100.   Which of the following statements about debt securities is *most likely* correct?
A. Insured bonds are bonds collateralized by an escrow of securities guaranteed by the U.S. government.
B. Tax-backed municipal bonds are supported through revenues generated from projects that are funded in whole or in part with the proceeds of the original bond issue.
C. A collateralized mortgage obligation is a derivative of a passthrough security with a payment structure that redistributes risk among investors in various tranches.

101.   An investor has a 1-year, semiannual, 10% coupon bond which is priced at $1,025. If the 6-month spot rate on a bond-equivalent basis is 8%, the 1-year theoretical spot rate as a BEY is:
A. 6.4%.
B. 7.3%.
C. 8.0%.

102.   The 3-year annual spot rate is 7%, the 4-year annual spot rate is 7.5%, and the 5-year annual spot rate is 8%. Based on the pure expectations theory of interest rates, the 1-year implied forward rate in four years is *closest* to:
A. 7%.
B. 9%.
C. 10%.

103.   A bond priced at par ($1,000) has a modified duration of 8 and a convexity of 50. If interest rates fall 50 basis points, the new price will be:
A. $1,041.25.
B. $958.75.
C. $875.00.

104.   Which of the following statements regarding mortgage-backed securities (MBS) and collateralized mortgage obligations (CMOs) is *most likely* correct?
A. MBS are created from CMOs.
B. Creating CMOs does not reduce the overall prepayment risk of a mortgage passthrough security.
C. The prepayment option of an MBS benefits the security holder.

105. Which of the following statements about embedded options is *least likely* correct?
    A. An investor benefits when a floating rate bond has an interest rate floor.
    B. The prepayment right granted with a mortgage favors the issuer/borrower.
    C. If the market value of a putable bond falls below the par value, the issuer will likely exercise the option.

106. A $1,000 par, semiannual-pay bond is trading for 89.14, has a coupon rate of 8.75%, and accrued interest of $43.72. The clean price of the bond is:
    A. $847.69.
    B. $891.40.
    C. $935.12.

107. Which of the following is *least likely* a reason that floating rate bonds may trade at prices different from their par values?
    A. A time lag exists between the rate change in the market and the time when the coupon rate is reset.
    B. The fixed quoted margin on the floating rate security may differ from the margin required by the market.
    C. Resetting interest rates makes floating rate bonds more susceptible to the price risk that results from changing interest rates.

108. For a domestic investor purchasing foreign bonds:
    A. appreciation of both the asset and the foreign currency benefits the domestic investor.
    B. depreciation of both the asset and the foreign currency benefits the domestic investor.
    C. appreciation of the asset and depreciation of the foreign currency benefit the domestic investor.

109. Reinvestment risk is *least likely*:
    A. minimized with zero-coupon bond issues.
    B. more problematic for those investors with longer time horizons.
    C. more problematic when the current coupons being reinvested are relatively small.

110. Which of the following statements regarding yield spreads is *least accurate*? The:
    A. option cost in percentage terms can be computed by subtracting the OAS from the zero-volatility spread.
    B. nominal yield spread measures the difference between the YTM on a risky bond and the YTM on a Treasury bond of similar maturity.
    C. zero-volatility spread is the constant spread that is added to each Treasury spot rate to equate the present value of a bond's cash flows to the price of an otherwise identical option-free bond.

The following 6 questions relate to Derivatives. (9 minutes)

111. Which of the following statements about call options is *least likely* correct?
    A. The buyer of a call option has an obligation to perform.
    B. A call option is in the money when the strike price is below the stock price.
    C. The lower the strike price relative to the stock's underlying price, the more the call option is worth.

112. Hessian Investments has a short position in a deliverable equity forward contract. The company now expects the underlying security to be worth more than the contract price at the expiration date. If Hessian wishes to avoid executing the contract at the settlement date, it:
    A. can renegotiate the contract.
    B. can enter into a long forward on an identical security at a higher price.
    C. has the option to pay cash equal to the difference between the security price and the contract price.

113. A 3-year annual-pay currency swap takes place between a New Zealand company with New Zealand dollars (NZD) and a U.S. company with U.S. dollars (USD). The New Zealand company swaps NZD for USD on which it makes end-of-period payments based on the rate in effect at the beginning of each period. The U.S. company makes fixed-rate payments in NZD.
    • The fixed swap rate at the initiation of the swap was 7%; at the end of the swap it was 8%.
    • The variable rate at the end of year 1 was 6%, at the end of year 2 was 8%, and at the end of year 3 was 7%.
    • At the beginning of the swap, one million USD were exchanged at a NZD/USD rate of 2.
    • At the end of the swap period, the exchange rate was NZD/USD 1.5.

    At the end of year 2, the:
    A. New Zealand company gives the U.S. company USD 60,000.
    B. U.S. company gives the New Zealand company USD 80,000.
    C. New Zealand company gives the U.S. company USD 80,000.

114. A dealer arranges an equity swap with a mutual fund. The notional principal on the swap is $50 million and quarterly payments have been scheduled. The mutual fund agrees to pay the dealer the return on the S&P 400 Midcap Index, which is currently at 1,038.4. Three months later it is 1,052.5. The dealer pays a fixed rate of 5.5% to the mutual fund, with payments made on the basis of 91 days in the period and 365 days in the year. What is the net payment and who makes it?
    A. Dealer pays $6,687.
    B. Dealer pays $1,364,546.
    C. Mutual fund pays $6,687.

115. Which of the following statements about futures and forwards is *most accurate*? Futures:
    A. are subject to default risk, but forwards are not.
    B. are individualized contracts, but forwards are standardized.
    C. require that traders post margin in order to trade, but forwards typically require no cash transaction until the delivery date.

116. Which of the following statements about futures markets is *most accurate*?
    A. Hedgers accept market risk in exchange for expected profits.
    B. The futures exchange establishes the minimum price fluctuation for each contract.
    C. The role of the clearinghouse is to take an active position in the market to maintain a fair and orderly market by providing liquidity when the normal flow of orders is not adequate.

The following 4 questions relate to Alternative Investments. (6 minutes)

117. Allison Fletcher is analyzing a real estate investment with the following characteristics:
    • Purchase price is $2.5 million.
    • Down payment is $500,000, financing at 10%, with 20 annual end-of-year payments.
    • Gross annual rents are $300,000.
    • Depreciation is $60,000 per year.
    • Maintenance and taxes are $35,000 per year.

    If Fletcher is in a 35% marginal income tax bracket, the first year after-tax cash flow is *closest* to:
    A. –$19,000.
    B. $5,000.
    C. $28,000.

118. Which of the following is *least likely* a benefit of fund of funds (FOF) investing?
    A. FOFs may permit access to otherwise closed hedge funds.
    B. FOFs allow investors to diversify the risks of holding a single hedge fund.
    C. The fee is generally quite reasonable since the investor only pays the manager of the FOF.

119. Open-end funds differ from closed-end funds in that:
    A. open-end funds stand ready to redeem their shares, while closed-end funds do not.
    B. closed-end funds require experienced fund managers, while open-end funds do not.
    C. open-end funds issue shares that are then traded in secondary markets, while closed-end funds do not.

120. Which of the following would be *least likely* to provide an effective hedge for an investor with a portfolio primarily in fixed-coupon bonds?
    A. Sell bond futures.
    B. Buy interest rate puts.
    C. Buy commodity-linked equities.

EXAM 1
AFTERNOON SESSION

Calculating Your Score

Topic	Maximum Score	Your Score
Ethical and Professional Standards	18	
Quantitative Methods	14	
Economics	12	
Financial Reporting and Analysis	24	
Corporate Finance	10	
Portfolio Management	6	
Equity Investments	12	
Fixed Income	14	
Derivatives	6	
Alternative Investments	4	
Total	120	

The morning and afternoon exams are identically weighted over the topics and readings. You can therefore treat the morning and afternoon exams as independent exams.

If you took more than three hours (180 minutes) to complete this portion of the exam, you should adjust your score downward by one point for each minute you ran over.

Remember: the real exam *will be more difficult* than these practice exams. The main reason for this is the general anxiety and stress that you will be feeling on exam day, coupled with the time pressure you will be under. Many of the questions on this practice exam and the real exam are not individually difficult, so if you take extra time to answer the questions on this practice exam, your score will go up significantly. However, if you want an accurate measure of your potential performance on the exam, adhere to the 3-hour time limit.

After you have finished grading your practice exam, you may find it useful to use the exam questions and recommended solutions for review. Many of these questions were specifically written for your use as study tools. Once again, I feel I should remind you not to rely on memorizing these questions; you are not likely to see them on the actual exam. What you will see on the exam, though, are the concepts, terms, and procedures presented in these questions.

Your actual exam will most likely look different than what you see in this book. Please remember, no study provider knows the content of the actual exam. These practice exams are our best guess as to the structure, content, and difficulty of an actual exam.

Test Answers

1.	Ⓐ	Ⓑ	Ⓒ	41.	Ⓐ	Ⓑ	Ⓒ	81.	Ⓐ	Ⓑ	Ⓒ
2.	Ⓐ	Ⓑ	Ⓒ	42.	Ⓐ	Ⓑ	Ⓒ	82.	Ⓐ	Ⓑ	Ⓒ
3.	Ⓐ	Ⓑ	Ⓒ	43.	Ⓐ	Ⓑ	Ⓒ	83.	Ⓐ	Ⓑ	Ⓒ
4.	Ⓐ	Ⓑ	Ⓒ	44.	Ⓐ	Ⓑ	Ⓒ	84.	Ⓐ	Ⓑ	Ⓒ
5.	Ⓐ	Ⓑ	Ⓒ	45.	Ⓐ	Ⓑ	Ⓒ	85.	Ⓐ	Ⓑ	Ⓒ
6.	Ⓐ	Ⓑ	Ⓒ	46.	Ⓐ	Ⓑ	Ⓒ	86.	Ⓐ	Ⓑ	Ⓒ
7.	Ⓐ	Ⓑ	Ⓒ	47.	Ⓐ	Ⓑ	Ⓒ	87.	Ⓐ	Ⓑ	Ⓒ
8.	Ⓐ	Ⓑ	Ⓒ	48.	Ⓐ	Ⓑ	Ⓒ	88.	Ⓐ	Ⓑ	Ⓒ
9.	Ⓐ	Ⓑ	Ⓒ	49.	Ⓐ	Ⓑ	Ⓒ	89.	Ⓐ	Ⓑ	Ⓒ
10.	Ⓐ	Ⓑ	Ⓒ	50.	Ⓐ	Ⓑ	Ⓒ	90.	Ⓐ	Ⓑ	Ⓒ
11.	Ⓐ	Ⓑ	Ⓒ	51.	Ⓐ	Ⓑ	Ⓒ	91.	Ⓐ	Ⓑ	Ⓒ
12.	Ⓐ	Ⓑ	Ⓒ	52.	Ⓐ	Ⓑ	Ⓒ	92.	Ⓐ	Ⓑ	Ⓒ
13.	Ⓐ	Ⓑ	Ⓒ	53.	Ⓐ	Ⓑ	Ⓒ	93.	Ⓐ	Ⓑ	Ⓒ
14.	Ⓐ	Ⓑ	Ⓒ	54.	Ⓐ	Ⓑ	Ⓒ	94.	Ⓐ	Ⓑ	Ⓒ
15.	Ⓐ	Ⓑ	Ⓒ	55.	Ⓐ	Ⓑ	Ⓒ	95.	Ⓐ	Ⓑ	Ⓒ
16.	Ⓐ	Ⓑ	Ⓒ	56.	Ⓐ	Ⓑ	Ⓒ	96.	Ⓐ	Ⓑ	Ⓒ
17.	Ⓐ	Ⓑ	Ⓒ	57.	Ⓐ	Ⓑ	Ⓒ	97.	Ⓐ	Ⓑ	Ⓒ
18.	Ⓐ	Ⓑ	Ⓒ	58.	Ⓐ	Ⓑ	Ⓒ	98.	Ⓐ	Ⓑ	Ⓒ
19.	Ⓐ	Ⓑ	Ⓒ	59.	Ⓐ	Ⓑ	Ⓒ	99.	Ⓐ	Ⓑ	Ⓒ
20.	Ⓐ	Ⓑ	Ⓒ	60.	Ⓐ	Ⓑ	Ⓒ	100.	Ⓐ	Ⓑ	Ⓒ
21.	Ⓐ	Ⓑ	Ⓒ	61.	Ⓐ	Ⓑ	Ⓒ	101.	Ⓐ	Ⓑ	Ⓒ
22.	Ⓐ	Ⓑ	Ⓒ	62.	Ⓐ	Ⓑ	Ⓒ	102.	Ⓐ	Ⓑ	Ⓒ
23.	Ⓐ	Ⓑ	Ⓒ	63.	Ⓐ	Ⓑ	Ⓒ	103.	Ⓐ	Ⓑ	Ⓒ
24.	Ⓐ	Ⓑ	Ⓒ	64.	Ⓐ	Ⓑ	Ⓒ	104.	Ⓐ	Ⓑ	Ⓒ
25.	Ⓐ	Ⓑ	Ⓒ	65.	Ⓐ	Ⓑ	Ⓒ	105.	Ⓐ	Ⓑ	Ⓒ
26.	Ⓐ	Ⓑ	Ⓒ	66.	Ⓐ	Ⓑ	Ⓒ	106.	Ⓐ	Ⓑ	Ⓒ
27.	Ⓐ	Ⓑ	Ⓒ	67.	Ⓐ	Ⓑ	Ⓒ	107.	Ⓐ	Ⓑ	Ⓒ
28.	Ⓐ	Ⓑ	Ⓒ	68.	Ⓐ	Ⓑ	Ⓒ	108.	Ⓐ	Ⓑ	Ⓒ
29.	Ⓐ	Ⓑ	Ⓒ	69.	Ⓐ	Ⓑ	Ⓒ	109.	Ⓐ	Ⓑ	Ⓒ
30.	Ⓐ	Ⓑ	Ⓒ	70.	Ⓐ	Ⓑ	Ⓒ	110.	Ⓐ	Ⓑ	Ⓒ
31.	Ⓐ	Ⓑ	Ⓒ	71.	Ⓐ	Ⓑ	Ⓒ	111.	Ⓐ	Ⓑ	Ⓒ
32.	Ⓐ	Ⓑ	Ⓒ	72.	Ⓐ	Ⓑ	Ⓒ	112.	Ⓐ	Ⓑ	Ⓒ
33.	Ⓐ	Ⓑ	Ⓒ	73.	Ⓐ	Ⓑ	Ⓒ	113.	Ⓐ	Ⓑ	Ⓒ
34.	Ⓐ	Ⓑ	Ⓒ	74.	Ⓐ	Ⓑ	Ⓒ	114.	Ⓐ	Ⓑ	Ⓒ
35.	Ⓐ	Ⓑ	Ⓒ	75.	Ⓐ	Ⓑ	Ⓒ	115.	Ⓐ	Ⓑ	Ⓒ
36.	Ⓐ	Ⓑ	Ⓒ	76.	Ⓐ	Ⓑ	Ⓒ	116.	Ⓐ	Ⓑ	Ⓒ
37.	Ⓐ	Ⓑ	Ⓒ	77.	Ⓐ	Ⓑ	Ⓒ	117.	Ⓐ	Ⓑ	Ⓒ
38.	Ⓐ	Ⓑ	Ⓒ	78.	Ⓐ	Ⓑ	Ⓒ	118.	Ⓐ	Ⓑ	Ⓒ
39.	Ⓐ	Ⓑ	Ⓒ	79.	Ⓐ	Ⓑ	Ⓒ	119.	Ⓐ	Ⓑ	Ⓒ
40.	Ⓐ	Ⓑ	Ⓒ	80.	Ⓐ	Ⓑ	Ⓒ	120.	Ⓐ	Ⓑ	Ⓒ

Exam 1
Afternoon Session

The following 18 questions relate to Ethical and Professional Standards.
(27 minutes)

1. York Investment Advisers, which has publicly adopted the CFA Institute® Standards of Professional Conduct, has recently published a new marketing brochure highlighting the accomplishments of its investment professionals. Which of the following statements made in York's marketing brochure is a violation of Standard VII(B) Reference to CFA Institute, the CFA Designation, and the CFA Program?
   A. Roger Langley, Chartered Financial Analyst, has been a portfolio manager with York for ten years and passed all three levels of the CFA examinations on his first attempts.
   B. Langley is one of three CFAs on staff with York. We expect that two more of our staff members will earn the right to use the designation in the future.
   C. Paul Yeng has retired from the firm after 25 years of service. Yeng was awarded the CFA charter in 1988. Much of the firm's past successes can be attributed to Yeng's efforts as an analyst and portfolio manager.

2. Hedge Funds Unlimited, a global hedge fund, has publicly acknowledged in writing that it has adopted the CFA Institute Code and Standards as its policies. Which of the following is *least likely* a violation of the firm's policies?
   A. An analyst at the firm working overseas uses material nonpublic information as allowed by local law to make investment decisions for discretionary client accounts.
   B. A junior analyst at the firm uses a subscription to his local newspaper and the opinions of his friends and colleagues to make investment recommendations for discretionary client accounts.
   C. A CFA candidate at the firm, who is registered for the Level 3 exam, includes reference to participation in the CFA program and her status as a Level 3 candidate in her biographical background.

3.   Ralph Malone, CFA, is an investment adviser at a multinational finance corporation. He has many wealthy individuals among his clients, including a trust account that benefits three of his immediate family members. The research department of Malone's firm issues a "buy" recommendation on a stock that would be a suitable investment for several client accounts, including the family trust account. Which of the following would be considered a violation of Standard VI(B) Priority of Transactions?
   A. After giving clients time to act on the new recommendation, the firm buys 100,000 shares for its own account.
   B. Malone trades on the family account shortly after his firm's clients have been informed of the buy recommendation.
   C. Malone waits to trade on the family account until four days after his firm's clients have been informed of the buy recommendation, when his employer's trades are entered.

4.   Linda Bryant, CFA, is an employee of Roomkin Investment House, which underwrites equity and debt offerings. She has been approached by SimthCo to consult on a private debt placement. According to CFA Institute Standards of Professional Conduct, before Bryant agrees to accept this job, she is required to:
   A. obtain written consent from Roomkin after submitting details of the arrangement.
   B. talk to her immediate supervisor and get her approval to take this consulting job.
   C. inform SimthCo in writing that she will accept the job and provide details of the arrangement to Roomkin in writing.

5.   To comply with the Code and Standards, analysts who send research recommendations to clients must:
   A. keep records of all the data and analysis that went into creating the report.
   B. send recommendations only to those clients for whom the investments are suitable.
   C. not send recommendations without including the underlying analysis and basic investment characteristics.

6. Marilyn Walters, CFA, supervises a large group of research analysts. Walters has delegated some of her supervisory responsibilities to her assistant, Amy Brooks, who is a CFA candidate. In carrying out her responsibilities, Brooks has discovered that the firm's compliance system is inadequate and that Walters is not very supportive of Brooks's efforts to correct the situation. According to CFA Institute Standards of Professional Conduct, Brooks should:
   A. resign because her firm is not in compliance with the CFA Institute Standards, leaving her open to legal action.
   B. decline in writing to accept supervisory responsibilities until a reasonable compliance system is adopted.
   C. take no action because her efforts to correct the situation have satisfied her obligation under CFA Institute Standards.

7. Jarrett Rogers, CFA, is a registered investment adviser and a principal for Macrovest Broker-Dealer. Rogers is the head of the firm's investment program and recommends certain investment advisers in the program to high net worth individuals looking for separately managed discretionary accounts. Investment advisers in the program pay Macrovest a portion of their investment management fees to participate in the program, some of which is paid to Rogers as compensation for client referrals. When a client inquires with Rogers about criteria for including managers in the Macrovest program, Rogers indicates that managers are selected based only on historical investment performance versus a universe of comparable peer investment managers, but he does not mention fees paid by investment advisers to be included in the program. Which of the following CFA Institute Standards of Professional Conduct has Rogers violated?
   A. Standard VI(C) Referral Fees.
   B. Standard I(C) Misrepresentation.
   C. Standard III(B) Fair Dealing.

8. Ken Toma, a CFA charterholder and securities analyst for the leisure services industry, has just completed an extensive review of the demand for beach vacations in Hawaii and concluded that the demand will far exceed the supply for the foreseeable future. Toma writes a research report stating, "Based on the fact that the demand for Hawaiian beach vacations will exceed the supply of rooms for the foreseeable future, I recommend the purchase of shares of the Hawaiian Fund, a diversified portfolio of Hawaiian beachfront resorts." If Toma presents this report to his clients, he will have violated the CFA Institute Standards:
   A. because he did not distinguish between fact and opinion.
   B. by failing to have a reasonable and adequate basis for his recommendation.
   C. because he did not consider the suitability of the investment for his clients.

9. Derek Stevens, CFA, manages the pension plan assets of Colors, Inc. When voting proxies on plan equities, Stevens owes a fiduciary duty to:
   A. the plan trustees who hired him.
   B. the plan participants and beneficiaries.
   C. the managers, stockholders, and bondholders of Colors, Inc. equally.

10. Dawn Shields, CFA, decides to change her recommendation on TelSky from "buy" to "sell." In the morning, she mails the revision to all her clients with a known interest in TelSky. That afternoon, one of these clients calls in an order to buy 15,000 shares of TelSky. According to Standard III(B) Fair Dealing, Shields:
    A. must accept the order without mentioning the change because the Standard requires her to inform all clients of the change in recommendation simultaneously.
    B. should advise her customer of the change in her recommendation before accepting the order.
    C. must not accept the order until the customer has had time to receive and read the new report.

11. Which of the following is one of the eight major sections of the GIPS standards?
    A. Venture capital.
    B. Private equity.
    C. Sub-advisers.

12. Patrick Wilcox was recently hired by SafeTrust Investments as a fixed-income portfolio manager. Wilcox is informed by the head of the fixed income desk that all security analysis done by SafeTrust employees must be generated through the SafeTrust model that was developed in-house. Wilcox has reviewed reports that are based upon the model and appear to be thoroughly and accurately researched, but since he does not know first-hand the assumptions that the SafeTrust model is based on, he would prefer to use the services of an outside vendor that he has used for years. If Wilcox uses the in-house model as instructed, he will:
    A. not violate Standard V(A) Diligence and Reasonable Basis because the firm has deemed the model reliable.
    B. violate Standard IV(A) Loyalty because he may cause harm to his employer by using a potentially unreliable model.
    C. violate Standard V(A) Diligence and Reasonable Basis because he does not have personal knowledge of the model's reliability.

13. Greg Hoffman, a Level 1 CFA candidate, works as an independent securities research consultant. Hoffman has been hired by managers of Hill Manufacturing, Inc. (HMI) to write a research report on their company. Hoffman performs a thorough analysis of the firm's financials, the industry in which it operates, and the overall market and economy. After conducting his due diligence, Hoffman writes a report on HMI with a strong "Buy" recommendation. Hoffman posts the report for purchase on a web site he created to support his consulting business but does not state either on the web site or in the report that HMI paid for the research. According to Standard I(B) Independence and Objectivity and Standard VI(A) Disclosure of Conflicts, Hoffman has violated:
    A. both of these Standards.
    B. neither of these Standards.
    C. only one of these Standards.

14. Rhonda Morrow, CFA, is an analyst for Waller & Madison, a brokerage and investment banking firm. Waller & Madison is a market maker for CorpEast, and Tim Waller, a principal in the firm, sits on CorpEast's board. Morrow has been asked to write a research report on CorpEast. According to Standard VI(A) Disclosure of Conflicts, Morrow:
    A. may write the report without disclosure of Waller's seat on CorpEast's board since he is not writing the report, but she must disclose that Waller & Madison is a market maker in CorpEast shares.
    B. must not write the report and must request that Waller & Madison put CorpEast on their restricted list.
    C. may write the report only if she discloses that Waller & Madison is a market maker in CorpEast shares and that Waller sits on the CorpEast board.

15. John Farr, CFA, has accumulated several pieces of nonpublic information about Cattle Corp. of Omaha from his contacts with the company. Although none of this information is material by itself, when Farr combines it with his own analysis, it leads him to conclude that Cattle Corp. will have an unexpectedly low earnings report this year. Cattle Corp. has not announced this information, and although Farr has contacted the company, it will not confirm his finding. According to CFA Institute Standards of Professional Conduct, Farr:
    A. can use the information to make investment recommendations and decisions.
    B. cannot legally invest, divest, or make recommendations based on this information.
    C. may use the information, but only if his company's compliance officer is able to verify with Cattle Corp. that the material he used was indeed nonmaterial.

16. According to the GIPS standards, which of the following is *least likely* correct?
    A. Firms are not required to obtain verification for a claim of GIPS compliance.
    B. Written documentation of policies and procedures used to establish and maintain compliance with GIPS must be maintained.
    C. To initially claim compliance with GIPS, a company must present a minimum of ten years (or since the firm's inception if less than ten years) of GIPS-compliant performance data.

17. Geno Hanson is a portfolio manager at Bigtime Investments. James Ward, an old friend of Hanson's, is an executive recruiter in the same city. Ward refers to Hanson's firm any high-level executives that Ward places locally. In return, Hanson allows Ward to play a round of golf at Hanson's country club for each new client referred. According to Standard VI(C) Referral Fees, Hanson is required to disclose the arrangement with Ward to:
    A. his employer, all clients, and all prospective clients.
    B. prospective clients referred by Ward.
    C. his employer and to prospective clients referred by Ward.

18. Yvette Michaelson, a junior analyst for Torborg Investments, covers healthcare and consumer discretionary stocks alongside a senior analyst at the firm. Michaelson inadvertently overhears a conversation between two executives regarding Collective Healthcare's proposed tender offer for Network Healthcare at a 12% premium, which will be announced next week. Michaelson has followed both companies extensively and feels consolidation would be very beneficial for both companies. She calls her senior analyst to recommend a 15% increase in Torborg's current position in Network. According to Standard II(A) Material Nonpublic Information, Michaelson's actions are:
    A. in violation of the Standard since she is acting on material nonpublic information.
    B. not in violation of the Standard since she is acting on an unofficial conversation between two executives who have not breached any duty in discussing the information.
    C. not in violation of the Standard under the mosaic theory since she has followed both companies extensively, and the tender offer information substantiates her beliefs about the benefits of consolidation.

The following 14 questions relate to Quantitative Methods. (21 minutes)

19. The odds for an event occurring are calculated by dividing:
    A. one by the probability that the event occurs.
    B. the probability that the event does not occur by the probability that an event occurs.
    C. the probability that the event occurs by the probability that the event does not occur.

20. A successful investor has decided to set up a scholarship fund for deserving students at her alma mater. Her plan is for the fund to be capable of awarding $25,000 annually in perpetuity. The first scholarship is to be awarded and paid out exactly four years from today. The funds will be deposited into an account immediately and will grow at a rate of 4%, compounded semiannually, for the foreseeable future. How much money must the investor donate today to fund the scholarship?
   A. $528,150.
   B. $549,487.
   C. $574,253.

21. Which of the following statements about return distributions is *least likely* correct?
   A. With positive skewness, the mean is greater than the median.
   B. If skewness is positive, the average magnitude of positive deviations from the mean is larger than the average magnitude of negative deviations from the mean.
   C. If a return distribution has positive excess kurtosis and the analyst uses statistical models that do not account for the fatter tails, the analyst will overestimate the likelihood of very bad or very good outcomes.

22. Excerpt from the cumulative *z*-table:

z	0.00
2.3	0.9893
2.4	0.9918
2.5	0.9938

An analyst collects figures for the attendance at each of his college's hockey games over the last five years. The minimum percentage of the distribution that lies within plus or minus 2.4 standard deviations of the mean is *closest* to:
   A. 82.60%.
   B. 98.36%.
   C. 99.18%.

23. Which of the following statements about covariance and the correlation coefficient is *least accurate*?
    A. Covariance is a measure of how the returns of two assets tend to move together over time.
    B. The correlation coefficient is computed by dividing the covariance of returns on two assets by the individual variances of returns for the two assets.
    C. The covariance of returns between two assets is equal to the correlation between the returns of the two assets, multiplied by the product of their standard deviations of returns.

24. Greg Goldman, research analyst in the fixed-income area of an investment bank, needs to determine the average duration of a sample of twenty 15-year fixed-coupon investment grade bonds. Goldman first categorizes the bonds by risk class and then randomly selects bonds from each class. After combining the bonds selected (bond ratings and other information taken as of March 31 of the current year), he calculates a sample mean duration of 10.5 years. Assuming that the actual population mean duration is 9.7 years, which of the following statements about Goldman's sampling process and sample is *least accurate*?
    A. Goldman is using time-series data.
    B. The sample mean is a random variable.
    C. The sampling error is 0.8 years.

25. Which of the following is *least likely* an assumption underlying technical analysis?
    A. Stock prices move in trends that persist for long periods of time.
    B. Shifts in supply and demand can be observed in market price behavior.
    C. Supply is driven by the rational behavior of firms offering their shares, while demand is driven by the irrational behavior of investors.

26. If Stock X has a standard deviation of returns of 18.9% and Stock Y has a standard deviation of returns equal to 14.73% and returns on the stocks are perfectly positively correlated, the standard deviation of an equally weighted portfolio of the two is:
    A. 10.25%.
    B. 14.67%.
    C. 16.82%.

27.   Over a sample period, an investor gathers the following data about three mutual funds.

Mutual Fund	Risk-Free Rate	Portfolio Return	Portfolio Standard Deviation	Portfolio Beta
P	5%	13%	18%	1.2
Q	5%	15%	20%	1.4
R	5%	18%	24%	1.8

Based solely on the Sharpe measure, an investor would prefer mutual fund:
A. P.
B. Q.
C. R.

28.   An investment manager wants to select three analysts from a group of six analysts to receive first-, second-, and third-place awards for outstanding performance. In how many ways can the investment manager make the three awards?
A. 20 ways.
B. 54 ways.
C. 120 ways.

29.   Which of the following statements about the central limit theorem is *least likely* correct? The:
A. standard deviation of the sample mean is called the standard error of the sample mean.
B. standard error of the sample mean can be estimated by dividing the population standard deviation by $\sqrt{n-1}$.
C. sample means for large sample sizes will have an approximately normal distribution regardless of the distribution of the underlying population.

30.   An investment analyst takes a random sample of 100 aggressive equity funds and calculates the average beta as 1.7. The sample betas have a standard deviation of 0.4. Using a 95% confidence interval and a z-statistic, which of the following statements about the confidence interval and its interpretation is *most accurate*? The analyst can be confident at the 95% level that the interval:
A. 1.580 to 1.820 includes the mean of the population beta.
B. 1.622 to 1.778 includes the mean of the population beta.
C. 1.634 to 1.766 includes the mean of the population beta.

31. Which is the correct test statistic for a test of the null hypothesis
     H_0: $\sigma^2 = \sigma^2_0$ versus H_a: $\sigma^2 \neq \sigma^2_0$?
     A. *F*-statistic.
     B. *t*-statistic.
     C. Chi-square statistic.

32. Which of the following regarding technical analysts is *least likely* correct?
     Technical analysts:
     A. do not rely on getting information first.
     B. depend heavily on accounting information.
     C. attempt to determine when to buy, not why investors are buying.

The following 12 questions relate to Economics. (18 minutes)

33. To benefit from price discrimination, a monopolist *least likely* needs to
     have:
     A. a higher-quality product at a premium price and a lower-quality
        alternative.
     B. a way to prevent reselling between types of consumers.
     C. two identifiable groups of consumers with different price
        elasticities of demand for the product.

34. Automatic stabilizers are government programs that tend to:
     A. automatically increase tax collections during a recession.
     B. reduce interest rates, thus stimulating aggregate demand.
     C. change the government budget balance in a manner counter-cyclical to
        economic growth without legislative action.

35. Under monopolistic competition, a firm is expending the optimal amount
     of resources on innovation if the:
     A. marginal cost of innovation equals the marginal revenue of
        additional innovation.
     B. marginal revenue of additional innovation exceeds the marginal
        cost of innovation.
     C. firm's managers believe the amount is optimal, since no
        quantitative criterion exists.

36. Notasled, Inc., a producer of cafeteria trays, operates in a perfectly
     competitive market. If the market price of a cafeteria tray is $3.25,
     Notasled will increase production so long as:
     A. marginal revenue is positive.
     B. marginal cost is less than $3.25.
     C. marginal revenue is greater than $3.25.

37. Utilitarianism, in reference to economic fairness, refers to the idea that:
     A. the greatest good occurs when wealth is equalized.
     B. equality of opportunity is an important measure of economic fairness.
     C. economic efficiency is greatest when the marginal social cost is just equal to the marginal social benefit.

38. Alice Costain operates a convenience store in the financial district of London. If Costain increases the price of an ice cream bar from £1.00 to £1.15, weekly sales decrease from 200 units to 180 units. Which of the following statements is *most accurate*?
     A. The price elasticity of demand is –0.66.
     B. The price increase will lead to an increase in total value of ice cream bars sold.
     C. Since the price elasticity of demand is less than one, the demand for ice cream bars is elastic.

39. Which of the following is *least likely* a condition that characterizes monopolistic competition?
     A. Large number of independent sellers.
     B. Each produces a differentiated product.
     C. Producers face horizontal demand curves.

40. The cash price consumers pay for a product is *most likely* to increase as the result of a:
     A. government subsidy to product producers.
     B. new law imposing high penalties for sales of the product.
     C. new law imposing high penalties for consumption of the product.

41. Which of the following events is *most likely* to increase short-run aggregate supply (shift the curve to the right)?
     A. Inflation that results in an increase in goods prices.
     B. High unemployment puts downward pressure on money wages.
     C. An increase in government spending intended to increase real output.

42. The combination of currency in circulation, banks' reserve deposits at the central bank, and coins issued by the Treasury is referred to as the:
     A. monetary base.
     B. M1 money supply.
     C. real money supply.

43. For which of the following natural resources does the appropriate model indicate that the price is determined by demand rather than by supply?
     A. Oil.
     B. Gold.
     C. Farm land.

44.   In the short run, the average product of labor:
    A. is increasing when the total product of labor is increasing.
    B. is at a maximum where it intersects the marginal product of labor curve.
    C. is upward-sloping if the firm is experiencing diminishing marginal returns to labor.

The following 24 questions relate to Financial Reporting and Analysis. (36 minutes)

45.   When the Rivers Company filed its corporate tax returns for the first quarter of the current year, it owed a total of $6.7 million in corporate taxes. Rivers paid $4.4 million of the tax bill, but still owes $2.3 million. It also received $478,000 in the second quarter as a down payment towards $942,000 in custom-built products to be delivered in the third quarter. Its financial accounts for the second quarter *most likely* show the $2.3 million and the $478,000 as:

	$2.3 million	$478,000
A.	Income tax payable	Unearned revenue
B.	Income tax payable	Accrued revenue
C.	Deferred tax liability	Accrued revenue

46.   Which of the following statements about the appropriate revenue recognition method to use, given the status of completion of the earning process and assurance of payment, is *least likely* accurate? Use the:
    A. completed contract method when the firm cannot reliably estimate the outcome of the project.
    B. percentage-of-completion method when ultimate payment is reasonably assured and revenue and costs can be reliably estimated.
    C. installment method when collectability of payments for a sale can be reasonably estimated.

47.   An analyst gathered the following data about a company:
- Collections from customers are $5,000.
- Depreciation is $800.
- Cash expenses (including taxes) are $2,000.
- Tax rate = 30%.
- Net cash increased by $1,000.

If inventory increases over the period by $800, cash flow from operations equals:
    A. $1,600.
    B. $2,400.
    C. $3,000.

48. Which of the following statements about the indirect method of calculating cash flow from operations is *least accurate*?
    A. Depreciation is added back to net income because it is an expense not requiring cash.
    B. No adjustment is needed to account for changes in accounts receivable because no cash is involved.
    C. No adjustment is needed for the payment of taxes because the tax payment is already in net income.

49. A company has debt equal to $35 million and total assets of $105 million. This company makes a commitment to acquire raw materials over the next three years by making annual purchases of $5 million that have a present value of $12 million. For purposes of analysis, the *best* estimate of the debt-to-equity ratio after the appropriate analyst adjustment of the balance sheet is:
    A. 0.343.
    B. 0.573.
    C. 0.671.

50. Which of the following statements about the LIFO and FIFO inventory accounting methods is *least accurate*?
    A. For purposes of inventory analysis, FIFO is preferred over LIFO.
    B. FIFO cost of goods sold = LIFO cost of goods sold – change in LIFO reserve.
    C. In periods of declining prices, LIFO debt-to-equity ratios are higher than FIFO debt-to-equity ratios.

51. Which of the following is *most likely* presented on a common-size balance sheet or common-size income statement?
    A. Total asset turnover.
    B. Operating profit margin.
    C. Return on common equity.

52. An analyst gathers the following data about a company:
    - The company had 1 million shares of common stock outstanding for the entire year.
    - The company's beginning stock price was $50, its ending price was $70, and its average price was $60.
    - The company had 100,000 warrants outstanding for the entire year. Each warrant allows the holder to buy one share of common stock at $50 per share.

    How many shares of common stock should the company use in computing its diluted earnings per share?
    A. 1,100,000.
    B. 1,083,333.
    C. 1,016,667.

53. Under U.S. GAAP, land owned by the firm is *most likely* to be reported on the balance sheet at:
    A. historical cost.
    B. fair market value minus selling costs.
    C. historical cost less accumulated depreciation.

54. Which of the following items is *least likely* to contain details about various accruals, adjustments, balances, and management assumptions?
    A. Income statement.
    B. Supplementary schedules.
    C. Discussion and analysis by management.

55. A firm presents the following income statement, which complies with the standards under which it must report:

Sales	20,535
Cost of goods sold	14,525
Operating expenses	2,530
Operating income	3,480
Income taxes	1,220
Income from continuing operations	2,260
Extraordinary items, net of tax	(525)
Net income	1,735

   Based on the differences between U.S. GAAP and International Financial Reporting Standards, this firm:
    A. must report any dividends received as operating cash flows.
    B. is permitted to recognize upward revaluations of long-lived assets.
    C. cannot have used LIFO as its inventory cost assumption.

56. A permanent difference in pretax and taxable income is *least likely* to result when:
    A. tax-exempt interest is received.
    B. the installment sales method is used.
    C. premiums are paid on life insurance of key employees.

57. Which of the following statements about the financial implications of capitalization versus expensing is *least accurate*?
    A. Capitalizing will result in smoother reported income than expensing, and expensing will result in higher leverage ratios than capitalizing.
    B. Cash flow from operations is not affected by the capitalizing versus expensing decision, but the investing and financing cash flows depend on the method the firm chooses.
    C. Total cash flows are the same regardless of whether a firm chooses capitalizing or expensing, but profitability is different depending on the method that the firm chooses.

58. If a company is investing in new assets, using straight-line depreciation instead of accelerated depreciation in the early years of an asset's life will lead to lower:
    A. assets and higher net income.
    B. turnover ratios and higher assets.
    C. return on equity and higher cash flow.

59. From the lessee's perspective, compared to an operating lease, a finance lease results in:
    A. higher asset turnover.
    B. a higher debt-to-equity ratio.
    C. lower operating cash flow.

60. A firm needs to adjust the financial statements for a change in the tax rate. Taxable income is $80,000 and pretax income is $100,000. The current tax rate is 50%, and the new tax rate is 40%. The difference in taxes payable between the two rates is *closest* to:
    A. $8,000.
    B. $9,000.
    C. $10,000.

61. While motive and opportunity both can lead to accounting fraud, a third important contributing factor is:
    A. poor financial controls.
    B. a justification of the fraudulent actions.
    C. pressure to meet earnings expectations.

62. Which of the following items for a financial services company is *least likely* to be considered an operating item on the income statement?
    A. Interest income.
    B. Financing expenses.
    C. Income tax expense.

63. Three firms in the same industry show the following ratios for the most recent year after all proper adjustments have been made for dilutive securities and differences in financial reporting standards:

	Earnings per Share	*Operating Cash Flow per Share*
Company Y	$3.50	$2.00
Company Z	$2.00	$3.00

Based on this information, the better financial performer of these two firms:
    A. is Company Y because it has the highest earnings per share.
    B. is Company Z because it generated the most operating cash flow per share.
    C. cannot be determined because per-share ratios are not comparable.

64. Granite, Inc. owns a machine with a carrying value of $3.0 million and a salvage value of $2.0 million. The present value of the machine's future cash flows is $1.7 million. The asset is permanently impaired. Granite should:
   A. immediately write down the machine to its salvage value.
   B. immediately write down the machine to its present value of future cash flows.
   C. write down the machine to its present value of future cash flows as soon as it is depreciated down to salvage value.

65. Yamaska Mining issued a 5-year, $50 million face, 6% semiannual bond when market interest rates were 7%. The market yield of the bonds was 8% at the beginning of the next year. What is the initial balance sheet liability, and what is the interest expense that the company should report for the first half of the second year of the bond's life (the third semiannual period)?

	Initial liability	Interest expense, first half of year 2
A.	$47,920,849	$1,689,853
B.	$47,920,849	$1,750,000
C.	$50,000,000	$1,500,000

66. A company's financial statement reads:

Current assets	$2,000
Fixed assets	3,000
Debt	3,000
Equity	2,000

   The company sold $500 in receivables, but a review of the footnotes to the financial statements reveals that the credit risk was not transferred on the sale. Which of the following adjustments is an analyst reviewing the company *least likely* to make?
   A. Decrease equity by $500.
   B. Increase debt (short-term liabilities) by $500.
   C. Increase current assets (accounts receivable) by $500.

67. In a period of rising prices and stable or increasing inventory quantities, use of the last-in, first-out inventory cost flow assumption is *least likely* to result in:
   A. lower net income than under first-in, first-out.
   B. higher cash flows than under first-in, first-out.
   C. higher income taxes than under first-in, first-out.

68.   A firm pays accrued wages with cash. Assuming a current ratio greater
        than one and a quick ratio that is less than one, what will be the impact on
        the current ratio and the quick ratio?
        A. Both ratios will remain the same.
        B. The current ratio will increase and the quick ratio will decrease.
        C. The current ratio will decrease and the quick ratio will increase.

The following 10 questions relate to Corporate Finance. (15 minutes)

69.   Responsibilities of a board of directors' nominations committee are *least
        likely* to include:
        A. recruiting qualified members to the board.
        B. selecting an external auditor for the company.
        C. preparing a succession plan for the company's executive management.

70.   The following data applies to LeVeit Company:
        •   LeVeit has a target debt-to-equity ratio of 0.5.
        •   LeVeit's bonds are currently yielding 10%.
        •   LeVeit is a constant growth (5%) firm that just paid a dividend of
            $3.00.
        •   LeVeit's stock sells for $31.50 per share.
        •   The company's marginal tax rate is 40%.

        The company's weighted after-tax cost of capital is *closest* to:
        A. 10.5%.
        B. 11.0%.
        C. 12.0%.

71.   Timely Taxis, Ltd. has signed a long-term lease for 20 underground
        parking spots at $150 each per month for its fleet of taxis. The firm
        currently has 18 taxis in operation and is performing an NPV analysis on
        the purchase of a 19th taxi. The cost of parking for the 19th taxi is *best*
        described as a(n):
        A. sunk cost.
        B. opportunity cost.
        C. incremental cost.

72.   If a firm uses the weighted average cost of capital (WACC) to discount
        cash flows of higher than average risk projects, which one of the following
        will *most likely* occur?
        A. Project NPVs will be understated.
        B. The firm will reject profitable projects.
        C. The overall risk of the firm's investments will rise over time.

73. Michael Robe, CFA, is a junior analyst for a large financial institution and has been preparing an analysis of United Mines, a coal mining company located in the United States. As part of his research, he examines the company's proxy voting and rules and practices. Which of the following policies would be considered the *most* restrictive to shareholders?
    A. Shareholders of United Mines are allowed to cast confidential votes but must be present to do so.
    B. Corporate policy prohibits the use of share blocking prior to United Mines' annual meetings.
    C. United Mines requires shareowner attendance to vote but coordinates the timing of its annual meeting to be held on the same day as other companies in the region.

74. Wreathfield, Inc. is choosing between two mutually exclusive projects. The cash flows for the two projects are below. The firm has a cost of capital of 12%, and the risk of the projects is equivalent to the average risk of the firm.

	0	1	2	3	4	5	6
A:	−12,000	4,000	5,000	6,000			
B:	−20,000	3,000	3,000	3,000	5,000	8,000	8,000

    Wreathfield should accept:
    A. Project A.
    B. Project B.
    C. Neither project A nor project B.

75. To finance a proposed project, Youngham Corporation would need to issue £25 million in common equity. Youngham would receive £23 million in net proceeds from the equity issuance. When analyzing the project, analysts at Youngham should:
    A. not consider the flotation cost because it is a sunk cost.
    B. add the £2 million flotation cost to the project's initial cash outflow.
    C. increase the cost of equity capital to account for the 8% flotation cost.

76. If firms Acme and Butler have the same amount of sales and equal quick ratios, but Acme's receivables turnover is higher, it is *most likely* that:
    A. Butler has better liquidity than Acme.
    B. Butler has a lower cash ratio than Acme.
    C. Acme's average days of receivables is higher than Butler's.

77. Two projects being considered by a firm are mutually exclusive and have the following projected cash flows:

Year	Project A Cash Flow	Project B Cash Flow
0	−$4.0	?
1	$3.0	$1.7
2	$5.0	$3.2
3	$2.0	$5.8

The crossover rate of the two projects' NPV profiles is 9%. What is the initial cash flow for Project B?
A. −$4.22.
B. −$4.51.
C. −$5.70.

78. A firm's optimal capital budget can be found by moving along its investment opportunity schedule until:
A. it exhausts its capital budget.
B. average project return is equal to average cost of capital.
C. the next project's return is less than the marginal cost of capital.

The following 6 questions relate to Portfolio Management. (9 minutes)

79. Which of the following equations is *least accurate*?

A. $\beta_{stock} = \rho_{stock, market} \left(\dfrac{\sigma_{stock}}{\sigma_{market}} \right)$.

B. Total risk = unsystematic risk + nondiversifiable risk.

C. Two-stock portfolio standard deviation $= w_1^2 \sigma_1^2 + w_2^2 \sigma_2^2 + 2 w_1 w_2 \sigma_1 \sigma_2 \rho_{1,2}$.

80. Which of the following is *least likely* an implication of risk aversion for the investment process?
A. The capital market line (CML) is upward-sloping.
B. The promised yield on AAA rated bonds is higher than on A rated bonds.
C. A positive relationship exists between expected return and expected risk.

81. Which of the following possible portfolios is *least likely* to lie on the efficient frontier?

Portfolio	Expected Return	Standard Deviation
X	9%	12%
Y	11%	10%
Z	13%	15%

A. Portfolio X.
B. Portfolio Y.
C. Portfolio Z.

82. An investor gathers the following information about two stocks:

	Scenario 1	Scenario 2	Scenario 3
Probability	0.5	0.3	0.2
Rate of return on:			
Security 1	25%	10%	–25%
Security 2	1%	–5%	35%

If the investor plans to invest $60,000 in Security 1 and $40,000 in Security 2, the expected return on the two-asset portfolio is *closest* to:
A. 5.8%.
B. 8.7%.
C. 12.2%.

83. When the underlying assumption of zero transactions costs is relaxed, the CAPM produces:
A. a capital market line that is no longer straight.
B. several different security market lines.
C. a band of returns instead of a security market line.

84. An analyst gathered the following data about three stocks:

Stock	Beta	Estimated Return
A	1.5	18.1%
B	1.1	15.7%
C	0.6	12.5%

If the risk-free rate is 8%, and the market risk premium is 7%, the analyst is *least likely* to recommend buying:
A. Stock A.
B. Stock B.
C. Stock C.

The following 12 questions relate to Equity Investments. (18 minutes)

85.   Which of the following statements regarding primary and secondary capital markets is *least accurate*?
    A. An underwriter provides origination, risk-bearing, and distribution services to an issuer.
    B. The secondary market is where new shares are issued by firms whose shares are already publicly traded.
    C. In call markets, bids and offers are accumulated and trades take place periodically at prices that clear the market.

86.   Martin Johnson, CFA, is a stock analyst at High Mountain Investments. He uses several methods and a variety of ratios to estimate the values of equity securities. Three ratios that he commonly uses are the price-to-book value (P/BV) ratio, the price-to-earnings (P/E) ratio, and the price-to-sales (P/S) ratio. Johnson recognizes that there are drawbacks associated with each of these measures. The two drawbacks that are of most concern to his current analysis are:
    • Drawback #1: Failure to capture differences in cost structures across companies.
    • Drawback #2: Inflation and technological change may make this ratio difficult to compare across firms.

    Which of the following ratios are *most* susceptible to each of these drawbacks?

Drawback #1	Drawback #2
A. P/S ratio	P/BV ratio
B. P/BV ratio	P/E ratio
C. P/E ratio	P/S ratio

87.   Which of the following results of event studies about market anomalies would *most likely* be a reason to reject the semi-strong form of the efficient market hypothesis? Tests showing that:
    A. stock splits do not result in short-run or long-run impacts on security returns.
    B. pricing adjustments for initial public offerings occur within one day of the offering.
    C. abnormal returns can be earned over a period of days after a stock is listed on a national exchange.

88.   Which of the following is *least likely* an advantage of using a price-to-sales (P/S) ratio for valuation purposes?
    A. Sales growth is the best measure of value creation.
    B. P/S ratios are more stable than price-to-earnings ratios.
    C. P/S ratios are positive even when price-to-book and price-to-earnings ratios are not.

89. An analyst gathered the following data about a company:
    - A historical earnings retention rate of 60% that is projected to continue into the future.
    - A sustainable return on equity of 10%.
    - A beta of 1.0.
    - The nominal risk-free rate is 5%.
    - The expected market return is 10%.

    If next year's EPS is $2 per share, what value would be placed on this stock?
    A. $20.00.
    B. $30.50.
    C. $35.45.

90. An analyst makes the following predictions for the coming year:
    - A stock's earnings per share will be $4.
    - The dividend payout will be 55%.
    - Return on equity will be 15%.
    - The required rate of return on the market will be 12%.

    Based on these estimates, the value of the stock is *closest* to:
    A. $32.
    B. $37.
    C. $42.

91. The top-down approach to security selection is *least likely* to include:
    A. analysis of the global and national economic environment.
    B. determination of the suitability of securities for an investor's portfolio based on the investor's requirements and constraints.
    C. identification of the industry effects of changes in demographics, lifestyles, technology, and politics and regulation.

92. Which of the following is a limitation of arbitrage in correcting anomalies?
    A. Arbitrageurs are sophisticated traders, but too few of them exist to contribute significantly to the correction of market anomalies.
    B. Arbitrage is not always riskless, so trading based on information that a security is undervalued or overvalued does not ensure a profit.
    C. There is no limitation of arbitrage in correcting anomalies because arbitrageurs will use their capital to pursue any trade that exploits a mispricing.

93. Which of the following statements about short selling is *least accurate*?
    A. A short seller is required to set up a margin account.
    B. A short sale involves securities the investor does not own.
    C. A short seller loses if the price of the stock sold short decreases.

94. Compared to an index of 100 U.S. exchange-traded stocks, an index of 100 U.S. government and corporate bonds will *most likely*:
    A. reflect more timely price data.
    B. be more difficult to build and maintain.
    C. have less turnover among the securities in the index.

95. Beth Knight, CFA, and David Royal, CFA, are independently analyzing the value of Bishop, Inc. stock. Bishop paid a dividend of $1 last year. Knight expects the dividend to grow by 10% in each of the next three years, after which it will grow at a constant rate of 4% per year. Royal also expects a temporary growth rate of 10% followed by a constant growth rate of 4%, but he expects the supernormal growth to last for only two years. Knight estimates that the required return on Bishop stock is 9%, but Royal believes the required return is 10%. Royal's valuation of Bishop stock is approximately:
    A. equal to Knight's valuation.
    B. $5 less than Knight's valuation.
    C. $5 greater than Knight's valuation.

96. Which of the following statements regarding growth companies and growth stocks is *least accurate*?
    A. A growth stock does not have to be the stock of a growth company.
    B. Management of a growth company has the ability to consistently choose projects with above-average returns.
    C. If growth opportunities are already incorporated into its price, a growth company's stock will earn above-average returns.

The following 14 questions relate to Fixed Income. (21 minutes)

97. Consider the following Treasury spot rates expressed as bond equivalent yields:

Maturity	Spot Rate
6 months	3.0%
1 year	3.5%
1.5 years	4.0%
2 years	4.5%

    If a Treasury note with two years remaining to maturity has a 5% semiannual coupon and is priced at $1,008, the note is:
    A. overpriced.
    B. underpriced.
    C. correctly priced.

98. Which of the following is an advantage of a callable bond (compared to an identical option-free bond) to an investor?
    A. Less reinvestment risk.
    B. Higher yield.
    C. More convexity.

99. An investor is considering the purchase of Security X, which matures in ten years and has a par value of $1,000. During the first five years, X has a 6% coupon with quarterly payments. During the remaining five years, X has an 8% coupon with quarterly payments. The face value is paid at maturity. A second 10-year security, Security Z, has a 6% semiannual coupon and is selling at par. Assuming that X has the same bond equivalent yield as Z, the price of Security X is *closest* to:
    A. $943.
    B. $1,036.
    C. $1,067.

100. A bond has a yield-to-maturity of 8%. If its effective duration is 7.41 years, a 25 basis point increase in rates will result in an approximate:
    A. 7.41% decrease in price.
    B. 1.85% decrease in price.
    C. 12.85% increase in price.

101. The full price of a bond:
    A. is the price that includes accrued interest.
    B. is also known as the "clean" price.
    C. includes commissions and taxes.

102. Which statement regarding sinking funds is *least likely* correct?
    A. Sinking fund provisions require the retirement of a portion of a bond issue in specified amounts prior to the maturity date.
    B. Sinking fund redemptions can be accomplished by making cash payment to the trustee who will then retire the required proportion of the bonds.
    C. If rates have declined since the bond was issued, companies are likely to choose to retire a proportion of the debt through the delivery of securities.

103. The bank discount yield for a $1,000 face value U.S. Treasury bill (T-bill) trading at $983.10 with 160 days to maturity is *closest* to:
    A. 1.69%.
    B. 1.72%.
    C. 3.80%.

104. Consider a 25-year, $1,000 par semiannual-pay bond with a 7.5% coupon and a 9.25% YTM. Based on a yield change of 50 basis points, the effective duration of the bond is *closest* to:
   A. 8.73.
   B. 10.03.
   C. 12.50.

105. For a bond currently priced at $1,018 with an effective duration of 7.48, if the market yield moved down 75 basis points, the new price would be approximately:
   A. $961.
   B. $1,075.
   C. $1,094.

106. Consider a $1,000-face value, 12-year, 8%, semiannual coupon bond with a YTM of 10.45%. The change in value for a decrease in yield of 38 basis points is:
   A. $21.18.
   B. $22.76.
   C. $23.06.

107. Which of the following statements about Treasury Inflation Protected Securities (TIPS) is correct?
   A. Inflation adjustments are made annually.
   B. Yields on TIPS are effectively real rates of interest.
   C. The coupon rate adjusts upward for inflation.

108. The minimum amount of data required to calculate the implied forward rate for three years beginning three years from now is:
   A. the 3-year and 6-year spot rates.
   B. spot rates at 1-year intervals for the 6-year period.
   C. spot rates at intervals for the 6-year period.

109. Consider three bonds that are identical in all features except those shown in the following table:

Bond	Embedded Option	Amount Outstanding
A	Call	$20 million
B	Call	$80 million
C	Put	$20 million

The bond *most likely* to have the largest spread to a comparable Treasury security is:
   A. Bond A.
   B. Bond B.
   C. Bond C.

110.   A 3-year, 6% coupon, semiannual-pay note has a yield to maturity of 5.5%. If an investor holds this note to maturity and earns a 4.5% return on reinvested coupon income, his realized yield on the note is *closest* to:
A. 5.46%.
B. 5.57%.
C. 5.68%.

The following 6 questions relate to Derivatives. (9 minutes)

111.   Janet Powers writes a covered call on a stock she owns, Billings, Inc. The current price of the stock is $45, and Powers writes the call at a strike price of $50. The call option premium is $3.50. Which of the following statements regarding Powers's covered call strategy is *most accurate*?
A. Powers is trading the stock's upside potential in exchange for current income.
B. The price of the stock must rise to at least $50 before Powers will lose money.
C. Powers is eliminating downside risk at the same time she is increasing her current income with the covered call strategy.

112.   A portfolio manager holds a long position on a forward contract on $20 million face value 80-day T-bills priced at 1.85% on a discount basis. At settlement, 80-day T-bills are priced at 1.95% on a discount basis. If the contract settles in cash, the amount the portfolio manager will pay or receive at settlement is *closest* to:
A. pay $4,500.
B. receive $4,500.
C. pay $20,000.

113.   When comparing the values of two otherwise identical in-the-money options on a stock that pays no dividend, it is *most likely* that a(n):
A. European call with a lower exercise price will have less value than a European call with a higher exercise price.
B. American put with a lower exercise price will have more value than an American put with a higher exercise price.
C. American call with a shorter time to expiration will have less value than an American call with a longer time to expiration.

114. An analyst determines that a portfolio with a 35% weight in Investment A and a 65% weight in Investment B will have a standard deviation of returns equal to zero.
     - Investment A has an expected return of 8%.
     - Investment B has a standard deviation of returns of 7.1% and a covariance with the market of 0.0029.
     - The risk-free rate is 5% and the market risk premium is 7%.

     If no arbitrage opportunities are available, the expected rate of return on the combined portfolio is *closest* to:
     A. 5%.
     B. 6%.
     C. 7%.

115. The time value of an option is *most accurately* described as:
     A. being greatest at the option's expiration date.
     B. the entire premium for an out-of-the-money option.
     C. the amount by which the intrinsic value exceeds the option premium.

116. An investor long a forward position in a Treasury bill is *most likely* to be concerned about:
     A. default risk.
     B. delivery options the short has.
     C. paying more than expected because the price of the bill rises.

The following 4 questions relate to Alternative Investments. (6 minutes)

117. Which of the following similarities between distressed security investing and venture capital investing is *least likely* correct? Both:
     A. asset classes are illiquid.
     B. assets have reasonably short expected investment horizons.
     C. assets may require significant involvement by investors in order to be successful.

118. An open-end fund has the following holdings at the end of the business day:
     - 500,000 shares of A valued at $20 each.
     - 100,000 shares of B valued at $10 each.
     - 200,000 shares of C valued at $15 each.
     - $1,000,000 in cash.
     - The fund currently has one million shares outstanding.

     The fund's net asset value per share is:
     A. $13.
     B. $14.
     C. $15.

119. An investor buys two gold futures contracts at $350 per ounce. Each gold futures contract is based on 5,000 ounces of gold. At the same time he collateralizes his position by buying the required amount of Treasury bills yielding 3%. Two months later the price of gold is $347.40 and the T-bills mature. The net gain or loss on the value of the investor's collateralized futures position is *closest* to:
   A. $8,500 loss.
   B. $26,000 loss.
   C. $34,500 gain.

120. A highly risk-averse investor with a long time horizon who worries about inflation is *most likely* to invest in:
   A. long-term corporate bonds.
   B. market-neutral hedge funds.
   C. commingled real estate funds.

EXAM 2
MORNING SESSION

Calculating Your Score

Topic	Maximum Score	Your Score
Ethical and Professional Standards	18	
Quantitative Methods	14	
Economics	12	
Financial Reporting and Analysis	24	
Corporate Finance	10	
Portfolio Management	6	
Equity Investments	12	
Fixed Income	14	
Derivatives	6	
Alternative Investments	4	
Total	120	

The morning and afternoon exams are identically weighted over the topics and readings. You can therefore treat the morning and afternoon exams as independent exams.

If you took more than three hours (180 minutes) to complete this portion of the exam, you should adjust your score downward by one point for each minute you ran over.

Remember: the real exam *will be more difficult* than these practice exams. The main reason for this is the general anxiety and stress that you will be feeling on exam day, coupled with the time pressure you will be under. Many of the questions on this practice exam and the real exam are not individually difficult, so if you take extra time to answer the questions on this practice exam, your score will go up significantly. However, if you want an accurate measure of your potential performance on the exam, adhere to the 3-hour time limit.

After you have finished grading your practice exam, you may find it useful to use the exam questions and recommended solutions for review. Many of these questions were specifically written for your use as study tools. Once again, I feel I should remind you not to rely on memorizing these questions; you are not likely to see them on the actual exam. What you will see on the exam, though, are the concepts, terms, and procedures presented in these questions.

Your actual exam will most likely look different than what you see in this book. Please remember, no study provider knows the content of the actual exam. These practice exams are our best guess as to the structure, content, and difficulty of an actual exam.

Test Answers

1.	Ⓐ	Ⓑ	Ⓒ	41.	Ⓐ	Ⓑ	Ⓒ	81.	Ⓐ	Ⓑ	Ⓒ
2.	Ⓐ	Ⓑ	Ⓒ	42.	Ⓐ	Ⓑ	Ⓒ	82.	Ⓐ	Ⓑ	Ⓒ
3.	Ⓐ	Ⓑ	Ⓒ	43.	Ⓐ	Ⓑ	Ⓒ	83.	Ⓐ	Ⓑ	Ⓒ
4.	Ⓐ	Ⓑ	Ⓒ	44.	Ⓐ	Ⓑ	Ⓒ	84.	Ⓐ	Ⓑ	Ⓒ
5.	Ⓐ	Ⓑ	Ⓒ	45.	Ⓐ	Ⓑ	Ⓒ	85.	Ⓐ	Ⓑ	Ⓒ
6.	Ⓐ	Ⓑ	Ⓒ	46.	Ⓐ	Ⓑ	Ⓒ	86.	Ⓐ	Ⓑ	Ⓒ
7.	Ⓐ	Ⓑ	Ⓒ	47.	Ⓐ	Ⓑ	Ⓒ	87.	Ⓐ	Ⓑ	Ⓒ
8.	Ⓐ	Ⓑ	Ⓒ	48.	Ⓐ	Ⓑ	Ⓒ	88.	Ⓐ	Ⓑ	Ⓒ
9.	Ⓐ	Ⓑ	Ⓒ	49.	Ⓐ	Ⓑ	Ⓒ	89.	Ⓐ	Ⓑ	Ⓒ
10.	Ⓐ	Ⓑ	Ⓒ	50.	Ⓐ	Ⓑ	Ⓒ	90.	Ⓐ	Ⓑ	Ⓒ
11.	Ⓐ	Ⓑ	Ⓒ	51.	Ⓐ	Ⓑ	Ⓒ	91.	Ⓐ	Ⓑ	Ⓒ
12.	Ⓐ	Ⓑ	Ⓒ	52.	Ⓐ	Ⓑ	Ⓒ	92.	Ⓐ	Ⓑ	Ⓒ
13.	Ⓐ	Ⓑ	Ⓒ	53.	Ⓐ	Ⓑ	Ⓒ	93.	Ⓐ	Ⓑ	Ⓒ
14.	Ⓐ	Ⓑ	Ⓒ	54.	Ⓐ	Ⓑ	Ⓒ	94.	Ⓐ	Ⓑ	Ⓒ
15.	Ⓐ	Ⓑ	Ⓒ	55.	Ⓐ	Ⓑ	Ⓒ	95.	Ⓐ	Ⓑ	Ⓒ
16.	Ⓐ	Ⓑ	Ⓒ	56.	Ⓐ	Ⓑ	Ⓒ	96.	Ⓐ	Ⓑ	Ⓒ
17.	Ⓐ	Ⓑ	Ⓒ	57.	Ⓐ	Ⓑ	Ⓒ	97.	Ⓐ	Ⓑ	Ⓒ
18.	Ⓐ	Ⓑ	Ⓒ	58.	Ⓐ	Ⓑ	Ⓒ	98.	Ⓐ	Ⓑ	Ⓒ
19.	Ⓐ	Ⓑ	Ⓒ	59.	Ⓐ	Ⓑ	Ⓒ	99.	Ⓐ	Ⓑ	Ⓒ
20.	Ⓐ	Ⓑ	Ⓒ	60.	Ⓐ	Ⓑ	Ⓒ	100.	Ⓐ	Ⓑ	Ⓒ
21.	Ⓐ	Ⓑ	Ⓒ	61.	Ⓐ	Ⓑ	Ⓒ	101.	Ⓐ	Ⓑ	Ⓒ
22.	Ⓐ	Ⓑ	Ⓒ	62.	Ⓐ	Ⓑ	Ⓒ	102.	Ⓐ	Ⓑ	Ⓒ
23.	Ⓐ	Ⓑ	Ⓒ	63.	Ⓐ	Ⓑ	Ⓒ	103.	Ⓐ	Ⓑ	Ⓒ
24.	Ⓐ	Ⓑ	Ⓒ	64.	Ⓐ	Ⓑ	Ⓒ	104.	Ⓐ	Ⓑ	Ⓒ
25.	Ⓐ	Ⓑ	Ⓒ	65.	Ⓐ	Ⓑ	Ⓒ	105.	Ⓐ	Ⓑ	Ⓒ
26.	Ⓐ	Ⓑ	Ⓒ	66.	Ⓐ	Ⓑ	Ⓒ	106.	Ⓐ	Ⓑ	Ⓒ
27.	Ⓐ	Ⓑ	Ⓒ	67.	Ⓐ	Ⓑ	Ⓒ	107.	Ⓐ	Ⓑ	Ⓒ
28.	Ⓐ	Ⓑ	Ⓒ	68.	Ⓐ	Ⓑ	Ⓒ	108.	Ⓐ	Ⓑ	Ⓒ
29.	Ⓐ	Ⓑ	Ⓒ	69.	Ⓐ	Ⓑ	Ⓒ	109.	Ⓐ	Ⓑ	Ⓒ
30.	Ⓐ	Ⓑ	Ⓒ	70.	Ⓐ	Ⓑ	Ⓒ	110.	Ⓐ	Ⓑ	Ⓒ
31.	Ⓐ	Ⓑ	Ⓒ	71.	Ⓐ	Ⓑ	Ⓒ	111.	Ⓐ	Ⓑ	Ⓒ
32.	Ⓐ	Ⓑ	Ⓒ	72.	Ⓐ	Ⓑ	Ⓒ	112.	Ⓐ	Ⓑ	Ⓒ
33.	Ⓐ	Ⓑ	Ⓒ	73.	Ⓐ	Ⓑ	Ⓒ	113.	Ⓐ	Ⓑ	Ⓒ
34.	Ⓐ	Ⓑ	Ⓒ	74.	Ⓐ	Ⓑ	Ⓒ	114.	Ⓐ	Ⓑ	Ⓒ
35.	Ⓐ	Ⓑ	Ⓒ	75.	Ⓐ	Ⓑ	Ⓒ	115.	Ⓐ	Ⓑ	Ⓒ
36.	Ⓐ	Ⓑ	Ⓒ	76.	Ⓐ	Ⓑ	Ⓒ	116.	Ⓐ	Ⓑ	Ⓒ
37.	Ⓐ	Ⓑ	Ⓒ	77.	Ⓐ	Ⓑ	Ⓒ	117.	Ⓐ	Ⓑ	Ⓒ
38.	Ⓐ	Ⓑ	Ⓒ	78.	Ⓐ	Ⓑ	Ⓒ	118.	Ⓐ	Ⓑ	Ⓒ
39.	Ⓐ	Ⓑ	Ⓒ	79.	Ⓐ	Ⓑ	Ⓒ	119.	Ⓐ	Ⓑ	Ⓒ
40.	Ⓐ	Ⓑ	Ⓒ	80.	Ⓐ	Ⓑ	Ⓒ	120.	Ⓐ	Ⓑ	Ⓒ

Exam 2
Morning Session

The following 18 questions relate to Ethical and Professional Standards. (27 minutes)

1. Adam Schute, CFA, is in the investment banking division of Worldwide Brokers, a full service brokerage firm. While on a conference call with the CFO of an investment banking client, Schute has his phone speaker on and his door open. Salesmen and traders from the brokerage side of the firm overhear the CFO describing problems with production target dates on an important new product line that have not been publicly disclosed. The salesmen make calls to relay this information to clients, and two traders who overheard the CFO reduce their positions in the stock. With respect to Standard II(A) Material Nonpublic Information, Schute has:
    A. not violated the Standard because he has not acted on the information, but the traders and salesmen have violated the Standard.
    B. violated the Standard because he should have taken steps to prevent the dissemination of the information.
    C. violated the Standard by not making the information public when he realized others had overheard the call.

2. Peter Wellington is a client relationship manager for Huntington Financial Services who references his status as a "CFA candidate" in current client presentation materials. Wellington completed the Level 2 CFA examination two years ago, regularly reads research materials prepared by CFA Institute, and attends continuing education seminars for employees who are CFA charterholders. Wellington plans to register for the Level 3 CFA exam next year. Wellington's reference to his status as a CFA candidate in presentation materials:
    A. does not violate any CFA Institute Standards of Professional Conduct.
    B. violates Standard VII(A) Conduct as a CFA Institute Member or CFA Candidate.
    C. violates Standard VII(B) Reference to the CFA Institute, the CFA Designation, and the CFA Program.

3.   Which of the following statements relating to the Global Investment Performance Standards (GIPS®) is *least accurate*?
     A. Only investment management firms may claim compliance with GIPS.
     B. GIPS represent standards to which members of CFA Institute and CFA candidates must adhere.
     C. To claim GIPS compliance, a firm must present at least five years (or since its inception if less than five years) of annual investment performance that complies with GIPS.

4.   Ed Michaels, CFA, is a compliance officer with oversight responsibilities for traders at Gaslight Broker-Dealer. Upon accepting the compliance officer position two years ago, Michaels wrote compliance procedures and made all covered employees aware of the procedures. He has recently been informed by an external auditor that, on several occasions over the past two years, two different employees have been trading in recommended securities ahead of trades made in managed client accounts. Michaels fires both employees in accordance with their employment agreements and recirculates the written compliance procedures that explain clearly which activities are prohibited. Michaels has violated:
     A. Standard IV(A) Loyalty by firing the employees instead of restricting their activities.
     B. Standard I(D) Misconduct because he was associated with the unethical activity.
     C. Standard IV(C) Responsibilities of Supervisors by failing to implement reasonable procedures to detect violations.

5.   Mitch Sherwood, CFA, is a portfolio manager for Oak Investments, a large hedge fund. He is considering leaving his current position and starting his own firm. Sherwood will need to make some preparations for his new business venture while he is still employed in his current position, including setting up offices, phones, and a web site. In addition, Sherwood is considering taking on client portfolios to manage on his own time to begin establishing his own investment track record. According to Standard IV(A) Loyalty (to employer), Sherwood:
     A. is prohibited from taking on the clients and from making preparations for his new business venture while still employed, without permission from Oak Investments.
     B. must disclose to and obtain Oak Investments' consent to take on the clients, but doesn't need to do either regarding the preparations to begin his own business.
     C. must disclose to Oak Investments the types of services to be performed, the duration of services, and the compensation to be received as a result of the consulting.

6. Patricia Nelson, CFA, was informed by one of her clients that if Nelson could get the performance of the client firm's pension portfolio above that of the Standard & Poor's average by year end, the client would give her a free trip to Singapore to visit the firm's offices. If Nelson agrees to this arrangement, which of the following actions complies with CFA Institute Standards of Professional Conduct? Nelson:
   A. must inform her employer orally of this agreement but does not need consent.
   B. may inform her employer by e-mail of this agreement and must receive written consent.
   C. may inform her employer orally of this agreement but must receive written consent.

7. John Anderson's company is participating in an acquisition. To speed up the process, his manager gives him a report from another company's analyst, also working on the project, and tells Anderson to put it on company letterhead and distribute the report by the end of the day. If Anderson, who is a CFA Institute member, complies, which of the following CFA Institute Standards of Professional Conduct will he have violated?
   A. Standard I(C) Misrepresentation.
   B. Standard II(A) Material Nonpublic Information.
   C. Standard V(B) Communication with Clients and Prospective Clients.

8. Roger Smith, CFA, has been invited to join a group of analysts in touring the riverboats of River Casino Corp. For the tour, River Casino has arranged chartered flights from casino to casino since commercial flight schedules are inconvenient and not practical for the group's time schedule. River Casino has also arranged to pay the hotel bill for the three nights of the tour. The trip is purely business. According to CFA Institute Standards of Professional Conduct, Smith:
   A. may accept the arrangements as they are.
   B. may accept the flight but must pay his own hotel bill.
   C. must offer to pay for his share of the airfare and his own hotel bill.

9. Samuel Parkin, a principal of Argor Advisers, is in charge of preparing the firm's performance history in accordance with GIPS. Parkin is careful to include every portfolio managed into a composite for reporting. At the end of each year, he assigns each portfolio to a single composite. He calculates the total return on each portfolio and averages them to calculate the composite performance for the year. With respect to his assignment of portfolios to composites and his calculation of composite total returns, has Parkin violated the requirements of GIPS?
   A. Both of these actions violate GIPS.
   B. Neither of these actions violates GIPS.
   C. Only one of these actions violates GIPS.

10. Susan Smart, CFA, is about to change her "buy" recommendation on RollinsCo to "sell." RollinsCo had been growing rapidly over the past year, but Smart believes the growth potential is now gone. Smart sells the shares held in her discretionary client accounts and in her own personal account before issuing her report. According to Standard III(B) Fair Dealing and Standard VI(B) Priority of Transactions, Smart violated:
    A. both of these Standards.
    B. neither of these Standards.
    C. only one of these Standards.

11. Matt Jacobs, CFA, is an investment adviser to several university endowment funds. Jacobs previously recommended to a client that he buy shares in Timeco. The shares have underperformed the market this year, and the client has spoken with Jacobs about closing out the position. Jacobs firmly believes Timeco is still a worthy investment and that the client should not sell. Since the stock is thinly traded, Jacobs buys 1,000 Timeco shares in his personal account in order boost the company's share price, with the intent of reversing the trade a few days later. After making the purchase, the share price rises, allowing Jacobs to convince his client to hold on to his Timeco shares. Has Jacobs violated Standard II(B) Market Manipulation?
    A. No, because he made the trades for the benefit of his client.
    B. Yes, because he intended to interfere with the market price of Timeco.
    C. Yes, because he failed to consider the stock's current price in relation to its true value.

12. William Rex, CFA, distributes materials referencing his performance results since he is the only portfolio manager at the firm he has founded. In the presentation, Rex includes five years of investment performance, four of which were with a previous employer. The presentation does not make a distinction between the first four years and the most recent year of performance. Also included in the presentation are simulated results of a stock selection model Rex has recently developed and tested. The fact that the results are simulated is disclosed in the presentation. Has Rex violated any CFA Institute Standards of Professional Conduct?
    A. No.
    B. Yes, failing to disclose that four years of his performance results were with another employer is a violation, but including the simulated results is acceptable.
    C. Yes, both failing to disclose that four years of his performance results were with another employer and including the simulated results are violations.

13. Tony Roberts, CFA, is a portfolio manager at Delta Securities. He suspects a colleague, who is not a member or candidate, of ongoing activities that, while not illegal under local law, violate CFA Institute Standards of Professional Conduct. Roberts and the colleague both report to the same managing director at Delta and are both currently being considered for a promotion to senior portfolio manager. According to the CFA Institute Standards of Professional Conduct, Roberts *least likely:*
    A. is required to dissociate from the activities that violate the Code and Standards if they continue.
    B. is governed by the Code and Standards and not local law in this situation.
    C. must report the suspected violations of the Code and Standards first to his supervisor and then to CFA Institute.

14. Judy Blush is a CFA candidate and is recommending the purchase of a mutual fund that invests solely in long-term U.S. Treasury bonds (T-bonds) to one of her clients. She states that, "Since the U.S. government guarantees payment of both the bond's principal and interest, risk of loss with this investment is virtually zero." Blush's actions violated:
    A. Standard I(C) Misrepresentation.
    B. Standard V(B) Communication with Clients and Prospective Clients.
    C. none of the CFA Institute Standards of Professional Conduct.

15. Which of the following actions is *least likely* a violation of Standard VII(A) Conduct as Members and Candidates in the CFA Program?
    A. A member anonymously posts a disparaging comment about CFA Institute policies on an internet message board.
    B. A member fails to disclose a formal complaint from a client on her annual Professional Conduct Statement.
    C. A candidate discusses specific questions from the June Level 1 CFA exam with a candidate for the December exam.

16. Lilly Marlow is an elderly widow with a moderate risk tolerance who depends on her investment portfolio to meet her living expenses. Marcus Pate, CFA, has been her investment adviser for years and has always managed Marlow's account to her satisfaction. Pate has a lunch meeting with Marlow quarterly and has always used their discussions as a basis for selecting investments for her account, over which he has full discretion to set the investment strategies. Pate often invests in risky derivative strategies to increase the return on Marlow's account. As Marlow's son is reviewing her recent year-end statement, he is shocked to discover that Pate has invested a significant amount of the account's assets in currency derivatives. According to the CFA Institute Standards, Pate is:
    A. in violation of Standard III(C) Suitability.
    B. in violation of Standard V(B) Communication with Clients and Prospective Clients.
    C. not in violation of any standard because Marlow has been satisfied with the portfolio performance to date.

17. Byland Advisors is an investment management firm that has reported performance results since 2000 in compliance with the Country Version of GIPS (CVG) applicable to their country, where they operate exclusively. There are differences between that CVG and the current version of GIPS, which became effective January 1, 2006. Which of the following *best* describes the requirements for this firm to present a compliant presentation for 2006 and later?
    A. The firm must recalculate performance for 2001 through 2005 in accordance with GIPS, and report performance for 2006 and later in accordance with GIPS.
    B. The firm must recalculate all prior performance in accordance with GIPS, and report performance for 2006 and later in accordance with GIPS.
    C. The firm may report performance from 2000 to 2005 as it was calculated under the CVG, and report performance for 2006 and later in accordance with GIPS.

18. Byron Bell, CFA, is an investment manager for Sally Fillmore, president of the local branch of First Bank. Fillmore, in a conversation with Bell's trading assistant, mentions that she is considering moving her account to another investment manager and confides that she has been diagnosed with the early signs of Alzheimer's disease. The trading assistant relays the conversation to Bell. According to the CFA Institute Code and Standards, the trading assistant is:
    A. not in violation of any Standard.
    B. in violation of Standard III(E) Preservation of Confidentiality by disclosing confidential client information.
    C. in violation of Standard III(A) Loyalty, Prudence, and Care by putting her employer's interests before the client's.

The following 14 questions relate to Quantitative Methods. (21 minutes)

19.   A client is celebrating his 50th birthday today and wants to start saving for his anticipated retirement at age 65. He wants to be able to withdraw $20,000 from his savings account on his 66th birthday and each year for 19 more years after that.

   After extensive research, the client determines that he can invest his money in an account that offers 5% interest per year with quarterly compounding. He wants to make equal annual payments on each birthday into the account—the first payment on his 51st birthday and the last on his 65th birthday.

   In addition, the client's employer will contribute $2,000 to the account each year (beginning on the client's 51st birthday) as part of the company's profit-sharing plan (a total of 15 contributions).

   The amount the client must deposit personally into the account each year on his birthday to enable him to make the desired withdrawals at retirement is *closest* to:
   A. $9,375.
   B. $9,459.
   C. $11,400.

20.   A company reports its past six years' earnings growth at 10%, 14%, 12%, 10%, –10%, and 12%. The company's average compound annual growth rate of earnings is *closest* to:
   A. 7.7%.
   B. 8.0%.
   C. 8.5%.

21.   The following table summarizes the results of a poll (hypothetically) taken of CFA charterholders and CFA candidates regarding the importance of a continuing education requirement after the CFA designation is obtained:

Group	In Favor of a Continuing Education Requirement	Against a Continuing Education Requirement
CFA charterholders	235	765
CFA candidates	180	820

   Given the information that a member of the group is in favor of a continuing education requirement, what is the probability that she is a CFA candidate?
   A. 37%.
   B. 43%.
   C. 50%.

22. Which of the following statements *best* describes what causes the Barron's Confidence Index to decrease?
    A. Defensive stocks are outperforming growth stocks.
    B. Average bond yields are increasing relative to high-quality bond yields.
    C. High-quality bond yields are increasing relative to average bond yields.

23. Which of the following statements about common probability distributions is *least likely* correct?
    A. A probability distribution specifies the probabilities of the possible outcomes of a random variable.
    B. In a binomial probability distribution, each observation has only two possible outcomes that are mutually exclusive.
    C. A normal distribution is a discrete symmetric probability distribution that is completely described by two parameters: its mean and variance.

24. For a binomial random variable with a 40% probability of success on each trial, the expected number of successes in 12 trials is *closest* to:
    A. 4.8.
    B. 5.6.
    C. 7.2.

25. Which of the following statements about the univariate, multivariate, and standard normal distributions is *least likely* correct?
    A. A univariate distribution describes a single random variable.
    B. A multivariate distribution specifies the probabilities for a group of related random variables.
    C. The standard normal random variable, denoted Z, has mean equal to one and variance equal to one.

26. An investor currently has $1.2 million and is considering investing in one of the three following portfolios:

Statistical Measures	Portfolio X	Portfolio Y	Portfolio Z
Expected annual return	12%	17%	22%
Standard deviation of return	14%	20%	25%

At the end of the year, the investor may need to take out $60,000 without invading the initial capital of $1.2 million. The optimal portfolio using Roy's safety-first criterion is:
    A. Portfolio X.
    B. Portfolio Y.
    C. Portfolio Z.

27. An analyst is testing the hypothesis that the variance of monthly returns for Index A equals the variance of monthly returns for Index B based on samples of 50 monthly observations. The sample variance of Index A returns is 0.085, whereas the sample variance of Index B returns is 0.084. Assuming the samples are independent and the returns are normally distributed, which of the following represents the *most appropriate* test statistic?

    A. $\dfrac{\text{sample variance of Index A}}{\text{sample variance of Index B}}$.

    B. $\dfrac{\text{variance of Index A} - \text{variance of Index B}}{\text{standard error of squared differences}}$.

    C. $\dfrac{(\text{degrees of freedom}) \times (\text{Index A sample variance})}{\text{Index B sample variance}}$.

28. An analyst plans to use the following test statistic: $t_{n-1} = \dfrac{\overline{x} - \mu_0}{s / \sqrt{n}}$.

    This test statistic is appropriate for a hypothesis about the:
    A. mean difference of two normal populations.
    B. population mean of a normal distribution with unknown variance.
    C. the equality of two population means of two normally distributed populations based on independent samples.

29. Alan Barnes, CFA, is interested in the expected quarterly return on FTSE 100 stock index. He has data for the last five years and calculates the average return on the index over the last 20 quarters. This average return:
    A. is different from the statistic he is trying to estimate by the amount of the sampling error.
    B. overstates the return because he should divide by the square root of 20 when using a mean value.
    C. overstates the expected return because he should have used the geometric mean and not the simple average.

30. Which of the following statements regarding the significance level of a hypothesis test is *most accurate*?
    A. Given a significance level of 5%, a test will reject a true null hypothesis 5% of the time.
    B. If the significance level of a test is 5%, it will yield the correct decision about the null hypothesis 95% of the time.
    C. If the significance level of a test is 95%, it will yield the correct decision about the null hypothesis 95% of the time.

31. A researcher needs to choose a probability distribution for the price of an asset that is quite volatile in order to simulate returns outcomes. She has a program that will generate random variables from any of a variety of distributions. The *most appropriate* distribution for her to select to generate the asset price distribution is a:
    A. normal distribution.
    B. lognormal distribution.
    C. binomial distribution.

32. An investor is interested in the following piece of property:
    - The property will cost $200,000 at time zero.
    - It will provide cash flows of $50,000 in year 1, $60,000 in year 2, $70,000 in year 3, and $80,000 in year 4.
    - A $20,000 investment will be required in year 5 as the property will have some environmental contamination and will have to be restored to its original condition.

    What is the NPV of the project if the investor's required rate of return is 10%?
    A. –$10,144.
    B. $14,693.
    C. $15,232.

The following 12 questions relate to Economics. (18 minutes)

33. If investors' expected future incomes increase and the demand for financial capital increases, other things equal, the:
    A. equilibrium interest rate will rise.
    B. equilibrium interest rate will fall.
    C. effects of the two changes on the equilibrium interest rate are opposite to each other.

34. Assume that the reserve requirement is 20%, and banks currently have no excess reserves. If the Federal Reserve then buys $100 million of Treasury bills from the banks, the money supply could potentially increase by:
    A. $20 million.
    B. $100 million.
    C. $500 million.

35. If a minimum wage is set above the equilibrium wage in the labor market, what is the *most likely* effect?
    A. The minimum wage will have no effect on the equilibrium quantity of labor.
    B. Firms will use less than the economically efficient amount of capital.
    C. There will be excess supply of labor, and unemployment will increase.

36. The firm's demand curve for labor is:
    A. identical to the supply curve of the output product.
    B. the mirror image of the supply curve of the output product.
    C. the downward sloping portion of the marginal revenue product of labor curve.

37. Which of the following is *least likely* an automatic stabilizer?
    A. Property taxes.
    B. Corporate profit taxes.
    C. Unemployment compensation.

38. If the government regulates a natural monopoly and enforces an average cost pricing, what are the effects on output quantity and price compared to an unregulated natural monopoly?
    A. Both are lower under average cost pricing.
    B. Both are higher under average cost pricing.
    C. One is higher and one is lower under average cost pricing.

39. The type of business organization that can survive the death of an owner and subjects its owners to unlimited liability is a:
    A. partnership.
    B. corporation.
    C. sole proprietorship.

40. Oligopolists have an incentive to cheat on collusive agreements in order to:
    A. avoid competitive practices.
    B. increase their individual share of the joint profit.
    C. restrict output and put upward pressure on price.

41. What long-run impact will higher rates of inflation have on real interest rates and on nominal interest rates?
    A. Both will increase in the long run.
    B. Neither will increase in the long run.
    C. Only one will increase in the long run.

42. Because copper producers are allowed to release harmful chemicals into the air, the industry supply curve is not the marginal social cost curve. Given this situation and a copper market that is otherwise competitive, copper producers will:
    A. produce less than the efficient amount of copper, resulting in a deadweight loss from underproduction.
    B. produce more than the efficient amount of copper, an example of the "free rider" problem.
    C. produce more than the efficient amount of copper, resulting in a deadweight loss from overproduction.

43. An individual sees her income rise from $80,000 to $88,000, and along with it, her consumption of Good X has decreased from eight dozen packages per year to six dozen packages per year. Good X should be classified as a(n):
    A. normal good.
    B. luxury good.
    C. inferior good.

44. The Keynesian view suggests that the government can diminish aggregate demand by using:
    A. restrictive fiscal policy to shift the government budget toward a surplus (or smaller deficit).
    B. restrictive fiscal policy to shift the government budget toward a deficit (or a smaller surplus).
    C. expansionary fiscal policy to shift the government budget toward a surplus (or a smaller deficit).

The following 24 questions relate to Financial Reporting and Analysis. (36 minutes)

45. Which of the following is *least likely* to be considered a barrier to developing one universally recognized set of reporting standards?
    A. Differences of opinion among various regulatory bodies.
    B. Reluctance of firms to adhere to a single set of reporting standards.
    C. Political pressure from stakeholders affected by reporting standards.

46. Which of the following items affects owners' equity but is not included as a component of net income?
    A. Depreciation.
    B. Dividends received on shares of another company classified as available for sale.
    C. Foreign currency translation gains and losses.

47. A company's financial statement data for the most recent year include the following:

• Net income	$100
• Depreciation expense	25
• Purchase of machine	50
• Sale of company trucks	30
• Sale of common stock	45
• Decrease in accounts receivable	10
• Increase in inventory	20
• Issuance of bonds	25
• Increase in accounts payable	15
• Increase in wages payable	10

    Based only on these items, cash flow from financing activities is *closest* to:
    A. $70.
    B. $85.
    C. $140.

48. A firm that rents DVDs to customers capitalizes the cost of newly released DVDs that it purchases and depreciates them over three years to a value of zero. Based on the underlying economics of the DVD rental business, the *most appropriate* method of depreciation for the firm to use on its financial statements is:
    A. straight-line.
    B. declining balance.
    C. units-of-production.

49. The item "minority interest" included as a component of equity represents the:
    A. firm's ownership of less than 50% of a subsidiary.
    B. portion of a subsidiary the firm does not own.
    C. firm's ownership of less than 30% of a subsidiary.

50. An analyst gathered the following information about a company:

• Cash flow from operations	$800
• Purchase of plant and equipment	40
• Sale of land	30
• Interest expense	80
• Depreciation and amortization	100
• The company has a tax rate of 35% and prepares its financial statements under U.S. GAAP.	

    The company's free cash flow to the firm (FCFF) is *closest* to:
    A. $840.
    B. $870.
    C. $940.

51. For which of the following balance sheet items is a change in market value *most likely* to affect net income?
    A. Debt securities issued by the firm.
    B. Debt securities that the firm intends to hold until maturity.
    C. Securities held with the intent to profit over the short term.

52. IFRS and U.S. GAAP are *most* similar in their requirements for:
    A. extraordinary items.
    B. discontinued operations.
    C. valuation of fixed assets.

53. A company using LIFO reports the following:
    - Cost of goods sold was $27,000.
    - Beginning inventory was $6,500, and ending inventory was $6,200.
    - The beginning LIFO reserve was $1,200.
    - The ending LIFO reserve was $1,400.

    The *best* estimate of the company's cost of goods sold on a FIFO basis would be:
    A. $21,300.
    B. $26,800.
    C. $27,500.

54. Which of the following items is *best* described as a listing of all the journal entries in order of their dates?
    A. Trial ledger.
    B. General ledger.
    C. General journal.

55. An analyst gathered the following data about a company:
    - 1,000,000 shares of common are outstanding at the beginning of the year.
    - 10,000 6% convertible bonds (conversion ratio is 20 to 1) were issued at par June 30 of this year.
    - The company has 100,000 warrants outstanding all year with an exercise price of $25 per share.
    - The average stock price for the period is $20, and the ending stock price is $30.

    If the convertible bonds are considered dilutive, the number of shares of common stock that the analyst should use to calculate diluted earnings per share is:
    A. 1,000,000.
    B. 1,100,000.
    C. 1,266,667.

56.   During periods of rising prices:
        A. LIFO COGS > Weighted Average COGS > FIFO COGS.
        B. LIFO COGS > Weighted Average COGS < FIFO COGS.
        C. LIFO COGS < Weighted Average COGS < FIFO COGS.

57.   Which of the following statements about the approaches for calculating earnings per share (EPS) in simple versus complex capital structure is *least* accurate?
        A. If convertible bonds are dilutive, the numerator in the diluted EPS calculation is increased by the interest expense on the bonds.
        B. If convertible preferred stock is dilutive, the convertible preferred dividends must be added back to the numerator to calculate diluted EPS.
        C. The denominator in the basic EPS equation contains the number of shares of common stock issued, weighted by the days that the shares have been outstanding.

58.   In periods of rising prices and stable or increasing inventory quantities, a company using last in, first out (LIFO) rather than first in, first out (FIFO) will report inventory turnover and net profit margin that are:

	Inventory turnover	Net profit margin
A.	Lower	Higher
B.	Lower	Lower
C.	Higher	Lower

59.   A junior analyst wants to understand the underlying components of the DuPont method to better see what changes are driving the changes in ROE. Which of the following items is a direct component of the original (three-part) DuPont equation?
        A. Asset turnover.
        B. Gross profit margin.
        C. Debt-to-equity ratio.

60.   Harding Corp. has a permanently impaired asset. The difference between its carrying value and the present value of its expected cash flows should be written down immediately and:
        A. reported as an operating loss.
        B. charged directly against retained earnings.
        C. reported as a non-operating loss as other comprehensive income.

61.   Two growing companies are identical except that Company X capitalized significant marketing costs in year 1, whereas Company Y expenses all marketing costs. For these two companies, which of the following statements about financial statement effects is *least* accurate? Company X will show:
   A. lower income variability over time and equal total cash flows compared to Company Y.
   B. lower debt-to-assets and debt-to-equity ratios and lower investing cash flows than Company Y.
   C. lower return on equity in year 1 and lower income variability over time than Company Y.

62.   Which of the following statements regarding deferred taxes is *least* accurate?
   A. A permanent difference is a difference between taxable income and pretax income that will not reverse.
   B. A deferred tax asset is created when a temporary difference results in taxable income that exceeds pretax income.
   C. Deferred tax assets and liabilities are not adjusted for changes in tax rates.

63.   A company has beginning gross investment of $400,000 and ending gross investment of $480,000 in a period when the depreciation expense was $25,000 and accumulated depreciation was $250,000. The average useful life of the company's assets is *closest* to:
   A. 10 years.
   B. 15 years.
   C. 20 years.

64.   At the end of its last fiscal year, Vintner's Supply Corp. reported retained earnings of $215,000. This year, Vintner's reported year-end retained earnings of $245,000 and net income of $20,000, paid dividends of $10,000, paid interest expense of $5,000, and received dividends of $5,000. Vintner's other comprehensive income for this year is *closest* to:
   A. $15,000.
   B. $20,000.
   C. $25,000.

65.   Which of the following statements regarding leasing is *least* accurate?
   A. Under an operating lease, the lessee treats the entire lease payment as a reduction to cash from operations.
   B. The lessee's current ratio is unaffected by the classification of a lease as an operating or a finance lease.
   C. Under a sales-type lease, the lessor recognizes gross profit equal to the present value of minimum lease payments minus the cost of the leased asset.

66. Of the following methods of examining the uncertainty of financial outcomes around point estimates, which answers hypothetical questions about the effect of changes in a single variable and which uses assumed probability distributions for key variables?

Hypothetical questions	Probability distributions
A. Sensitivity analysis	Simulation
B. Scenario analysis	Simulation
C. Scenario analysis	Sensitivity analysis

67. Information about a company's financial position at a point in time is *most likely* found in the:
    A. balance sheet.
    B. income statement.
    C. cash flow statement.

68. Which of the following is *least likely* a type of off-balance-sheet financing?
    A. Sale of receivables with recourse.
    B. Issuance of debt with warrants to finance expansion.
    C. Use of take-or-pay agreements to ensure the long-term availability of raw materials and other inputs necessary for operations.

The following 10 questions relate to Corporate Finance. (15 minutes)

69. The following information applies to a corporation:
    • The company has $200 million in equity and $100 million in debt.
    • The company recently issued bonds at 9%.
    • The corporate tax rate is 30%.
    • The company's beta is 1.125.

    If the risk-free rate is 6% and the expected return on the market portfolio is 14%, the company's after-tax weighted average cost of capital is *closest* to:
    A. 10.5%.
    B. 11.2%.
    C. 12.1%.

70. An analyst gathered the following information about a capital budgeting project:
    • The proposed project cost $10,000.
    • The project is expected to increase pre-tax net income and cash flow by $3,000 in each of the next eight years.
    • The company has 50% of its capital in equity at a cost of 12%.
    • The pretax cost of debt capital is 6%.
    • The company's tax rate is 33%.

    The project's net present value is *closest* to:
    A. $1,551.
    B. $6,604.
    C. $7,240.

71. In order to properly protect shareholders' long-term interests, the *most appropriate* characteristic for a board is that:
    A. the board meets regularly with management present.
    B. the majority of board members are not firm executives.
    C. board members represent firm suppliers, customers, and/or pension advisers.

72. The amount of a company's optimal capital budget is *most accurately* determined by the point on the company's investment opportunity schedule:
    A. where the amount of new capital raised is at its minimum.
    B. where it intersects the company's marginal cost of capital curve.
    C. where the expected return on the next potential project is at its maximum.

73. A company is *most likely* faced with a drag on liquidity if its:
    A. weighted average collection period increases from 42 days to 46 days.
    B. largest vendor changes its invoice terms from "3/10 net 30" to "3/10 net 60."
    C. inventory turnover was below the industry average last year and is above the industry average this year.

74. Grove Industries has a target capital structure of 30% debt, 40% common equity, and 30% preferred equity, and its marginal tax rate is 34%. Grove has $1.6 million of retained earnings available for investment, and its investment bankers have stated that they can sell up to $1.5 million in new bonds at a YTM of 8.3% but will have to increase the yield to 9% to issue new bonds in excess of that amount. Grove's marginal cost of capital schedule will reflect an increase in its WACC at a total amount of investment of:
    A. $1.6 million.
    B. $3.0 million.
    C. $5.0 million.

75. Faye Harlan, CFA, is estimating the cost of common equity for Cyrene Corporation. She prepares the following data for Cyrene:
    - Price per share = $50.
    - Expected dividend per share = $3.
    - Expected retention ratio = 30%.
    - Expected return on equity = 20%.
    - Beta = 0.89.
    - Yield to maturity on outstanding debt = 10%.
    - The expected market rate of return is 12% and the risk-free rate is 3%.

    Based on these data, Harlan determines that Cyrene's cost of common equity is 14%. Harlan *most likely* arrived at this estimate by using the:
    A. dividend discount model approach.
    B. capital asset pricing model approach.
    C. bond yield plus risk premium approach.

©2009 Kaplan, Inc.

76. Quixote Co. and Sisyphus Co., two similar-sized competitors, have had stable operating cycles of 180 days and cash conversion cycles of 140 days over the past several years. Sisyphus' operating and cash conversion cycles remained at these levels in the most recent year, but Quixote's cash conversion cycle contracted to 120 days while its operating cycle remained at 180 days. Relative to Sisyphus, Quixote has *most likely* begun:
    A. taking more time to pay its suppliers.
    B. operating with less inventory on hand.
    C. offering easier credit terms to its customers.

77. A company prepares a chart with the net present value (NPV) profiles for two mutually exclusive projects with equal lives of five years. Project Jones and Project Smith have the same initial cash outflow and total undiscounted cash inflows, but 75% of the cash inflows for Project Jones occur in years 1 and 2, while 75% of the cash inflows for Project Smith occur in years 4 and 5. Which of the following statements is *most accurate* regarding these projects?
    A. Project Smith has a higher internal rate of return than Project Jones.
    B. There is a range of discount rates in which the optimal decision is to reject both projects.
    C. There is a range of discount rates in which the company should choose Project Jones and a range in which it should choose Project Smith.

78. There are several important requisite skills a qualified board member should possess. Many qualities are critical. Which of the following is a sign of a well-qualified board member?
    A. Major supplier to the firm.
    B. Has other board experience.
    C. Does not have a significant stock position.

The following 6 questions relate to Portfolio Management. (9 minutes)

79. An analyst gathers the following information about three stocks.

	Stock X	Stock Y	Stock Z
Estimated return	8.0%	18.0%	22.5%
Beta	0.6	1.2	1.8

    The analyst estimates that the risk-free rate is 5%, and the return on the market portfolio is 12%. Based on the above inputs and the capital asset pricing model (CAPM), the analyst is *least likely* to recommend buying:
    A. Stock X.
    B. Stock Y.
    C. Stock Z.

80.   An investment policy statement is important to the portfolio management process because it:
       A. forces the investor and adviser to articulate the investment strategy they will employ.
       B. creates a record of the benchmark against which performance will be judged.
       C. provides a clear understanding of the level of risk a client is willing to accept.

81.   The investment objective of earning a return on an investment that is at least equal to the inflation rate is called:
       A. total return.
       B. current income.
       C. capital preservation.

82.   Davis Samuel, CFA, is meeting with one of his portfolio management clients, Joseph Pope, to discuss Pope's investment constraints. Samuel has established that:
       • Pope plans to retire from his job as a bond salesman in 17 years, after which this portfolio will be his primary source of income.
       • Pope has sufficient cash available that he will not need this portfolio to generate cash outflows until he retires.
       • Pope, as a registered securities representative, is required to have Samuel send a copy of his account statements to the compliance officer at Pope's employer.
       • Pope opposes certain policies of the government of Lower Pannonia and does not wish to own any securities of companies that do business with its regime.

       To complete his assessment of Pope's investment constraints, Samuel still needs to inquire about Pope's:
       A. tax concerns.
       B. liquidity needs.
       C. unique needs and preferences.

83.   When a risk-free asset is combined with a portfolio of risky assets, which of the following is *least accurate*?
       A. The standard deviation of the return for the newly created portfolio is the standard deviation of the returns of the risky asset portfolio multiplied by its portfolio weight.
       B. The expected return for the newly created portfolio is the weighted average of the return on the risk-free asset and the expected return on the risky asset portfolio.
       C. The variance of the resulting portfolio is a weighted average of the returns variances of the risk-free asset and of the portfolio of risky assets.

84. Which of the following is *most likely* to result in a capital market line (CML) that is kinked?
    A. Taxes are added to the model.
    B. Borrowing rate exceeds the lending rate.
    C. Positive transaction costs are added to the model.

The following 12 questions relate to Equity Investments. (18 minutes)

85. Characteristics of a well-functioning market are *least likely* to include:
    A. prices that adjust quickly to new information.
    B. small changes in price from one transaction to the next.
    C. complete information about supply and demand conditions.

86. To ensure the continuity of a value-weighted index when one of the stocks in the index is split:
    A. no adjustment is necessary.
    B. only the denominator must be adjusted for the split.
    C. both the numerator and the denominator must be adjusted for the split.

87. Robert Higgins is estimating the price-earnings (P/E) ratio that will be appropriate for an index at the end of next year. He has estimated that:
    • Expected annual dividends will increase by 10% compared to this year.
    • Expected earnings per share will increase by 10% compared to this year.
    • The expected growth rate of dividends will be the same as the current estimate of 5%.
    • The required rate of return will rise from 8% to 11%.

    Compared to the current P/E, the end-of-the-year P/E will be:
    A. 50% lower.
    B. 2% higher.
    C. 10% higher.

88. An analyst gathered the following data about a stock:
    • The stock paid a $1 dividend last year.
    • Next year's dividend is projected to be 10% higher.
    • The stock is projected to sell for $25 at the end of the year.
    • The risk-free rate of interest is 8%.
    • The expected return on the market is 13%.
    • The stock's beta is 1.2.

    The value of the stock today is *closest* to:
    A. $19.45.
    B. $22.89.
    C. $26.74.

89. The strong form of the efficient market hypothesis (EMH) states that:
    A. stock prices fully reflect all market information, and that investors cannot achieve excess returns using technical analysis.
    B. security prices already include all market and nonmarket public information, and event studies can be used to test this form of the EMH.
    C. stock prices already reflect all information from public and private sources, and professional money managers are not able to outperform a buy-and-hold strategy on average.

90. Which of the following statements regarding the role of arbitrageurs in correcting pricing anomalies is *least accurate*?
    A. Arbitrageurs can be restricted by limits on trading and position sizes placed by those who provide capital.
    B. Even if arbitrageurs correctly identify a pricing anomaly, they face the risk that mispricings might persist or increase.
    C. Because the funds available to arbitrageurs are virtually unlimited, arbitrage trading tends to correct all but the smallest pricing errors.

91. A firm has a constant growth rate of 7% and just paid a dividend of $6.25. If the required rate of return is 12%, what will the stock sell for two years from now based on the dividend discount model?
    A. $133.75.
    B. $149.80.
    C. $153.13.

92. Which of the following statements about the tests used to examine different forms of the Efficient Market Hypothesis (EMH) is *least accurate*?
    A. Statistical and trading rule tests generally support the weak form of the EMH.
    B. The superior historical performance of exchange specialists and corporate insiders is inconsistent with the semi-strong form of the EMH.
    C. Event studies on stock splits and announcements of accounting changes are tests of the semi-strong form of the EMH.

93. Which of the following statements about measures of relative value is *least likely* correct?
    A. Companies with low price/book value (P/BV) ratios tend to outperform high P/BV ratio firms on a risk-adjusted basis.
    B. P/BV and price/cash flow (P/CF) ratios should be used in conjunction with price/earnings (P/E) ratios in fundamental analysis.
    C. A major benefit to relative valuation methods such as P/BV and price/sales (P/S) is the ability to utilize them in comparing firms from different industries.

94. Assume the Wansch Corporation is expected to pay a dividend of $2.25 per share this year. Sales and profit for Wansch are forecasted to grow at a rate of 20% for two years after that, then grow at 5% per year forever. Dividend and sales growth are expected to be equal. If Wansch's shareholders require a 15% return, the per-share value of Wansch's common stock based on the dividend discount model is *closest* to:
    A. $22.75.
    B. $26.00.
    C. $28.50.

95. Assuming all other factors remain unchanged, a company's earnings multiplier would decrease as a result of an increase in the:
    A. dividend growth rate.
    B. dividend payout ratio.
    C. required rate of return.

96. The sustainable dividend growth rate is estimated as the:
    A. retention ratio × return on equity.
    B. retention ratio × return on assets.
    C. dividend payout ratio × return on equity.

The following 14 questions relate to Fixed Income. (21 minutes)

97. Compared to the underlying MBS, a collateralized mortgage obligation (CMO):
    A. has lower duration.
    B. may have more or less prepayment risk.
    C. allows an investor to select an exact maturity.

98. An analyst collects the following spot rates, stated as annual BEYs:
    - 6-month spot rate = 6%.
    - 12-month spot rate = 6.5%.
    - 18-month spot rate = 7%.
    - 24-month spot rate = 7.5%.

    Given only this information, the price of a 2-year, semiannual-pay, 10% coupon bond with a face value of $1,000 is *closest* to:
    A. $918.30.
    B. $1,000.00.
    C. $1,046.77.

99. A bond has an effective duration of 7.5. If the bond yield changes by 100 basis points, the price of the bond will change by:
    A. exactly 0.75%.
    B. approximately 7.5%.
    C. approximately 0.75%.

100. Which of the following *best* describes the motivation for a corporation to issue an asset-backed security? Securitization of specific assets by a corporation enables the corporation to:
   A. improve the recovery rate in the event of default.
   B. use the assets as collateral for additional borrowing.
   C. get a credit rating on the ABS that will result in a lower cost of borrowing.

101. An analyst is considering two bonds: Bond A yields 7.5%, and Bond B yields 7.0%. Using Bond B as the reference bond, the yield ratio for Bond A is *closest* to:
   A. 0.93.
   B. 1.07.
   C. 7.14.

102. In contrast to the full valuation approach to measuring interest rate risk, the duration/convexity approach:
   A. accounts for the curvature of the price-yield relation.
   B. provides a more accurate assessment of interest rate risk.
   C. simplifies the process of estimating the value impact of changes in yield.

103. An analyst collects the following information regarding spot rates of interest:
   • 1-year rate = 4%.
   • 2-year rate = 5%.
   • 3-year rate = 6%.
   • 4-year rate = 7%.

   Utilizing the pure expectations theory of the term structure of interest rates, the expected annualized 2-year interest rate two years from today is *closest* to:
   A. 7.02%.
   B. 8.03%.
   C. 9.04%.

104. A $1,000 par value, 10% semiannual, 20-year debenture is currently selling for $1,100. The bond's current yield is:
   A. 8.9%.
   B. 9.1%.
   C. 10.0%.

105. An analyst is comparing two bonds and has collected the following data:
- Bond A: Nominal spread of 125 basis points, zero-volatility spread of 125 basis points, and option-adjusted spread of 65 basis points.
- Bond B: Nominal spread of 95 basis points, zero-volatility spread of 95 basis points, and option-adjusted spread of 95 basis points.

Each bond is similar in all respects except that Bond A is a mortgage passthrough security and Bond B is a noncallable corporate bond. Based only on this information, which of the following statements is *most accurate*?
A. The yield curve is flat.
B. Bond A is preferred to Bond B because its nominal spread is 30 basis points higher.
C. Bond A is preferred to Bond B because the embedded option in Bond A returns the investor an additional 65 basis points.

106. Which of the following is *least likely* allowed if a bond is non-refundable? A corporation:
A. refunds bonds by issuing preferred stock.
B. calls its nonrefundable bonds and issues common equity in their place.
C. issues zero coupon bonds at a yield that is lower than the current rate on their bonds and redeems the old bond issue.

107. CureAll General Hospital has been forced to file for bankruptcy protection. The company managing the hospital has been allowed to reorganize under the name United Hospital of Hope. The courts have specified that a new indenture should be written to accompany a planned new bond issue. The issue would have ten years to maturity and carry a 10% coupon that would be paid annually. The new agreement would relieve the company of the obligation to make interest payments during the first five years after the bond is issued. For the remaining five years, regular interest payments would resume. Finally, at maturity, the principal ($1,000) plus the interest that was not paid during the first five years would be paid. However, no additional interest would be payable on the deferred interest. If the bond's YTM is 10%, its value is *closest* to:
A. $778.
B. $814.
C. $856.

108   Which of the following statements regarding the term structure of interest rates is *least accurate*?
   A. Forward interest rates are the best estimates of future short-term interest rates under the pure expectations theory.
   B. The observed yield curve likely contains elements of liquidity preference, market segmentation, and expectations theories.
   C. Under the market segmentation theory, a flat yield curve is likely to become positively sloped if the demand for long-term bonds exceeds supply and if the supply of short-term bonds exceeds demand.

109.   A floating-rate security is *most likely* to trade at a discount to its par value because the:
   A. next reset date is in three months.
   B. security's yield premium for credit risk decreases.
   C. floating rate includes a margin over LIBOR to compensate for the issue's liquidity risk.

110.   The price value of a basis point (PVBP) for a bond is *most accurately* described as:
   A. the product of a bond's value and its duration.
   B. the change in the price of the bond when its yield changes by 0.01%.
   C. an estimate of the curvature of the price-yield relationship for a small change in yield.

The following 6 questions relate to Derivatives. (9 minutes)

111.   Which of the following statements about interest rate swaps and currency swaps is *least likely* correct?
   A. A plain-vanilla interest rate swap involves trading fixed interest rate payments for floating-rate payments.
   B. A fixed-for-floating currency swap involves trading floating-rate interest payments on one currency for fixed-rate interest payments on another currency.
   C. In a currency swap, the net difference between the notional principal amounts is exchanged at the beginning and termination of the swap. Full interest rate payments are exchanged on each settlement date.

112.   An investor with a variable-rate loan who wants to protect herself from an increase in interest rates without sacrificing potential gains from an interest rate decrease should purchase:
   A. a bond call option.
   B. an interest rate cap.
   C. an interest rate cap and sell an interest rate floor.

113. An investor has a call option on a stock that is currently selling for $35. The call option is in the money by $3. The call option's strike price is:
    A. $32.
    B. $35.
    C. $38.

114. An investor is short a portfolio of stocks that has volatility and return characteristics similar to that of the S&P 500. Which of the following strategies would *best* hedge the market risk of the short portfolio position?
    A. Buy a put option on the S&P 500.
    B. Write a call option on the S&P 500.
    C. Write a put option and buy a call option on the S&P 500.

115. A put on a stock with a strike price of $50 is priced at $4 per share, while a call with a strike price of $50 is priced at $6. What is the maximum per share loss to the writer of the put?
    A. $46.
    B. $50.
    C. Unlimited.

116. A major bank has entered into a 4-year, annual-pay, 6% plain-vanilla interest rate swap with a notional principal value of $10,000,000 as the fixed-rate payer. The following spot and forward rates are observed and expected:
    - 1-year LIBOR today = 5%.
    - Expected 1-year LIBOR in one year = 6%.
    - Expected 1-year LIBOR in two years = 7%.

    Based solely on this information, the expected net payment in 24 months (for the fixed-rate payer) will be:
    A. $100,000 inflow.
    B. $0.
    C. $100,000 outflow.

The following 4 questions relate to Alternative Investments. (6 minutes)

117. Supplying capital to companies that are just moving into operation, but do not as yet have a product or service available to sell, is a description that best relates to which of the following stages of venture capital investing?
    A. Seed stage.
    B. Second stage.
    C. Early stage.

118. An apartment complex would earn $2 million annually if fully occupied. The complex has a 10% vacancy rate and annual operating expenses of $200,000 a year. The interest costs of financing the purchase of the building would be $150,000 a year. The investor's marginal tax rate is 40%. The investor wants to earn 10% on this investment. Using the income approach, the value the investor would place on the office building would be *closest* to:
    A. $8,700,000.
    B. $14,500,000.
    C. $16,000,000.

119. The creation and redemption of "in-kind" shares by authorized participants is a feature that's unique to which of the following types of securities?
    A. Hedge funds.
    B. Closed-end funds.
    C. Exchange-traded funds.

120. Which of the following is *least accurate* regarding the cost approach to valuing real estate?
    A. The approach may be problematic because obtaining a land appraisal may not be straightforward.
    B. The approach is reliable since there is generally a negligible difference between construction cost and market value of an existing property.
    C. It is similar to using the replacement cost of total assets in equity valuation.

Exam 2
Afternoon Session

Calculating Your Score

Topic	Maximum Score	Your Score
Ethical and Professional Standards	18	
Quantitative Methods	14	
Economics	12	
Financial Reporting and Analysis	24	
Corporate Finance	10	
Portfolio Management	6	
Equity Investments	12	
Fixed Income	14	
Derivatives	6	
Alternative Investments	4	
Total	120	

The morning and afternoon exams are identically weighted over the topics and readings. You can therefore treat the morning and afternoon exams as independent exams.

If you took more than three hours (180 minutes) to complete this portion of the exam, you should adjust your score downward by one point for each minute you ran over.

Remember: the real exam *will be more difficult* than these practice exams. The main reason for this is the general anxiety and stress that you will be feeling on exam day, coupled with the time pressure you will be under. Many of the questions on this practice exam and the real exam are not individually difficult, so if you take extra time to answer the questions on this practice exam, your score will go up significantly. However, if you want an accurate measure of your potential performance on the exam, adhere to the 3-hour time limit.

After you have finished grading your practice exam, you may find it useful to use the exam questions and recommended solutions for review. Many of these questions were specifically written for your use as study tools. Once again, I feel I should remind you not to rely on memorizing these questions; you are not likely to see them on the actual exam. What you will see on the exam, though, are the concepts, terms, and procedures presented in these questions.

Your actual exam will most likely look different than what you see in this book. Please remember, no study provider knows the content of the actual exam. These practice exams are our best guess as to the structure, content, and difficulty of an actual exam.

Test Answers

1.	(A)	(B)	(C)		41.	(A)	(B)	(C)		81.	(A)	(B)	(C)
2.	(A)	(B)	(C)		42.	(A)	(B)	(C)		82.	(A)	(B)	(C)
3.	(A)	(B)	(C)		43.	(A)	(B)	(C)		83.	(A)	(B)	(C)
4.	(A)	(B)	(C)		44.	(A)	(B)	(C)		84.	(A)	(B)	(C)
5.	(A)	(B)	(C)		45.	(A)	(B)	(C)		85.	(A)	(B)	(C)
6.	(A)	(B)	(C)		46.	(A)	(B)	(C)		86.	(A)	(B)	(C)
7.	(A)	(B)	(C)		47.	(A)	(B)	(C)		87.	(A)	(B)	(C)
8.	(A)	(B)	(C)		48.	(A)	(B)	(C)		88.	(A)	(B)	(C)
9.	(A)	(B)	(C)		49.	(A)	(B)	(C)		89.	(A)	(B)	(C)
10.	(A)	(B)	(C)		50.	(A)	(B)	(C)		90.	(A)	(B)	(C)
11.	(A)	(B)	(C)		51.	(A)	(B)	(C)		91.	(A)	(B)	(C)
12.	(A)	(B)	(C)		52.	(A)	(B)	(C)		92.	(A)	(B)	(C)
13.	(A)	(B)	(C)		53.	(A)	(B)	(C)		93.	(A)	(B)	(C)
14.	(A)	(B)	(C)		54.	(A)	(B)	(C)		94.	(A)	(B)	(C)
15.	(A)	(B)	(C)		55.	(A)	(B)	(C)		95.	(A)	(B)	(C)
16.	(A)	(B)	(C)		56.	(A)	(B)	(C)		96.	(A)	(B)	(C)
17.	(A)	(B)	(C)		57.	(A)	(B)	(C)		97.	(A)	(B)	(C)
18.	(A)	(B)	(C)		58.	(A)	(B)	(C)		98.	(A)	(B)	(C)
19.	(A)	(B)	(C)		59.	(A)	(B)	(C)		99.	(A)	(B)	(C)
20.	(A)	(B)	(C)		60.	(A)	(B)	(C)		100.	(A)	(B)	(C)
21.	(A)	(B)	(C)		61.	(A)	(B)	(C)		101.	(A)	(B)	(C)
22.	(A)	(B)	(C)		62.	(A)	(B)	(C)		102.	(A)	(B)	(C)
23.	(A)	(B)	(C)		63.	(A)	(B)	(C)		103.	(A)	(B)	(C)
24.	(A)	(B)	(C)		64.	(A)	(B)	(C)		104.	(A)	(B)	(C)
25.	(A)	(B)	(C)		65.	(A)	(B)	(C)		105.	(A)	(B)	(C)
26.	(A)	(B)	(C)		66.	(A)	(B)	(C)		106.	(A)	(B)	(C)
27.	(A)	(B)	(C)		67.	(A)	(B)	(C)		107.	(A)	(B)	(C)
28.	(A)	(B)	(C)		68.	(A)	(B)	(C)		108.	(A)	(B)	(C)
29.	(A)	(B)	(C)		69.	(A)	(B)	(C)		109.	(A)	(B)	(C)
30.	(A)	(B)	(C)		70.	(A)	(B)	(C)		110.	(A)	(B)	(C)
31.	(A)	(B)	(C)		71.	(A)	(B)	(C)		111.	(A)	(B)	(C)
32.	(A)	(B)	(C)		72.	(A)	(B)	(C)		112.	(A)	(B)	(C)
33.	(A)	(B)	(C)		73.	(A)	(B)	(C)		113.	(A)	(B)	(C)
34.	(A)	(B)	(C)		74.	(A)	(B)	(C)		114.	(A)	(B)	(C)
35.	(A)	(B)	(C)		75.	(A)	(B)	(C)		115.	(A)	(B)	(C)
36.	(A)	(B)	(C)		76.	(A)	(B)	(C)		116.	(A)	(B)	(C)
37.	(A)	(B)	(C)		77.	(A)	(B)	(C)		117.	(A)	(B)	(C)
38.	(A)	(B)	(C)		78.	(A)	(B)	(C)		118.	(A)	(B)	(C)
39.	(A)	(B)	(C)		79.	(A)	(B)	(C)		119.	(A)	(B)	(C)
40.	(A)	(B)	(C)		80.	(A)	(B)	(C)		120.	(A)	(B)	(C)

EXAM 2
AFTERNOON SESSION

The following 18 questions relate to Ethical and Professional Standards.
(27 minutes)

1. Courtney Johnson, CFA, is an investment advisor in independent practice and provides investment services for equity securities. Johnson refers clients seeking fixed-income investments to the fixed-income department at Reliable Securities. Reliable Securities, in turn, provides Johnson with equity research. Johnson has not informed her clients of the arrangement with Reliable. Johnson's clients often praise her for obtaining such quality research and for referring them to Reliable for fixed-income investments that have consistently performed well. Has Johnson violated any CFA Institute Standards of Professional Conduct?
    A. Yes, because the soft dollars generated by the arrangement don't benefit all the clients.
    B. No, because Johnson recommended high-quality fixed income managers.
    C. Yes, because her clients are unable to evaluate any partiality inherent in Johnson's recommendation of Reliable's services.

2. Russell Finley, CFA, is a managing director at Wilson Brothers, a regional brokerage firm. Finley manages the institutional fixed-income desk and is responsible for 20 employees in both the trading and sales departments. Finley recently called a meeting with the head of trading and the head of sales to review the firm's policies regarding trading by employees in their personal accounts. He instructed the two to review the information with the employees they supervise. A week after the meeting, Finley discovered that a sales assistant made personal trades during a firm "blackout" period on a restricted security. According to the Standards of Professional Conduct, Standard IV(C) Responsibilities of Supervisors, the *least appropriate* action for Finley to take is to:
    A. speak directly to the employee and attain assurance that the violation will not be repeated.
    B. begin an investigation to determine the extent of the wrongdoing.
    C. increase the monitoring of the employee's activities at the firm.

3. Charlotte Stein, a CFA candidate, obtained a copy of a computerized stock selection model designed by a former MBA classmate who is a Wall Street analyst. After spending some time reviewing the program and making some adjustments, Stein showed the new model to her supervisor. Her supervisor said she did a great job and told Stein to incorporate the new model in her next industry review. She called her old classmate for permission, and he told her to go ahead and use the model, which she did without reference to its origin. Stein has:
   A. violated Standard I(C) Misrepresentation.
   B. violated Standard V(B) Communication with Clients and Prospective Clients.
   C. not violated CFA Institute Standards of Professional Conduct.

4. Justin Matthews, CFA, is the CFO of a regional bank and serves on the bank's investment committee. The investment committee is considering the appropriate actions to take with regard to the bank's temporary surplus of cash. The committee, composed of analysts and investment personnel, recommends to the bank's CEO that the cash be invested in intermediate-term Treasury notes. Matthews feels that the recommendation is too conservative. However, Matthews is the only member of the independent committee who disagrees with the recommendation. In accordance with CFA Institute Standard of Professional Conduct, Matthews should, *most* appropriately:
   A. decline to be associated with the recommendation.
   B. privately express his concerns to his supervisor.
   C. document his difference of opinion with the committee.

5. Howard Klein, CFA, supervises a group of research analysts, none of whom is a CFA charterholder or CFA candidate. He has attempted on several occasions to get his firm to adopt a compliance system to ensure that applicable laws and regulations are followed. The firm's principals, however, have never adopted his recommendations. According to CFA Institute Standards of Professional Conduct, Klein at this point:
   A. should decline in writing to accept supervisory responsibility until his firm adopts reasonable compliance procedures.
   B. needs to take no action because the employees are not CFA charterholders or CFA candidates.
   C. must resign from the company and document in writing his reasons for doing so.

6.   Lisa Crocker, CFA, manages several pension accounts and directs most of her trades through the Zeta Brokerage House. Crocker does this because she believes she gets expedient and low-cost trade execution, and Zeta provides her with excellent research reports used in the management of these accounts. Regional, a small discount brokerage house, has just approached Crocker and said it will execute her trades at half of Zeta's cost. However, Regional does not have a research department. If Crocker declines to switch her business to Regional, has she violated any CFA Institute Standards of Professional Conduct?
     A. Yes, because she has not obtained explicit permission from her clients to use Zeta.
     B. No, if the higher commissions are commensurate with the value of the research services she receives.
     C. Yes, because Standard III(A) Loyalty, Prudence, and Care states that she must minimize trade expenses.

7.   Katrina Anderson, CFA, is an investment advisor for Ringfellow Investments, an institutional investment manager with $5 billion in assets under management. Prior to joining Ringfellow, Anderson was in a similar position with a boutique firm that had $500 million in assets under management. Anderson left her previous employer on good terms, did not sign a non-compete agreement, and took no firm materials with her. According to CFA Institute Standards of Professional Conduct, Anderson:
     A. must seek permission from her previous employer before contacting her previous clients at that firm.
     B. may contact clients of her previous firm immediately after ending her employment there.
     C. should not contact clients from her previous employment at all because it would harm her previous employer.

8.   Richard Chambers, CFA, is a registered representative for Global Brokers. Chambers, who was a leading revenue producer in the firm's New York office, moved last week to the firm's new Botwari office to establish a revenue source in Asia. To develop a strong client base, Chambers follows firm practices and takes advantage of a local law allowing brokers to pay prospective clients as an inducement to gain their personal business. Chambers sometimes pays local accountants significant sums for referring wealthy clients to him as well, and he discloses this to the clients. Has Chambers violated CFA Institute Standards of Professional Conduct?
     A. No, Chambers has not violated the Code and Standards.
     B. Yes, Chambers is violating U.S. law, which puts him in violation of Standard I(D) Misconduct.
     C. Yes, Chambers has violated Standard VI(C) Referral Fees.

9. Isabelle Burns, CFA, is an investment advisor for a firm whose client base is composed of high net worth individuals. In her personal portfolio, Burns has an investment in Torex, a company that has developed software to speed up internet browsing. Burns has thoroughly researched Torex and believes the company is financially strong yet currently significantly undervalued. According to the CFA Institute Standards of Professional Conduct, Burns may:

   A. not recommend Torex as long as she has a personal investment in the stock.
   B. recommend Torex to a client, but she must disclose her investment in Torex to the client.
   C. recommend Torex to a client without disclosure as long as it is a suitable investment for the client.

10. Christopher Kim, CFA, is a research analyst for Batts Brothers, an investment banking firm in New York. Kim follows the energy industry and has frequent contact with industry executives. A CEO of a large oil and gas corporation that has previously employed Batts Brothers to underwrite a stock issue has invited Kim to his office to discuss a secondary offering of the company's stock. The CEO wants Batts Brothers to underwrite the stock issue. As an incentive to place the issue quickly with institutional investors, the CEO offers Kim the opportunity to fly on his private jet to his ranch in Texas for an exotic game hunting expedition if Kim's firm can complete the underwriting within one month. According to CFA Institute Standards of Conduct, Kim:

    A. must not accept such lavish benefits, in order to maintain his objectivity.
    B. must obtain written consent from Batts Brothers before accepting the invitation.
    C. may accept the invitation without consent only if he discloses the trip to Batts Brothers before accepting.

11. When GIPS and local laws conflict, in order to be in compliance with GIPS, the investment firm must:

    A. follow local law but disclose the conflict with GIPS.
    B. follow local law, and no additional disclosure is required.
    C. follow GIPS but disclose that this is in conflict with local laws.

12. Kim Vance, a CFA candidate, tells a prospective client, "I may not have a long-term track record, but I am sure you will be satisfied with my performance. Over the three years I have been in the business, my equity-oriented clients have averaged a total return of more than 20% a year." The statement is accurate, but Vance only has a few equity clients, and one of these took a large position in a penny stock (against Vance's advice) and realized a huge gain. This large return caused the average of all of Vance's clients to exceed 20% per year. Without this one investment, the average gain would have been 10% per year. Has Vance violated CFA Institute Standards of Professional Conduct?

A. Yes, because the statement misrepresents Vance's track record.

B. No, because it is true and Vance has not assured such returns in the future.

C. Yes, because the equities composite she mentions does not qualify as a composite.

13. Joseph Drake, CFA, is a portfolio manager for Best Investments. The fixed-income desk at Best has developed a new structured product that produces positive returns in a very wide range of interest rate scenarios. Drake thoroughly reads and evaluates an analytical report about the product and is impressed by its return profile. He faxes the cover page of the analysis, which includes the name of the author, to a client with objectives similar to those that the structured product is designed to meet, and handwrites a note to the client saying, "I think you should act quickly on this!" When the client calls requesting the entire report, Drake informs him that the research is proprietary and cannot be released. With respect to Standard V(B) Communication with Clients and Prospective Clients and Standard III(C) Suitability, Drake is in violation of:

A. both of these Standards.

B. neither of these Standards.

C. only one of these Standards.

14. Brian Farley, CFA, is an independent portfolio manager. Currently, Farley's only client is a $75 million university endowment fund. A representative of the endowment fund calls Farley and places a "Sell" order on a portfolio holding whose management has just issued a negative earnings forecast. Farley also owns the security in his retirement account and immediately decides to sell his position. He places simultaneous "Sell" orders for both the client and his personal account. According to Standard III(B) Fair Dealing and Standard VI(B) Priority of Transactions, Farley is in violation of:

A. both of these Standards.

B. neither of these Standards.

C. only one of these Standards.

15. Franklin Murphy is a trader and CFA Level 3 candidate who works for Wellington & Worrel Advisers. When selecting brokers for client trades, Murphy usually selects between Casanova Broker-Dealer (where he receives discounts on personal securities transactions) and Cedrock Brokers (where he receives investment research used in managing client portfolios). Both Casanova and Cedrock charge higher commission rates than other brokers used by Wellington & Worrel, and Cedrock provides more efficient trade execution than other brokers. According to Standard III(A) Loyalty, Prudence, and Care, Murphy violates the Standard by directing trades to:
    A. Casanova and Cedrock.
    B. Cedrock but not Casanova.
    C. Casanova but not Cedrock.

16. Art Dodd, CFA, is a registered representative with Owens Securities. He is currently in a dispute with one client, Madge Phillips, CFP, about a limit order for her IRA account that she feels was entered incorrectly, resulting in a loss (in her opinion) of $500. Dodd has been allocated 1,000 shares of a new issue that is oversubscribed. He suggests to Phillips that he will give her 250 shares of his allocation if she forgets about the supposed trade error. Further, he offers to buy her dinner at a very nice restaurant that serves an excellent salmon Kulebyaka, which he suggests they pair with a nice 1997 white Cheval-Blanc Signé. According to the Standards of Practice, Dodd has *most likely* violated:
    A. Standard I(D) Misconduct.
    B. Standard III(B) Fair Dealing.
    C. Standard IV(B) Additional Compensation Arrangements.

17. Which of the following is *least likely* one of the eight major topics of the CFA Institute Global Investment Performance Standards (GIPS)?
    A. Real Estate.
    B. Private Equity.
    C. Venture Capital.

18.   Graham Carson has served as investment advisor to Ron Grayson, a
      wealthy philanthropist, for one year. Grayson has called a meeting with
      Carson to discuss his disappointment with two of the portfolio stocks
      Carson had chosen last year. Grayson feels that, in both cases, the
      individual securities possessed greater risk than he had agreed to in the
      investment policy statement. Carson reviews his notes and files pertaining
      to the account and sees that, according to his analysis at the time of
      the recommendations, the portfolio he recommended to Grayson was
      consistent with the risk and return objectives as well as the constraints of
      Grayson's portfolio as detailed in Grayson's most recent investment policy
      statement (IPS). The individual securities, however, were each quite risky
      and appeared even more so now, since they had performed so poorly.
      According to Standard III(C) Suitability and Standard V(A) Diligence and
      Reasonable Basis, Carson is in violation of:
      A. both of these Standards.
      B. neither of these Standards.
      C. only one of these Standards.

The following 14 questions relate to Quantitative Methods. (21 minutes)

19.   Five years ago, an investor borrowed $5,000 from a financial institution
      that charged a 6% annual interest rate, and he immediately took his family
      to live in Nepal. He made no payments during the time he was away.
      When he returned, he agreed to repay the original loan plus the accrued
      interest by making five end-of-year payments starting one year after he
      returned. If the interest rate on the loan is held constant at 6% per year,
      what annual payment must the investor make in order to retire the loan?
      A. $1,338.23.
      B. $1,588.45.
      C. $1,638.23.

20.   If an investment of $4,000 will grow to $6,520 in four years with monthly
      compounding, the effective annual interest rate will be *closest* to:
      A. 11.2%.
      B. 12.3%.
      C. 13.0%.

21. An analyst constructs a histogram and frequency polygon of monthly returns for aggressive equity funds over a 20-year period. Which of the following statements about these displays is *most accurate*?
    A. The height of each bar in a frequency polygon represents the absolute frequency for each return interval.
    B. Both a histogram and a frequency polygon provide a graphical display of data found in a frequency distribution.
    C. To construct a histogram, the analyst would plot the midpoint of the return intervals on the x-axis and the absolute frequency for that interval on the y-axis, connecting neighboring points with a straight line.

22. An investor holds a portfolio consisting of one share of each of the following stocks:

Stock	Price at the Beginning of the Year	Price at the End of the Year	Cash Dividend During the Year
X	$20	$10	$0
Y	$40	$50	$2
Z	$100	$105	$4

For the 1-year holding period, the portfolio return is *closest* to:
    A. 6.9%.
    B. 9.1%.
    C. 13.1%.

23. An analyst takes a sample of yearly returns of aggressive growth funds resulting in the following data set: 25, 15, 35, 45, and 55. The mean absolute deviation (MAD) of the data set is *closest* to:
    A. 12.
    B. 16.
    C. 20.

24. A security has annual returns of 5%, 10%, and 15%. The coefficient of variation of the security (using the population standard deviation) is *closest* to:
    A. 0.3.
    B. 0.4.
    C. 0.5.

25. If an analyst concludes that the distribution of a large sample of returns is positively skewed, which of the following relationships involving the mean, median, and mode is *most likely*?
    A. Mean > median > mode.
    B. Mean < median < mode.
    C. Mean > median < mode.

26. An analyst has been hired to evaluate a high-risk project. The analyst estimates the probability that the project will fail in the first year as well as the conditional probability of failure for each of the remaining four years of the project, as follows:

Year	1	2	3	4	5
Failure probability	0.25	0.20	0.20	0.15	0.10

The project will have no payoff if it fails, but it will have a payoff of $20,000 at the end of the fifth year if it succeeds. Because of its high risk, the required rate of return for an investment in this project is 25%. Based on this information, the expected present value of the project is *closest* to:
A. $2,400.
B. $3,010.
C. $5,900.

27. An investor opens an account by purchasing 1,000 shares of stock at $42 per share. One year later, these shares are trading at $55 per share, and the investor purchases 1,000 more shares. At the end of the second year, the shares are trading at $54. The time-weighted rate of return on the account is *closest* to:
A. 7.7%.
B. 13.4%.
C. 16.4%.

28. Which of the following distributions is *most likely* a discrete distribution?
A. A normal distribution.
B. A univariate distribution.
C. A binomial distribution.

29. An investment has a mean return of 15% and a standard deviation of returns equal to 10%. If the distribution of returns is approximately normal, which of the following statements is *least likely* correct? The probability of obtaining a return:
A. less than 5% is about 16%.
B. greater than 35% is about 2.5%.
C. between 5% and 25% is about 95%.

30. Which of the following statements about the central limit theorem is *least likely* correct?
A. The central limit theorem has limited usefulness for skewed distributions.
B. The mean of the population and the mean of all possible sample means are equal.
C. When the sample size is large, the sampling distribution of the sample means is approximately normal.

31. An analyst takes a random sample of the returns on 225 stocks from a population with a known variance of returns of 100. The standard error of the sample mean return is *closest* to:
    A. 0.44.
    B. 0.67.
    C. 2.26.

32. Which of the following statements about hypothesis testing involving a *z*-statistic is *least accurate*?
    A. The *p*-value is the smallest significance level at which the null hypothesis can be rejected.
    B. A *z*-test is theoretically acceptable in place of a *t*-test for tests concerning a mean when sample size is small.
    C. If the confidence level is set at 95%, the chance of rejecting the null hypothesis when in fact it is true is 5%.

The following 12 questions relate to Economics. (18 minutes)

33. According to the crowding-out effect, the sale of government bonds used to finance excess government spending is *least likely* to:
    A. increase the real interest rate.
    B. reduce private investment spending.
    C. increase the profitability of corporate investment projects.

34. If currency held is 5% of deposits, a reserve requirement of 20% implies a money multiplier *closest* to:
    A. 4.0.
    B. 4.2.
    C. 5.0.

35. External benefits lead to an inefficient allocation of resources because:
    A. there is an over-allocation of resources to the producers creating the external benefit.
    B. the demand curve does not represent the marginal benefit to society of the good or service.
    C. the equilibrium quantity produced and consumed will be greater than the efficient quantity.

36. Technically, an individual is unemployed when he is actively seeking employment or is:
    A. a retiree.
    B. a discouraged worker.
    C. waiting to return to a job from which he was just laid off.

37. The long-run production decision differs from the short-run production decision in that:
    A. fixed costs can be changed in the long run but not the short run.
    B. variable costs can be changed in the long run but not the short run.
    C. variable costs can be changed in the short run but not the long run.

38. Which of the following statements about elasticity of demand is *least likely* correct?
    A. If the cross elasticity of demand is negative, the goods are complements.
    B. In the short run, if the price of gasoline increases, consumption of gasoline will decrease by a smaller percentage.
    C. In the short run, if the price of a brand of flour increases, consumption of that brand of flour will decrease by a smaller percentage.

39. Which of the following statements about a monopolist is *least accurate*?
    A. The monopolist faces a downward sloping demand curve.
    B. Unlike an oligopolist, a monopolist will always be able to earn economic profit.
    C. A profit-maximizing monopolist will expand output until marginal revenue equals marginal cost.

40. A market has the following characteristics: a large number of independent sellers, each producing a differentiated product; low barriers to entry; producers facing downward sloping demand curves; and demand that is highly elastic. This description *most* closely describes:
    A. an oligopoly.
    B. pure competition.
    C. monopolistic competition.

41. Regarding the cost-push and demand-pull inflation processes, which requires repeated expansionary actions by policymakers?
    A. Both require repeated expansionary actions.
    B. Neither requires repeated expansionary actions.
    C. Only one requires repeated expansionary actions.

42. Accounting profit is often an unsatisfactory performance measure from an economic point of view because it:
    A. does not consider depreciation.
    B. considers marginal costs rather than average costs.
    C. does not consider the opportunity costs of equity capital.

43. The Taylor rule for monetary policy:
    A. emphasizes price level stability at every stage of the business cycle.
    B. uses the growth rate of the monetary base as its primary policy variable.
    C. attempts to reduce differences between real GDP and potential real GDP.

44. The *most likely* effects of the imposition of an effective increase in the minimum wage include:
    A. an increase in the real wage, gains in efficiency, and a decrease in inflation.
    B. increased unemployment, an excess supply of labor at the new wage rate, and a decrease in economic efficiency.
    C. a reduction in non-monetary labor benefits, excess demand for labor, and a shortage of highly skilled workers.

The following 24 questions relate to Financial Reporting and Analysis. (36 minutes)

45. Normal Corp. has a current ratio above 1 and a quick ratio less than 1. Which of the following actions will increase the current ratio and decrease the quick ratio? Normal Corp.:
    A. buys fixed assets on credit.
    B. uses cash to purchase inventory.
    C. pays off accounts payable from cash.

46. A company has a cash conversion cycle of 70 days. If the company's payables turnover decreases from 11 to 10 and days of sales outstanding increase by 5, the company's cash conversion cycle will:
    A. decrease by approximately 8 days.
    B. decrease by approximately 3 days.
    C. increase by approximately 2 days.

47. The IASB states that the role of financial reporting is "to provide information about the financial position (and) performance…that is useful to a wide range of users." Which of the following financial statements would *best* provide information about a firm's "performance," as used here?
    A. Balance sheet.
    B. Income statement.
    C. Cash flow statement.

48. Which of the following is *least likely* to be considered an objective of financial market regulation according to the International Organization of Securities Commissions (IOSCO)?
    A. Reduce systemic risk.
    B. Ensure the fairness, efficiency, and transparency of markets.
    C. Develop individual financial regulatory standards for each country to reflect the unique needs of each market.

49.   Napa Corp. sells 1-year memberships to its Fine Wine Club for $180.
        Wine Club members each receive a bottle of white wine and a bottle of red
        wine, selected by the club director, four times each year at the beginning
        of each quarter. To properly account for sales of Wine Club memberships,
        Napa will record:
        A. an asset for prepaid sales.
        B. a liability for accrued expenses.
        C. a liability for unearned revenue.

50.   An analyst gathered the following data about a company:
        •   Net sales $4,000
        •   Dividends declared   170
        •   Cost of goods sold   2,000
        •   Inventory increased by   100
        •   Accounts payable increased by   300
        •   Cash expenses for other inputs   500
        •   Long-term debt principal repayment   250
        •   Cash tax payments   200
        •   Purchase of new equipment   300

        The company's cash flow from operations, based on these data only, is:
        A. $1,200.
        B. $1,500.
        C. $1,575.

51.   Jennifer Frye, CFA, is comparing the financial performance of a firm that
        presents its results under IFRS to that of a firm that complies with U.S.
        GAAP. The U.S. firm uses the LIFO method for inventory accounting,
        and the other firm uses the FIFO method. If Frye performs the appropriate
        adjustments to make the U.S. firm's financial statements comparable to the
        firm that reports under IFRS, her adjustments are *least likely* to change the
        firm's:
        A. quick ratio.
        B. debt-to-equity ratio.
        C. cash conversion cycle.

52.   Two growing firms are identical except that Alfred Company capitalizes
        costs for some long-lived assets that Canute Company expenses. For
        these two firms, which of the following financial statement effects is *most
        likely*? Alfred will show:
        A. greater investing cash flow than Canute.
        B. greater solvency ratios than Canute.
        C. less volatile return on assets than Canute.

53.   The following data pertains to a company's common-size financial
        statements.
        - Current assets   40%
        - Total debt   40%
        - Net income   16%
        - Total assets $2,000
        - Sales $1,500
        - Total asset turnover ratio   0.75
        - The firm has no preferred stock in its capital structure.

        The company's after-tax return on common equity is *closest* to:
        A. 15%.
        B. 20%.
        C. 25%.

54.   Which of the following statements about the calculation of earnings per
        share (EPS) is *least accurate*?
        A. Shares issued after a stock split must be adjusted for the split.
        B. Options outstanding may have no effect on diluted EPS.
        C. Reacquired shares are excluded from the computation from the date of
           reacquisition.

55.   A company has 1,000,000 warrants outstanding at the beginning of the
        year, each convertible into one share of stock with an exercise price of
        $50. No new warrants were issued during the year. The average stock
        price during the period was $60, and the year-end stock price was $45.
        What adjustment for these warrants should be made, under the treasury
        stock method, to the number of shares used to calculate diluted earnings
        per share (EPS)?
        A. 0.
        B. 166,667.
        C. 200,000.

56.   Which of the following statements about financial ratios is *most accurate*?
        A. A company with a high debt-to-equity ratio will have a return on
           asssets that is greater than its return on equity.
        B. Any firm with a high net profit margin will have a high gross profit
           margin and vice versa.
        C. A company that has an inventory turnover of 6 times, a receivables
           turnover of 9 times, and a payables turnover of 12 times will have a
           cash conversion cycle of approximately 71 days.

57.   In periods of rising prices and stable or increasing inventory quantities,
        FIFO inventory accounting, compared to the LIFO method, is *most likely*
        to result in:
        A. lower net income and lower taxes paid.
        B. higher working capital and lower cost of goods sold.
        C. higher cost of goods sold and lower inventory value.

58. During an accounting period, a company has the following sequence of transactions with a beginning inventory of zero:

Purchases	Sales
100 units at $210	80 units at $240
90 units at $225	90 units at $250

The company's cost of goods sold (COGS) using FIFO for inventory accounting, and its ending inventory using LIFO, are *closest* to:

	FIFO COGS	LIFO ending inventory
A.	$36,750	$4,200
B.	$37,050	$4,200
C.	$37,050	$4,500

59. On January 2, a company acquires some state-of-the-art production equipment at a net cost of $14 million. For financial reporting purposes, the firm will depreciate the equipment over a 7-year life using straight-line depreciation and a zero salvage value; for tax reporting purposes, however, the firm will use 3-year accelerated depreciation. Given a tax rate of 35% and a first-year accelerated depreciation factor of 0.333, by how much will the company's deferred tax liability increase in the first year of the equipment's life?
   A. $931,700.
   B. $1,064,800.
   C. $1,730,300.

60. Patch Grove Nursery uses the LIFO inventory accounting method. Maria Huff, president, wants to determine the financial statement impact of changing to the FIFO accounting method. Selected company information follows:
   - Year-end inventory $22,000
   - Year-end LIFO reserve $4,000
   - Beginning of year LIFO reserve $3,000
   - LIFO cost of goods sold $18,000
   - After-tax income $2,000
   - Tax rate 40%

Under FIFO, the nursery's ending inventory and after-tax profit for the year would have been:

	FIFO ending inventory	FIFO after-tax profit
A.	$18,000	$2,600
B.	$26,000	$1,400
C.	$26,000	$2,600

61. Which of the following statements about capitalizing and expensing the cost of a long-lived asset is *least accurate*?
    A. A company that capitalizes the cost will have lower debt-to-asset and debt-to-equity ratios than a company that expenses the cost.
    B. A company that expenses the cost will show the same total cash flows as the capitalizing firm, but will show higher profitability early in the asset's life.
    C. In the early years of the asset's life, a company that expenses the cost will have lower profitability ratios, such as return on assets and return on equity, than a company that capitalizes the cost.

62. Maritza Inc. is involved in an exchange of debt for equity. In which of the following sections of the cash flow statement would Maritza record this transaction?
    A. Investing activities section.
    B. Financing activities section.
    C. Footnotes to the cash flow statement.

63. A company using straight-line depreciation has an ending gross investment in fixed assets of $750, an accumulated depreciation of $300, and an annual depreciation expense of $150. The average depreciable life of the fixed assets and the average age of the plant and equipment are *closest* to:

	Depreciable life	Avg. age of P&E
A.	2 years	7 years
B.	5 years	2 years
C.	7 years	5 years

64. Analysts reviewing Amber, Inc.'s and Bold, Inc.'s long-term contracting activities observe that Amber's contracts are being accounted for under the percentage-of-completion method while Bold's are being accounted for under the completed contract method. This difference is *least likely* to affect the two companies':
    A. income statements.
    B. statements of cash flows.
    C. assets on the balance sheets.

65. Which of the following statements regarding an audit and a standard auditor's opinion is *most accurate*?
    A. The objective of an audit is to enable the auditor to provide an opinion on the numerical accuracy of the financial statements.
    B. To provide an independent review of a company's financial statements, an independent certified public accounting firm is appointed by the company's management.
    C. The absence of an explanatory paragraph in the audit report relating to the going concern assumption suggests that there are no serious problems that require a close examination of that assumption by the analyst.

66. A firm issues discount bonds during a period of increasing interest rates. From an analyst's perspective, this firm's statement of cash flows will *most likely*:
    A. understate cash flows from financing over the bond's life.
    B. understate cash flows from operations over the bond's life.
    C. not require adjustments to operating, investing, or financing cash flows.

67. A company has a long-term "take or pay" commitment with its major supplier. When calculating the company's financial ratios, a financial analyst should:
    A. add the present value of the minimum future commitment to the company's debt only.
    B. add the present value of the minimum future commitment to both the company's debt and assets.
    C. subtract the present value of the minimum future commitment from the company's debt and assets.

68. Which of the following statements about the treatment of leases on the lessor's financial statements is *least accurate*?
    A. If the present value of the payments on a finance lease is greater than the carrying value of the asset, the lease is a sales-type lease on the books of the lessor.
    B. In a direct financing lease, the lessor recognizes gross profit at the lease inception, while in a sales-type lease it does not.
    C. To be a finance lease for the lessor, collectibility must be reasonably certain and the lessor must have substantially completed performance.

The following 10 questions relate to Corporate Finance. (15 minutes)

69. A company's outstanding 20-year, annual-pay 6% coupon bonds are selling for $894. At a tax rate of 40%, the company's after-tax cost of debt capital is *closest* to:
    A. 4.2%.
    B. 5.1%.
    C. 7.0%.

70. Weights to be used in calculating a company's weighted average cost of capital are *least appropriately* based on:
    A. information from the company about its target capital structure.
    B. the average capital structure weights for companies of a similar size.
    C. the average capital structure weights for companies in the same industry.

71. An accounts receivable aging schedule is *best* used to:
    A. determine how the receivables turnover ratio has changed over time.
    B. identify trends in how well the firm is doing at collecting receivables and converting them to cash.
    C. compare a company's receivables management to those of the average for its industry or for a group of peer companies.

72. Managers of Smith Corporation are reviewing a section of the firm's code of ethics that relates to Board members. Vice president Susan Klepp argues, "Drawing upon the expertise of our Board members by hiring them as consultants is in the shareholders' best interests. However, personal use of company assets by Board members should be limited to those instances that align the incentives of the Board members with those of the firm." With respect to the provisions that should be included in a strong corporate code of ethics, Klepp is:
    A. correct about both provisions.
    B. correct about only one of these provisions.
    C. incorrect about both provisions.

73. An ice hockey club is considering the purchase of an ice resurfacing machine for $25,000. Using the machine would save the club $5,000 per year in labor costs, after taxes. The machine's useful life is estimated at ten years with no salvage value. If the club's cost of capital is 12%, the club:
    A. should buy the machine.
    B. should not buy the machine.
    C. will be no better or worse off with the machine.

74. Ron's Organic Markets has limited access to borrowed funds and must choose among ten independent projects with returns greater than their cost of capital. All the projects under consideration have the same required investment of $2 million, and Ron's has $10 million available for capital investments this year. Which of the following selection criteria is *least likely* to identify the five projects that will produce the greatest expected increase in the value of the firm? Choose the five projects with:
    A. the highest IRRs.
    B. the greatest total NPV.
    C. the largest sum of profitability indexes.

75. Randox Industries has the following investment policy statement: "In order to achieve the safety and liquidity necessary in the investment of excess cash balances, the CFO or his designee may invest excess cash balances in 30-day U.S. Treasury bills, or in banker's acceptances with maturities of less than 31 days or 30-day certificates of deposit, where the credit rating of the issuing bank is A+ or higher." This policy statement is:
    A. inappropriate because it is too restrictive.
    B. appropriate because these are all safe, liquid securities.
    C. inappropriate because both banker's acceptances and certificates of deposit are illiquid.

76.   Which of the following is *least* relevant in determining project cash flow
       for a capital investment?
       A. Sunk costs.
       B. Tax impacts.
       C. Opportunity costs.

77.   From a liquidity management perspective, an increase in the number of
       days of payables is *best* described as:
       A. liquidity neutral.
       B. a drag on liquidity.
       C. a source of liquidity.

78.   Which of the following characteristics is *least likely* required to ensure
       that a company's Board of Directors Audit Committee is adequately
       representing shareowner interests?
       A. Any conflicts between the external auditor and the firm are resolved in
          a manner that favors shareholders.
       B. The shareholders vote on whether to approve of the Board's selection
          of the external auditor.
       C. The committee regularly reviews the performance, independence,
          skills, and experience of existing board members.

The following 6 questions relate to Portfolio Management. (9 minutes)

79.   From a theoretical perspective, even though the assumption that investors
       can borrow and lend at the same (risk-free) rate is violated, a straight-line
       capital market line can still be constructed if:
       A. investors are risk neutral.
       B. there are no transaction costs.
       C. a zero-beta portfolio exists and yields more than the risk-free rate.

80.   Which of the following is *least likely* among the usual investment
       constraints that should be considered?
       A. Legal and regulatory factors.
       B. Unique needs and preferences.
       C. Adherence to the Standards of Practice.

81. Given the following correlation matrix, a risk-averse investor would *least* prefer which of the following 2-stock portfolios (all else equal)?

Stock	W	X	Y	Z
W	+1			
X	−0.2	+1		
Y	+0.6	−0.1	+1	
Z	+0.8	−0.3	+0.5	+1

   A. W and Y.
   B. X and Y.
   C. X and Z.

82. Which type of risk is positively related to expected excess returns according to the CAPM?
   A. Unique.
   B. Systematic.
   C. Diversifiable.

83. Which of the following statements about the security market line (SML) and capital market line (CML) is *most accurate*?
   A. The SML involves the concept of a risk-free asset, but the CML does not.
   B. The SML uses beta, but the CML uses standard deviation as the risk measure.
   C. Both the SML and CML can be used to explain a stock's expected return.

84. The percentage of the variation in returns for a single portfolio that can be explained by differences in target asset allocations is *approximately*:
   A. 30%.
   B. 70%.
   C. 90%.

The following 12 questions relate to Equity Investments. (18 minutes)

85. An index is composed of three stocks. Their performance in a recent period is as follows:

Stock	Number of Shares Outstanding (Thousands)	Beginning Price	Ending Price	Percent Change
X	100	160	136	−15%
Y	100	80	100	+25%
Z	1,000	60	66	+10%

None of the stocks split during the period. This index will have the smallest percentage increase for the period if it is a(n):
A. value-weighted index.
B. price-weighted index.
C. unweighted index using the geometric mean.

86. M. Gomez has purchased 100 shares of each of the stocks in a price-weighted index and intends to reinvest cash dividends in additional shares. Assuming there are no stock splits, stock dividends, or changes in the makeup of the index, how will Gomez's portfolio return based on its initial value compare with that of the index? His portfolio:
A. will have higher returns than the index.
B. performance relative to the index will depend on how low-price stocks perform relative to high-price stocks.
C. may do better or worse than the index depending on whether the overall market goes up or down.

87. In the top-down valuation process, the analyst performs the following four actions:

1. Analyze the prospects for various industries.
2. Analyze the individual firms in the industries.
3. Pick the best stocks in the best industries under the economic forecast.
4. Examine the influence of the general economy on the securities markets.

In what order should the analyst perform these actions?
A. 1, 2, 3, 4.
B. 3, 2, 4, 1.
C. 4, 1, 2, 3.

88. Which form of the efficient markets hypothesis (EMH) implies that an investor can achieve positive abnormal returns on average by using technical analysis?
    A. None.
    B. Weak form.
    C. Weak form or semistrong form.

89. A stock has a steady 5% growth rate in dividends. The required rate of return for stocks of this risk class is 15%. The stock is expected to pay a $1 dividend this coming year. The expected value of the stock at the end of the fourth year is:
    A. $12.16.
    B. $14.21.
    C. $16.32.

90. Which of the following statements about financial market anomalies is *most accurate*?
    A. Restrictions on short sales can cause securities to remain undervalued by making arbitrage trades that would correct the mispricing unprofitable.
    B. Mispricings of small-company stocks can persist because arbitrage traders often cannot establish large enough positions to generate meaningful profits.
    C. A profitable arbitrage opportunity exists if an anomaly is persistent, is backed by sound theory, is not the result of measurement bias, and results in a strategy that generates positive abnormal returns that exceed the transactions costs.

91. If all other factors remain unchanged, which of the following would *most likely* reduce a company's price/earnings ratio?
    A. The dividend payout ratio increases, and the dividend growth rate increases.
    B. The dividend growth rate increases, and the required rate of return decreases.
    C. The required rate of return increases, and the dividend payout ratio decreases.

92. An analyst is asked to calculate the trailing P/E for AdMicro Systems (AMS) on November 15, 20X3, when the share price is $27.50. The company's fiscal year ended December 31, 20X2. Financial statements indicate that the earnings per share (EPS) for 20X2 were $1.27, which included a nonrecurring item amounting to $0.12 per share. As of October 31, 20X3, the trailing 12 months' EPS was $1.45 based on three quarters in 20X3 and one quarter in 20X2. When various nonrecurring and extraordinary items are taken into account, the adjusted EPS for the most recent 12 months is $1.10. Based on this information, the P/E estimate the analyst should use for AMS is *closest* to:
    A. 19.
    B. 22.
    C. 25.

93. An analyst wants to determine a country risk premium for use in estimating the required return for foreign equities. Which of the following risks would the analyst be *least likely* to include in the country risk premium?
    A. Default risk.
    B. Political risk.
    C. Liquidity risk.

94. A stop buy order is *most likely*:
    A. used to limit the potential losses on a short sale.
    B. executed if the market price is less than or equal to the specified level.
    C. an order to purchase a security if the price decreases to a specified level.

95. Beachballs, Inc., expects abnormally high earnings for the next three years due to the forecast of unusually hot summers. After the 3-year period, their growth will level off to its normal rate of 6%. Dividends and earnings are expected to grow at 20% for years 1 and 2 and 15% in year 3. The last dividend paid was $1.00. If an investor requires a 10% return on Beachballs, the price she is willing to pay for the stock is *closest* to:
    A. $26.00.
    B. $36.50.
    C. $50.00.

96. If stock markets are semistrong-form efficient, a portfolio manager is *least likely* to create value for investors by:
    A. monitoring clients' needs and circumstances.
    B. allocating invested funds among asset classes.
    C. analyzing financial statements to select undervalued stocks.

The following 14 questions relate to Fixed Income. (21 minutes)

97. Which of the following statements about how various embedded options benefit the issuers or the bondholders is *least accurate*?
    A. The accelerated sinking fund provision favors the issuers.
    B. The conversion provision favors the bondholders.
    C. The option-adjusted spread measures the spread, including the effect of the embedded option.

98. For an option-free bond, what are the effects of the convexity adjustment on the magnitude (absolute value) of the approximate bond price change in response to an increase in yield and to a decrease in yield?

	Decrease in yield	Increase in yield
A.	Increase in magnitude	Decrease in magnitude
B.	Increase in magnitude	Increase in magnitude
C.	Decrease in magnitude	Increase in magnitude

99. Which of the following statements about different types of bonds is *least likely* correct?
    A. Municipal bonds are traded primarily on the New York Stock Exchange.
    B. Tax-backed bonds are backed by the full faith and credit of the issuer.
    C. Government agency issues of federally related institutions are typically backed by the full faith and credit of the U.S. government.

100. A 10%, 10-year bond is sold to yield 8%. One year passes, and the yield remains unchanged at 8%. Holding all other factors constant, the bond's price during this period will have:
    A. increased.
    B. decreased.
    C. remained constant.

101. An investor purchases a $1,000 face, 4.50%, semiannual coupon bond with seven years to maturity priced to yield 6.50% for $888.94. The reinvestment income that must be generated over the life of the bond for the investor to realize a yield of 6.5% is *closest* to:
    A. $72.
    B. $76.
    C. $80.

102. Exactly one year ago, an investor purchased a $1,000 face value, zero-coupon bond with 11 years remaining to maturity. The YTM (semiannual) was 8.0%. Now, one year later, with market rates unchanged, an investor purchases an annuity that pays $40 every six months for 10 years. The combined value of the two investments based on the 8% semiannual yield is *approximately*:
    A. $966.
    B. $1,000.
    C. $1,456.

103. An analyst gathered the following information about a 15-year bond:
   - 10% semiannual coupon.
   - Effective duration of 7.6 years.

   If the market yield rises 75 basis points, the bond's approximate price change is a:
   A. 5.4% decrease.
   B. 5.4% increase.
   C. 5.7% decrease.

104. Which of the following relationships is *least accurate*?
   A. Premium bond: nominal yield > current yield; current yield > yield to maturity.
   B. Discount bond: coupon rate < yield to maturity; nominal yield < yield to maturity.
   C. Discount bond: current yield < yield to maturity; nominal yield > yield to maturity.

105. An investor most concerned with reinvestment risk would be *least likely* to:
   A. prefer a noncallable bond to a callable bond.
   B. prefer a lower coupon bond to a higher coupon bond.
   C. eliminate reinvestment risk by holding a coupon bond until maturity.

106. For an asset-backed security (ABS), a special purpose vehicle:
   A. sells an asset to the issuing corporation, which then proceeds to issue the ABS.
   B. is a legal entity used to separate assets used as collateral from those of the company seeking financing through an ABS.
   C. acts as an intermediary that purchases an asset from the company issuing an ABS and then resells it to obtain sufficient liquid funds to provide collateral for the ABS.

107. The following interest rate information is observed:

	Spot Rates
1 year	10%
2 years	11%
3 years	12%

   Based on this data, the 2-year forward rate one year from now is *closest* to:
   A. 12%.
   B. 13%.
   C. 14%.

108. Which of the following statements about theories of the yield curve is *most likely* correct?
    A. A liquidity preference is not consistent with a flat term structure of interest rates.
    B. The pure expectations theory suggests that an upward-sloping term structure of interest rates is a consequence of investors expecting short-term rates to remain unchanged for a period of time, followed by investors expecting short-term rates to rise for a period of time.
    C. The liquidity preference theory suggests that a downward-sloping term structure of interest rates is due to declining expected short-term rates, and although there is a maturity premium to consider, it is not large enough to offset the expected decline in short-term rates.

109. An analyst makes the following two statements about putable bonds:

    Statement 1: As yields rise, the price of putable bonds will fall more quickly than similar option-free bonds (beyond a critical point) due to the decline in value of the embedded put option.

    Statement 2: As yields fall, the price of putable bonds will rise more quickly than similar option-free bonds (beyond a critical point) due to the increase in value of the embedded put option.

    Are the analyst's statements correct?
    A. Both statements are correct.
    B. Neither statement is correct.
    C. Only one of the statements is correct.

110. An investor who is calculating the arbitrage-free value of a Treasury security should discount each cash flow using the:
    A. risk-free rate.
    B. Treasury spot rate that is specific to its maturity.
    C. Treasury note yield that is specific to its maturity.

The following 6 questions relate to Derivatives. (9 minutes)

111. The payoff to the long position in a forward rate agreement (FRA) can be duplicated by which of the following combinations of interest rate options?

	Interest rate call	Interest rate put
A.	Long	Long
B.	Long	Short
C.	Short	Long

112. Which of the following statements about equity forward contracts is *least likely* correct?
    A. The primary risk managed by equity forwards is the uncertainty about dividend yields.
    B. An asset manager can effectively lock in the price of a specific stock at a particular point in time if he can arrange for the sale of a forward contract on the stock through a reputable dealer.
    C. A pension fund manager who wants to sell a specific group of stocks in the future can accomplish this either by selling a forward contract on each of the stocks, or by selling a single forward contract on the portfolio of stocks she wants to sell.

113. An investor buys a stock for $40 per share and simultaneously sells a call option on the stock with an exercise price of $42 for a premium of $3 per share. Ignoring dividends and transaction costs, what is the maximum profit the writer of this covered call can earn at expiration?
    A. $2.
    B. $3.
    C. $5.

114. Which of the following derivatives positions is *least accurately* characterized as a legally binding obligation?
    A. Short position in an equity call option.
    B. Long position in an interest rate put option.
    C. Fixed-rate receiver position in an interest rate swap.

115. Which of the following statements about futures margins is *least likely* correct?
    A. The initial margin is set by the clearinghouse based on the volatility of the price of the underlying asset.
    B. If the balance of the margin account exceeds the initial margin requirement, the trader can remove the excess funds from the account.
    C. If the margin account balance falls below the maintenance margin level, the account balance must be brought back up to the maintenance level.

116. What are the minimum values of an American-style and a European-style 3-month call option with a strike price of $80 on a non-dividend-paying stock trading at $86 if the risk-free rate is 3%?

	American	European
A.	$6.00	$6.00
B.	$6.59	$6.00
C.	$6.59	$6.59

The following 4 questions relate to Alternative Investments. (6 minutes)

117.   The yield on a long-only commodity futures position that is dependent on whether the contract is in contango or backwardation is the:
A.   collateral yield.
B.   roll yield.
C.   contract yield.

118.   The term "mezzanine financing" is used to describe the financing that:
A.   provides capital preceding an initial public offering.
B.   represents capital provided to initiate commercial manufacturing.
C.   provides capital that supports product development and market research.

119.   Which of the following statements about valuation techniques for real estate is *least likely* correct?
A.   The cost approach to valuation is based on what it would cost to rebuild the property at today's prices.
B.   The sales comparison approach to valuation is based on the sales price of properties similar to the subject property.
C.   The income approach to valuation calculates the property's value as the present value of its future annual after-tax cash flows, ignoring financing costs.

120.   Biggs, Inc., is considering a real estate investment that provides gross revenues (if fully occupied) of $250,000, a vacancy rate of 4%, and operating expenses of $15,000. The property costs $1,000,000, and the depreciation expense on the property is 2.6% of the cost in the first year and 1.3% of the cost over the next several years. The marginal tax rate is 35%. The after-tax cash flow in year 1 if the property is purchased for cash is:
A. $69,650.
B. $129,350.
C. $155,350.

Exam 3
Morning Session

Calculating Your Score

Topic	Maximum Score	Your Score
Ethical and Professional Standards	18	
Quantitative Methods	14	
Economics	12	
Financial Reporting and Analysis	24	
Corporate Finance	10	
Portfolio Management	6	
Equity Investments	12	
Fixed Income	14	
Derivatives	6	
Alternative Investments	4	
Total	120	

The morning and afternoon exams are identically weighted over the topics and readings. You can therefore treat the morning and afternoon exams as independent exams.

If you took more than three hours (180 minutes) to complete this portion of the exam, you should adjust your score downward by one point for each minute you ran over.

Remember: the real exam *will be more difficult* than these practice exams. The main reason for this is the general anxiety and stress that you will be feeling on exam day, coupled with the time pressure you will be under. Many of the questions on this practice exam and the real exam are not individually difficult, so if you take extra time to answer the questions on this practice exam, your score will go up significantly. However, if you want an accurate measure of your potential performance on the exam, adhere to the 3-hour time limit.

After you have finished grading your practice exam, you may find it useful to use the exam questions and recommended solutions for review. Many of these questions were specifically written for your use as study tools. Once again, I feel I should remind you not to rely on memorizing these questions; you are not likely to see them on the actual exam. What you will see on the exam, though, are the concepts, terms, and procedures presented in these questions.

Your actual exam will most likely look different than what you see in this book. Please remember, no study provider knows the content of the actual exam. These practice exams are our best guess as to the structure, content, and difficulty of an actual exam.

Test Answers

1.	Ⓐ	Ⓑ	Ⓒ
2.	Ⓐ	Ⓑ	Ⓒ
3.	Ⓐ	Ⓑ	Ⓒ
4.	Ⓐ	Ⓑ	Ⓒ
5.	Ⓐ	Ⓑ	Ⓒ
6.	Ⓐ	Ⓑ	Ⓒ
7.	Ⓐ	Ⓑ	Ⓒ
8.	Ⓐ	Ⓑ	Ⓒ
9.	Ⓐ	Ⓑ	Ⓒ
10.	Ⓐ	Ⓑ	Ⓒ
11.	Ⓐ	Ⓑ	Ⓒ
12.	Ⓐ	Ⓑ	Ⓒ
13.	Ⓐ	Ⓑ	Ⓒ
14.	Ⓐ	Ⓑ	Ⓒ
15.	Ⓐ	Ⓑ	Ⓒ
16.	Ⓐ	Ⓑ	Ⓒ
17.	Ⓐ	Ⓑ	Ⓒ
18.	Ⓐ	Ⓑ	Ⓒ
19.	Ⓐ	Ⓑ	Ⓒ
20.	Ⓐ	Ⓑ	Ⓒ
21.	Ⓐ	Ⓑ	Ⓒ
22.	Ⓐ	Ⓑ	Ⓒ
23.	Ⓐ	Ⓑ	Ⓒ
24.	Ⓐ	Ⓑ	Ⓒ
25.	Ⓐ	Ⓑ	Ⓒ
26.	Ⓐ	Ⓑ	Ⓒ
27.	Ⓐ	Ⓑ	Ⓒ
28.	Ⓐ	Ⓑ	Ⓒ
29.	Ⓐ	Ⓑ	Ⓒ
30.	Ⓐ	Ⓑ	Ⓒ
31.	Ⓐ	Ⓑ	Ⓒ
32.	Ⓐ	Ⓑ	Ⓒ
33.	Ⓐ	Ⓑ	Ⓒ
34.	Ⓐ	Ⓑ	Ⓒ
35.	Ⓐ	Ⓑ	Ⓒ
36.	Ⓐ	Ⓑ	Ⓒ
37.	Ⓐ	Ⓑ	Ⓒ
38.	Ⓐ	Ⓑ	Ⓒ
39.	Ⓐ	Ⓑ	Ⓒ
40.	Ⓐ	Ⓑ	Ⓒ

41.	Ⓐ	Ⓑ	Ⓒ
42.	Ⓐ	Ⓑ	Ⓒ
43.	Ⓐ	Ⓑ	Ⓒ
44.	Ⓐ	Ⓑ	Ⓒ
45.	Ⓐ	Ⓑ	Ⓒ
46.	Ⓐ	Ⓑ	Ⓒ
47.	Ⓐ	Ⓑ	Ⓒ
48.	Ⓐ	Ⓑ	Ⓒ
49.	Ⓐ	Ⓑ	Ⓒ
50.	Ⓐ	Ⓑ	Ⓒ
51.	Ⓐ	Ⓑ	Ⓒ
52.	Ⓐ	Ⓑ	Ⓒ
53.	Ⓐ	Ⓑ	Ⓒ
54.	Ⓐ	Ⓑ	Ⓒ
55.	Ⓐ	Ⓑ	Ⓒ
56.	Ⓐ	Ⓑ	Ⓒ
57.	Ⓐ	Ⓑ	Ⓒ
58.	Ⓐ	Ⓑ	Ⓒ
59.	Ⓐ	Ⓑ	Ⓒ
60.	Ⓐ	Ⓑ	Ⓒ
61.	Ⓐ	Ⓑ	Ⓒ
62.	Ⓐ	Ⓑ	Ⓒ
63.	Ⓐ	Ⓑ	Ⓒ
64.	Ⓐ	Ⓑ	Ⓒ
65.	Ⓐ	Ⓑ	Ⓒ
66.	Ⓐ	Ⓑ	Ⓒ
67.	Ⓐ	Ⓑ	Ⓒ
68.	Ⓐ	Ⓑ	Ⓒ
69.	Ⓐ	Ⓑ	Ⓒ
70.	Ⓐ	Ⓑ	Ⓒ
71.	Ⓐ	Ⓑ	Ⓒ
72.	Ⓐ	Ⓑ	Ⓒ
73.	Ⓐ	Ⓑ	Ⓒ
74.	Ⓐ	Ⓑ	Ⓒ
75.	Ⓐ	Ⓑ	Ⓒ
76.	Ⓐ	Ⓑ	Ⓒ
77.	Ⓐ	Ⓑ	Ⓒ
78.	Ⓐ	Ⓑ	Ⓒ
79.	Ⓐ	Ⓑ	Ⓒ
80.	Ⓐ	Ⓑ	Ⓒ

81.	Ⓐ	Ⓑ	Ⓒ
82.	Ⓐ	Ⓑ	Ⓒ
83.	Ⓐ	Ⓑ	Ⓒ
84.	Ⓐ	Ⓑ	Ⓒ
85.	Ⓐ	Ⓑ	Ⓒ
86.	Ⓐ	Ⓑ	Ⓒ
87.	Ⓐ	Ⓑ	Ⓒ
88.	Ⓐ	Ⓑ	Ⓒ
89.	Ⓐ	Ⓑ	Ⓒ
90.	Ⓐ	Ⓑ	Ⓒ
91.	Ⓐ	Ⓑ	Ⓒ
92.	Ⓐ	Ⓑ	Ⓒ
93.	Ⓐ	Ⓑ	Ⓒ
94.	Ⓐ	Ⓑ	Ⓒ
95.	Ⓐ	Ⓑ	Ⓒ
96.	Ⓐ	Ⓑ	Ⓒ
97.	Ⓐ	Ⓑ	Ⓒ
98.	Ⓐ	Ⓑ	Ⓒ
99.	Ⓐ	Ⓑ	Ⓒ
100.	Ⓐ	Ⓑ	Ⓒ
101.	Ⓐ	Ⓑ	Ⓒ
102.	Ⓐ	Ⓑ	Ⓒ
103.	Ⓐ	Ⓑ	Ⓒ
104.	Ⓐ	Ⓑ	Ⓒ
105.	Ⓐ	Ⓑ	Ⓒ
106.	Ⓐ	Ⓑ	Ⓒ
107.	Ⓐ	Ⓑ	Ⓒ
108.	Ⓐ	Ⓑ	Ⓒ
109.	Ⓐ	Ⓑ	Ⓒ
110.	Ⓐ	Ⓑ	Ⓒ
111.	Ⓐ	Ⓑ	Ⓒ
112.	Ⓐ	Ⓑ	Ⓒ
113.	Ⓐ	Ⓑ	Ⓒ
114.	Ⓐ	Ⓑ	Ⓒ
115.	Ⓐ	Ⓑ	Ⓒ
116.	Ⓐ	Ⓑ	Ⓒ
117.	Ⓐ	Ⓑ	Ⓒ
118.	Ⓐ	Ⓑ	Ⓒ
119.	Ⓐ	Ⓑ	Ⓒ
120.	Ⓐ	Ⓑ	Ⓒ

Exam 3
Morning Session

The following 18 questions relate to Ethical and Professional Standards. (27 minutes)

1. Which of the following statements about the CFA Institute's Professional Conduct Program (PCP) is *least accurate*?
    A. Possible sanctions include condemnation by a member's peers or suspension of a candidate's participation in the CFA Program.
    B. If the Designated Officer determines that a sanction against a member is warranted, the member must either accept the sanction or lose the right to use the CFA designation.
    C. Members who cooperate with a PCP inquiry by providing confidential client information to PCP staff are not in violation of Standard III(E) Preservation of Confidentiality.

2. Robert Miguel, CFA, is a portfolio manager for a large investment advisory firm. In appreciation of his impressive portfolio returns last quarter, one of his clients, Kevin Goodman, has invited Miguel and his wife to be his guests at his luxury suite for a major league baseball playoff game. Miguel, a baseball fan, accepts the invitation and attends the game. The next day at work, Miguel doesn't mention to his supervisor that he attended the game as a guest of the client. According to Standard I(B) Independence and Objectivity and Standard I(A) Knowledge of the Law, Miguel's actions are in violation of:
    A. both of these Standards.
    B. neither of these Standards.
    C. only one of these Standards.

3. Ann Smith, CFA, calls Bill Jones, CFA, and tells him that her research shows that Biokem Company is underpriced and that earnings will exceed $3.00 this year. Jones had never heard of Biokem before her call but knows that Smith is widely considered to be the best analyst in her sector. The report has been released publicly, and Smith tells Jones he's "welcome to it." After their conversation, Jones arranges a conference call with his firm's portfolio managers for whom Biokem is suitable and announces that Biokem is underpriced and will likely earn over $3.00 this year. During the call with the portfolio managers, Jones does not reference his conversation with Smith. According to Standard I(C) Misrepresentation and Standard V(A) Diligence and Reasonable Basis, Jones violated:
   A. both of these Standards.
   B. neither of these Standards.
   C. only one of these Standards.

4. Doug Watson, CFA, serves in a sales position at Sommerset Brokerage, a registered investment adviser. As part of his employment, he is expected to entertain clients from time to time with dinners, professional sporting events, and golf outings. Frequently at these client outings, Watson drinks excessively. On one occasion, after dropping off a client, Watson was cited by local police for misdemeanor public intoxication. According to Standard I(A) Knowledge of the Law and Standard I(D) Misconduct, Watson is in violation of:
   A. both of these Standards.
   B. neither of these Standards.
   C. only one of these Standards.

5. Kevin Richards is a performance analyst for Reliable Advisors, a retail investment advisory and consulting firm. Richards, who is a Level 1 CFA candidate, was hired as part of the firm's efforts to attract CFA candidates into critical areas of the firm, such as performance measurement and attribution. Richards' supervisor instructs him to reference the firm's compliance with GIPS in marketing materials to attract more clients. For Richards' reference to the firm's GIPS compliance to be accurate, Reliable is *least likely* required to:
   A. apply GIPS compliance firmwide and not only to the specific asset classes mentioned in the marketing materials.
   B. claim compliance with GIPS only if it has a compliant performance history of five years or more.
   C. include all discretionary fee-paying accounts in composites based on their investment objectives and/or strategies.

6. Peter Taylor, a CFA charterholder and an analyst for a large investment firm, has been offered an all-expense-paid trip by Sweet Pineapple Co. to visit the firm's processing plants in Maui, Oahu, and Kauai. Taylor, a food industry analyst, has been following Sweet's stock for several years and recently issued a "buy" recommendation on the stock. Taylor believes a review of the firm's processing facilities during its busy January harvest period would be an excellent opportunity for him to assess the firm's productive capacity and learn even more about their business. According to Standard I(B) Independence and Objectivity, it is recommended that Taylor:
    A. pay for his air travel and hotel expenses.
    B. obtain written permission from his employer before he accepts this offer.
    C. pay for all his travel expenses, including the cost of meals and incidental items.

7. Ruth Brett, a Level 1 CFA candidate, is a research analyst for a large investment firm. Due to a demanding work schedule with long hours, Brett was unable to attend any sort of exam preparation class, and has only been able to study sporadically. Feeling nervous and unprepared the night before the exam, Brett writes a few key notes on the bottom of her shoe. At the exam, Brett sees the large number of proctors present and decides not to risk getting caught and does not look at her shoe. According to the CFA Institute Code of Ethics and Standards of Professional Conduct, Brett is:
    A. not in violation of any Standard or the Code of Ethics because she did not use the notes.
    B. in violation of the Code of Ethics for bringing the notes into the examination room but is not in violation of any Standard because she did not use the notes.
    C. in violation of both the Code of Ethics and Standard VII(A) Conduct as Members and Candidates in the CFA Program for taking the notes into the examination room.

8. Which of the following is *least likely* included in the CFA Code of Ethics? Members of CFA Institute must:
    A. place their clients' interests before their employer's interests.
    B. strive to maintain and improve the competence of others in the profession.
    C. use reasonable care and exercise independent professional judgment.

9.   In formulating her report on GammaCorp's common stock, Barb Kramer, CFA, did a complex series of statistical tests on the company's past sales and earnings. Based on this statistical study, Kramer stated in her report that, "GammaCorp's earnings growth for the next five years will average 15% per year." Her conclusion was based in part on a regression analysis with a high level of statistical significance. Has Kramer violated Standard V(B) Communication with Clients and Prospective Clients?

A. Yes, because she didn't give complete details of the statistical model used.

B. Yes, because she failed to indicate that 15% growth is an estimate.

C. No, because her statistical studies were carefully done, and her projections are within the generally accepted bounds of statistical accuracy.

10.   Alpha Advisors Inc. is an investment management firm that has a client base that ranges from individuals to large foundations. Many of the firm's personnel responsible for managing larger accounts feel that Alpha must give these accounts "special service" in order to retain their business. Some of these employees have been responsible for developing and revising the firm's policies over time. Concerned that the policies might violate the CFA Institute Standards of Professional Conduct, the president of Alpha has been reviewing the firm's policies and procedures. Which of the following policies is *least appropriate* under the Standards? Alpha:

A. monitors the personal trading activity of firm personnel and requires them to pre-clear personal trades through the compliance office.

B. regularly calls larger accounts first after changes in investment recommendations have been faxed to all clients.

C. excludes client accounts of family members of employees from participating in IPOs.

11.   Dudley Thompson is a bond salesman for a small broker/dealer in London. His firm is the lead underwriter on a new junk bond issue for the Ibex Corporation. In order to stimulate sales of the new issue, Thompson calls all of his accounts over £1,000,000, many of which belong to elderly clients with low risk tolerances, and tells them that the Ibex issue is a fantastic opportunity for high returns that is not to be missed. Thompson also posts overly optimistic projections for Ibex's performance on several Internet "chat rooms" in order to increase the price of the bond issue and enhance his clients' returns on the investment. According to Standard II(B) Market Manipulation and Standard III(C) Suitability, Watson is in violation of:

A. both of these Standards.

B. neither of these Standards.

C. only one of these Standards.

12. Rob Elliott, a CFA candidate, is an analyst with a large asset management firm. His personal portfolio includes a large amount of common stock of TECH Inc., a semiconductor company which his firm does not currently follow. The director of the research department has just asked Elliott to analyze TECH and write a report about its investment potential, which will be distributed to clients and prospective clients. Based on the CFA Institute Standards of Professional Conduct, the *most appropriate* course of action for Elliot to take would be to:
   A. sell his shares of TECH before completing the report.
   B. decline to write the report.
   C. disclose the ownership of the stock to his employer and in the report if he writes it.

13. Antonio Mendoza, CFA, is an investment manager in private practice under the name Mendoza Investments. He manages small- to medium-sized accounts for individual investors. Mendoza solicits new business by making brief presentations at area senior citizen centers, touting his investment performance record and compliance with the Global Investment Performance Standards. At each presentation, he makes available a 1-page information sheet that outlines his performance history for the past ten years. His telephone number is on the sheet for prospective clients who wish to contact him for additional information. At the bottom of the sheet the following is stated: "Mendoza Investments has prepared and presented this report in compliance with the Global Investment Performance Standards (GIPS®)." Mendoza's presentation:
   A. does not comply with GIPS.
   B. violates Standard III(D) Performance Presentation.
   C. complies with both the Standards and GIPS.

14. Anne Franklin, CFA, is an analyst who covers technology stocks for Medallion Investments. Franklin frequently meets with company management and makes site visits to company facilities. Cynthia Lucas, chief technology officer for Level Tech, tells several analysts, including Franklin, during a conference call that overseas shipments of the company's important new product are going to be delayed due to manufacturing defects, which she expects are correctable. This information has not been released in any other format. Medallion manages discretionary accounts for Lucas and Franklin. Subsequent to her meeting, Franklin sends a note to Medallion's investment personnel telling them to "sell the stock in all client accounts," as the shipment information is significant and contrary to recent earnings guidance from the company. Franklin's use of the information received from Lucas:

   A. violates the Code and Standards, as Franklin received material nonpublic information that should not have been acted upon.
   B. violates the Code and Standards, since she directed the sale in all client accounts instead of acting in the best interests of her own clients.
   C. does not violate the Code and Standards, as Franklin was adhering to her fiduciary duty to Medallion's clients by sharing the information and recommending a "Sell."

15. R. J. Young is meeting with a new client for the first time. At this meeting, he will be gathering information about the client in order to assess the client's investment objectives and constraints. As he does for all of his clients, Young will then prepare a written investment policy statement (IPS). According to the recommended procedures for complying with Standard III(C) Suitability, which of the following statements regarding an IPS is *least accurate*?

   A. An IPS should describe the roles and responsibilities of the adviser and client.
   B. A member or candidate is not responsible for financial information withheld by the client.
   C. A client's IPS must be updated at least quarterly to reflect any changes in their investment profile.

16. Sue Johnson, CFA, has an elderly client with a very large asset base. The client intends to start divesting her fortune to various charities. Johnson is on the Board of a local charitable foundation. Johnson *most appropriately*:

   A. must not discuss anything regarding her client and her client's intentions with the charitable foundation without permission.

   B. can discuss her client's situation with the charitable foundation as long as she informs other local charities of her client's intentions.

   C. can make this known to the charitable foundation so that they can solicit the client, since it is the client's wish to divest assets to charities in the future.

17. According to Standard III(A) Loyalty, Prudence, and Care, which of the following statements regarding the voting of proxies on client holdings is *least accurate*?

   A. Proxies have economic value to a client.

   B. An investment management firm should vote all proxies on client holdings unless the client reserves that right.

   C. Members and candidates should explicitly disclose the firm's proxy voting policies to clients.

18. Alvin Gold, CFA, resides in Country A and does business as an investment advisor primarily in Country B. Country A allows trading on non-public information and does not require disclosure of referral fees. Country B prohibits trading on non-public information only if it is gained by illegal means and requires disclosure of referral fees of over $100 (U.S. equivalent). Gold accepts a referral fee of $75, and in the course of a meeting with two other analysts and the firm's CFO, Gold receives material non-public information. To comply with the Code and Standards, Gold:

   A. need not disclose the referral fee but cannot trade on the non-public information.

   B. must disclose the referral fee and cannot trade on the non-public information.

   C. must disclose the referral fee but may trade on the non-public information.

The following 14 questions relate to Quantitative Methods. (21 minutes)

19. Three years from now, an investor will deposit the first of eight $1,000 payments into a special fund. The fund will earn interest at the rate of 5% per year until the third deposit is made. Thereafter, the fund will return a reduced interest rate of 4% compounded annually until the final deposit is made. How much money will the investor have in the fund at the end of ten years assuming no withdrawals are made?
    A. $8,872.93.
    B. $9,251.82.
    C. $9,549.11.

20. An investor places $5,000 in an account. The stated annual interest rate is 6% compounded monthly. The value of the account at the end of three years is *closest* to:
    A. $5,970.
    B. $5,978.
    C. $5,983.

21. Compared to a *t*-distribution with 10 degrees of freedom, and compared to a normal distribution, a *t*-distribution with 20 degrees of freedom and the same variance has:

	Compared to df = 10	Compared to normal
A.	thinner tails	fatter tails
B.	fatter tails	thinner tails
C.	fatter tails	fatter tails

22. The initial market value of a portfolio was $100,000. One year later the portfolio was valued at $90,000 and two years later at $99,000. The geometric mean annual return excluding any dividend income is *closest* to:
    A. −0.5%.
    B. 0.0%.
    C. +0.5%.

23. A college endowment fund has $150 million. The fund manager intends to withdraw $2 million from the fund for operations, and she has a minimum year-end acceptable level of $151 million. The fund has two choices for the portfolio. The endowment manager can choose Portfolio X, which has an expected return of 10% and a standard deviation of 14%, or Portfolio Y, which has an expected return of 12% and a standard deviation of 20%. Given this scenario, which of the following statements regarding Roy's safety-first criterion is *most accurate*?
    A. Portfolio Y should be chosen because it has a safety-first ratio of 0.50.
    B. Portfolio X should be chosen because it has a safety-first ratio of 0.57.
    C. Portfolios X and Y are both acceptable because the safety-first ratios fall in the acceptable range.

24. An investor purchases 500 shares of Nevada Industries common stock for $22.00 per share today. At t = 1 year, this investor receives a $0.42 per share dividend (which is not reinvested) on the 500 shares and purchases an additional 500 shares for $24.75 per share. At t = 2 years, he receives another $0.42 (not reinvested) per share dividend on 1,000 shares and purchases 600 more shares for $31.25 per share. At t = 3 years, he sells 1,000 of the shares for $35.50 per share and the remaining 600 shares at $36.00 per share, but receives no dividends. Assuming no commissions or taxes, the money-weighted rate of return received on this investment is *closest* to:
    A. 14.3%.
    B. 17.6%.
    C. 18.5%.

25. The "up-move factor" in a binomial tree is *best* described as:
    A. the probability that the variable increases in any period.
    B. one minus the "down-move factor" for the binomial tree.
    C. one plus the percentage change in the variable when it increases.

26. Jane Acompora is calculating equivalent annualized yields based on the 1.3% holding period yield of a 90-day loan. The correct ordering of the annual money market yield (MMY), effective yield (EAY), and bond equivalent yield (BEY) is:
    A. MMY < EAY < BEY.
    B. MMY < BEY < EAY.
    C. BEY < EAY < MMY.

27.   An analyst develops the following probability distribution for the states of the economy and market returns.

Unconditional Probability P(A)		Conditional Probability P(B × A)	
Good economy	60%	Bull market	50%
		Normal market	30%
		Bear market	20%
Poor economy	40%	Bull market	20%
		Normal market	30%
		Bear market	50%

Which of the following statements about this probability distribution is *least accurate*?
A. The unconditional probability of a normal market is 0.30.
B. The joint probability of having a good economy and a bear market is 0.20.
C. Given that the economy is poor, the probability of a normal or a bull market is 0.50.

28.   An analyst estimates a stock has a 40% probability of earning a 10% return, a 40% probability of earning a 12.5% return, and a 20% probability of earning a 30% return. The stock's standard deviation of returns based on this returns model is *closest* to:
A. 3.74%.
B. 5.75%.
C. 7.58%.

29.   An investment manager has a pool of five security analysts he can choose from to cover three different industries. In how many different ways can the manager assign one analyst to each industry?
A. 15.
B. 60.
C. 125.

30.   Shortfall risk is the:
A. risk due to possible earnings shortfalls.
B. probability of failing to make a contractually promised payment.
C. probability that portfolio value will fall below some minimum level at a future date.

31. If a two-tailed hypothesis test has a 5% probability of rejecting the null hypothesis when the null is true, it is *most likely* that the:
    A. power of the test is 95%.
    B. confidence level of the test is 95%.
    C. probability of a Type I error is 2.5%.

32. Which of the following statements about hypothesis testing is *least accurate*?
    A. Rejecting a true null hypothesis is a Type I error.
    B. The power of a test is the probability of rejecting the null hypothesis when it is false.
    C. For a one-tailed test involving X, the null hypothesis would be $H_0: X = 0$, and the alternative hypothesis would be $H_A: X \neq 0$.

The following 12 questions relate to Economics. (18 minutes)

33. The problem associated with managers making decisions that benefit themselves at the expense of stockholders is called the:
    A. shirking problem.
    B. asymmetric benefits problem.
    C. principal-agent problem.

34. A loss of economic efficiency from price regulation is *least likely* to result from a:
    A. rent ceiling that effectively increases renters' search times for available units.
    B. minimum wage that is greater than the equilibrium wage for unskilled workers.
    C. maximum price for electricity set at a price level at which the quantity of electricity supplied is greater than the quantity demanded.

35. The classification system used by the U.S. Bureau of Labor Statistics would *least likely* consider someone unemployed who:
    A. was terminated from his last job.
    B. is disabled and unable to return to work.
    C. was laid off and is waiting to return to a previous job.

36. If the admission price for a rock concert is raised from $25 to $30, causing ticket sales to drop from 60,000 to 40,000, the price elasticity of demand for tickets is:
    A. –0.25.
    B. –1.67.
    C. –2.20.

37. Which of the following statements about monopolists is *most likely* correct?
     A. Monopolists have imperfect information about demand.
     B. Without government intervention, monopolists will always earn economic profits.
     C. A monopolist maximizes total revenue where marginal revenue equals marginal cost.

38. Which of the following statements about the characteristics of a monopoly and those of an oligopoly is *least accurate*?
     A. Both monopoly and oligopoly markets are characterized by high barriers to entry.
     B. In an oligopoly, the output decisions of each seller are independent of the policies followed by competitors.
     C. In a monopoly, there is a single seller of a well-defined product for which no good substitutes exist.

39. Which of the following statements regarding the money supply and determination of short-term interest rates is *least accurate*?
     A. On balance, financial innovation has decreased the demand for money.
     B. If the short-term interest rate is greater than the equilibrium rate, there will be excess supply of real money balances.
     C. An increase in the real money supply from an initial equilibrium situation will cause households and businesses to sell interest-bearing securities.

40. What are the *most likely* effects on aggregate demand in the current period of an increase in expected future incomes and of an increase in the money supply?
     A. Both increase aggregate demand.
     B. Both decrease aggregate demand.
     C. One increases aggregate demand and one decreases aggregate demand.

41. Which of the following is included in both the M1 and M2 measures of money?
     A. Time deposits.
     B. Savings deposits.
     C. Travelers' checks.

42. Which of the following statements regarding the supply of labor is *least accurate*?
    A. The income effect of a wage increase is to decrease the amount of labor supplied.
    B. The substitution effect leads to greater consumption of leisure time when the wage rate falls.
    C. Other things equal, an increase in the wage rate will lead to an increase in the amount of labor an individual will supply.

43. Competitive markets are *least likely* to produce more than the efficient quantity of a good if producing that good:
    A. generates external costs.
    B. uses a common resource as a factor input.
    C. generates a producer surplus that is greater than the consumer surplus.

44. Which of the following statements about elasticity is *least accurate*?
    A. Both demand and supply are more elastic in the long run than in the short run.
    B. When demand is inelastic, an increase in price will cause a decrease in the total expenditure on a good.
    C. When the price of a product increases, consumers will reduce their consumption by a larger amount in the long run than in the short run.

The following 24 questions relate to Financial Reporting and Analysis. (36 minutes)

45. Which of the following statements about nonrecurring items is *most accurate*?
    A. The correction of an accounting error is reported net of taxes below extraordinary items on the income statement.
    B. Discontinued operations are classified as unusual or infrequent and are reported as a component of net income from continuing operations.
    C. Uninsured losses from earthquakes and expropriations by foreign governments can be classified as extraordinary items under U.S. GAAP but not under IFRS.

46. On January 31, Dowling Inc. borrowed funds to purchase capital equipment for its business operations. On the same day, it also recorded the cost of salaries incurred to January 31, which will be paid on February 6. When these two transactions are recorded on January 31, the financial statement item that will increase the most is:
    A. assets.
    B. expenses.
    C. liabilities.

47. Under U.S. GAAP, which of the following statements about classifying cash flows is *least accurate*?
    A. Cash received from issuing long-term debt or stock is considered a financing cash flow.
    B. All income taxes paid are considered operating cash flows, even if some arise from financing and investing activities.
    C. Dividend payments made are financing cash flows, while interest payments received are investing cash flows.

48. Kimberwick Technologies reported the following information for the year ending December 31.

Data	
Net sales	50,000
Cash expenses	3,250
Cash inputs	17,000
Cash taxes	7,000
Increase in receivables	500
Depreciation expense	1,000
Cash flow from investing	–5,000
Cash flow from financing	–4,250

If the cash balance increased $13,000 over the year, cash flow from operations (CFO) is *closest* to:
    A. $21,250.
    B. $21,750.
    C. $22,250.

49. A company has a cash conversion cycle of 80 days. If the company's average receivables turnover increases from 11 to 12, the company's cash conversion cycle:
    A. decreases by approximately 3 days.
    B. increases by approximately 3 days.
    C. decreases by approximately 1 day.

50.   Which of the following statements about a corporation's annual reports, SEC filings, and press releases is *most accurate*?
      A. Annual and quarterly SEC filings must be audited.
      B. Interim SEC filings typically update the major financial statements and footnotes.
      C. Annual reports to shareholders are generally viewed as the most factual and objective source of information about a company.

51.   A company had the following changes in its stock:
      •   The company had 2 million shares outstanding on December 31, 20X6.
      •   On March 31, 20X7, the company paid a 10% stock dividend.
      •   On June 30, 20X7, the company sold $10 million face value of 7% convertible debentures, convertible into common at $5 per share.
      •   On September 30, 20X7, the company issued and sold 100,000 shares of common stock.

      The company should compute its 20X7 basic earnings per share based on:
      A. 2,225,000 shares.
      B. 2,250,000 shares.
      C. 3,225,000 shares.

52.   When a used delivery truck is sold, the gain or loss on disposal is *most accurately* stated as:
      A. fair market value – book value.
      B. selling price – original cost – accumulated depreciation.
      C. selling price – original cost + accumulated depreciation.

53.   Haltata Turf & Sod currently uses the first in, first out (FIFO) method to account for inventory. Due to significant tax-loss carryforwards, the company has an effective tax rate of zero. Prices are rising and inventory quantities are stable. If the company were to use last in, first out (LIFO) instead of FIFO:
      A. net income would be lower, and cash flows would be higher.
      B. cash flow would remain the same, and working capital would decrease.
      C. gross margin would increase, and average stockholder's equity would decrease.

54. Which of the following effects is *most likely* to occur when using ratio screens for high dividend yield stocks and low P/E stocks, respectively?

High dividend yield	Low P/E ratios
A. Include too many financial services firms	Exclude too many growth firms
B. Exclude too many financial services firms	Include too many growth firms
C. Include too many financial services firms	Include too many growth firms

55. The ratio of operating cash flow to net income (the cash flow earnings index) would *least likely* be an "accounting red flag" when it is:
A. less than one.
B. declining over time.
C. highly variable.

56. Which of the following statements regarding capitalization and expensing of intangible assets is *least accurate*? Based on U.S. GAAP:
A. purchased intangible assets are always amortized.
B. research and development costs are expensed when incurred.
C. computer software development costs to establish the technological or economic feasibility of software are expensed, but subsequent costs may be capitalized.

57. Which of the following statements about the role of depreciable lives and salvage values in the computation of depreciation expenses for financial reporting is *least accurate*?
A. Estimates of the useful life of the same depreciable asset can differ between companies.
B. Companies are required to disclose data about estimated salvage values in the footnotes to the financial statements.
C. Depreciable lives and salvage values are chosen by management and allow for the possibility of income manipulation.

58. A company owns an asset with the following characteristics:
     - Net book value of $500,000 (original cost of $1,300,000 less accumulated depreciation of $800,000).
     - Undiscounted expected future cash flows of $470,000.
     - Present value of expected future cash flows of $380,000.

     Which of the following statements about the accounting treatment of this asset is *least accurate*?
     A. The asset is impaired because the present value of expected future cash flows is less than the carrying value.
     B. Recognizing an impairment in the current period will tend to increase net income, asset turnover ratios, and leverage ratios in subsequent years.
     C. If an impairment is recognized, the company will report a $120,000 write-off in income from continuing operations.

59. Acme Corp. purchased a new stamping machine for $100,000, paid $10,000 for shipping, and paid $5,000 to have it installed in their plant. Based on an estimated salvage value of $25,000 and an economic life of six years, the difference between straight-line depreciation and double-declining balance depreciation in the second year of the asset's life is *closest* to:
     A. $7,220.
     B. $10,556.
     C. $16,666.

60. How will a firm's operating cash flow be affected by a decrease in accounts receivable and by an increase in accounts payable?
     A. Both will increase operating cash flow.
     B. Both will decrease operating cash flow.
     C. One will increase operating cash flow and one will decrease operating cash flow.

61. Which of the following statements about accounting for long-term debt is *least accurate*?
     A. Issuing zero-coupon bonds has no impact on cash flow from operations over the life of the bonds.
     B. For a bond issued at par, interest expense equals the coupon rate multiplied by the face value.
     C. A firm will have greater interest expense if it issues bonds priced at a premium, compared to issuing discount bonds to raise the same proceeds.

62.   In general, as compared to companies with operating leases, companies
       with finance leases report:
       A. lower working capital and asset turnover.
       B. higher debt to equity and return on equity ratios (in the early years).
       C. higher expenses in the early years and over the life of the lease.

63.   Longboat, Inc. sold a luxury passenger boat from its inventory on
       December 31 for $2,000,000. It is estimated that Longboat will incur
       $100,000 in warranty expenses during its 5-year warranty period.
       Longboat's tax rate is 30%. To account for the tax implications of the
       warranty obligation prior to incurring warranty expenses, Longboat
       should:
       A. record a deferred tax asset of $30,000.
       B. record a deferred tax liability of $30,000.
       C. make no entry until actual warranty expenses are incurred.

64.   During 20X3, Rory, Inc., reported net income of $15,000 and had
       2,000 shares of common stock outstanding for the entire year.
       Rory also had 2,000 shares of 10%, $50 par value preferred stock
       outstanding during 20X3. During 20X1, Rory issued 100, $1,000 par,
       6% bonds for $100,000. Each of these is convertible to 50 shares of
       common stock. Rory's tax rate is 40%. Assuming these bonds are
       dilutive, 20X3 diluted EPS for Rory is *closest* to:
       A. $0.71.
       B. $1.23.
       C. $2.50.

65.   The category of items on the balance sheet that typically offers
       an analyst the best information on a non-financial firm's investing
       activities is:
       A. current assets.
       B. current liabilities.
       C. noncurrent assets.

66.   A firm issues a 4-year semiannual-pay bond with a face value of $10
       million and a coupon rate of 10%. The market interest rate is 11%
       when the bond is issued. The balance sheet liability at the end of the
       first semiannual period is *closest* to:
       A. $9,650,700.
       B. $9,683,250.
       C. $9,715,850.

67.   The presentation format of balance sheet data that standardizes the
       first-year values to 1.0 and presents subsequent years' amounts relative
       to 1.0 is a(n):
       A. indexed balance sheet.
       B. vertical common-size balance sheet.
       C. horizontal common-size balance sheet.

68. Debt covenants to protect bondholders are *least likely* to:
    A. restrict the issuance of new debt.
    B. require sinking fund redemptions.
    C. prohibit bond repurchases at a premium to par.

The following 10 questions relate to Corporate Finance. (15 minutes)

69. Paul Haggerty, CFA, is analyzing the accounts receivable for Williams Computers and has collected the information below for the most recent four quarters:

Days Outstanding	1st Qtr	2nd Qtr	3rd Qtr	4th Qtr
< 31 days	30.0%	28.5%	27.0%	26.3%
31-60 days	27.5%	28.0%	28.5%	28.8%
61-90 days	23.8%	24.0%	24.8%	25.0%
> 90 days	18.8%	19.5%	19.8%	20.0%
Weighted Average Collection Period	61.6	62.7	63.5	63.9

Based on this information, Haggerty can *most* accurately conclude that over the past year, Williams':
    A. sales have increased.
    B. collections have accelerated.
    C. collections have slowed.

70. A strong corporate code of ethics is *most likely* to permit:
    A. the company to award consulting contracts to board members.
    B. board members to simultaneously sit on the board of another firm.
    C. finder's fees for merger or acquisition targets to be paid to relatives of board members.

71. The greatest amount of detailed capital budgeting analysis is typically required when deciding whether to:
    A. expand production capacity.
    B. introduce a new product or develop a new market.
    C. replace a functioning machine with a newer model to reduce costs.

72. When using the CAPM to estimate the cost of common equity for a company in a developing country, an analyst should *most appropriately*:
    A. add a country risk premium to the market risk premium.
    B. add the sovereign yield spread to the CAPM cost of common equity.
    C. make no adjustments because country risk is reflected in the equity's beta.

73. The type of short-term financing for which the financing cost is *most closely* tied to the creditworthiness of a firm's customers is:
    A. factoring.
    B. issuing commercial paper.
    C. an uncommitted line of credit.

74. In the U.S., which of the following short-term investment alternatives receives beneficial corporate tax treatment on the income it generates?
    A. Corporate bonds.
    B. Adjustable-rate preferred stock.
    C. Short-term federal agency securities.

75. If flotation costs are treated correctly in calculating the net present value of a project that will begin in the current period, the flotation costs are *most likely*:
    A. included in the initial outlay.
    B. reflected in the discount rate used for the project.
    C. included in the cost of the capital raised.

76. In a net present value (NPV) profile, the internal rate of return is represented as the:
    A. point where two NPV profiles intersect.
    B. intersection of the NPV profile with the vertical axis.
    C. intersection of the NPV profile with the horizontal axis.

77. Thompson Products has seen its marginal tax rate increase from 28% to 34% over the last two years and believes the change is permanent. The effects of this change on Thompson's current WACC and on its financial leverage over time are *most likely* a(n):
    A. increase in both.
    B. decrease in both.
    C. increase in one and a decrease in the other.

78. The audit committee of a company's Board of Directors is *most likely* to act in the interests of shareholders when:
    A. a company officer other than the CEO controls the audit budget.
    B. a reliable communication "firewall" is in place between the committee and the company's internal auditors.
    C. the committee has authority to prevent the company from engaging in non-audit business relationships with its external auditors.

The following 6 questions relate to Portfolio Management. (9 minutes)

79. Martin Dean, CFA, is a portfolio manager who is writing an investment policy statement (IPS) for Albert Francis, a new client. The *least likely* reason why Dean should prepare an IPS is to:
    A. comply with Standard III(C) Suitability.
    B. specify a benchmark against which to measure Dean's performance.
    C. set the target asset allocation.

80. Without the introduction of a risk-free asset or a zero-beta portfolio, the optimal portfolio on the efficient frontier for each investor is represented by:
    A. the market portfolio.
    B. any point where an indifference curve intersects the efficient frontier.
    C. the point where the investor's highest indifference curve is tangent to the efficient frontier.

81. When an investor can borrow and invest at the risk-free rate, which of the following statements is *least likely* correct?
    A. The capital market line (CML) is straight.
    B. The x-axis measurement of risk is the standardized covariance.
    C. Investors who borrow the risk-free asset to lever their portfolio will move their portfolios to the right of the market portfolio on the CML.

82. An analyst determines that four stocks have the following characteristics:

Stock	Beta	Estimated Return
X	1.0	10%
Y	1.6	16%
Z	2.0	16%

    If the risk-free rate is 4% and the expected return on the market is 10%, which of the following statements is *least accurate*?
    A. Stock X is properly valued.
    B. Stock Y is undervalued.
    C. Stock Z is overvalued.

83. Which of the following is one of the assumptions of capital market theory?
    A. Investors have heterogeneous expectations.
    B. Any asset or portfolio may be purchased in discrete shares.
    C. There are no taxes or transaction costs involved in buying or selling assets.

84. The risk-free rate is 5% and the expected market risk premium is 10%. A portfolio manager is projecting a return of 20% on a portfolio with a beta of 1.5. After adjusting for its systematic risk, this portfolio is expected to:
    A. equal the market's performance.
    B. outperform the market.
    C. underperform the market.

The following 12 questions relate to Equity Investments. (18 minutes)

85. An analyst determines that a company has a return on equity of 16% and pays 40% of its earnings in dividends. If the firm recently paid a $1.50 dividend and the stock is selling for $40, what is the required rate of return on the stock if it is priced according to the dividend discount model?
    A. 9.6%.
    B. 10.2%.
    C. 13.7%.

86. An investor buys a stock for $50. The initial margin requirement is 50%, and the maintenance margin requirement is 25%. The price below which the investor would receive a margin call would be:
    A. $25.00.
    B. $33.33.
    C. $37.50.

87. A securities market exhibits internal efficiency if it offers:
    A. low transaction costs.
    B. prices that respond rapidly to new information.
    C. rates of return proportional to risk.

88. A stock index consists of two stocks:
    - Company A has 50 shares outstanding valued at $2 each.
    - Company B has 10 shares outstanding valued at $10 each.
    - The price-weighted index is 6, and the value-weighted index is 100.

    If the price of Company A's stock increases to $4 per share, and Company B's stock splits two-for-one and is priced at $5, the value of the price-weighted index and the value-weighted index are:

	Price-weighted	Value-weighted
A.	7	150
B.	7	125
C.	4.5	150

89. Pam Robers, CFA, is performing a valuation analysis on the common stock of Allstare Inc. The stock's beta is 1.1, the risk-free rate is 5%, and the market risk premium is expected to be 8%. Allstare's ROE is expected to be constant at 18%, and its dividend payout ratio has been fairly constant over time at 40%. The forward-earnings multiplier that Robers should use to estimate the current value of the shares is *closest* to:
    A. 7.
    B. 13.
    C. 20.

90. An investor purchased stock in a company for $20 at the end of a year for which the company reported EPS of $4.00. Due to capital investment needs, the company retains 75% of earnings and intends to maintain this retention rate in the future. Return on equity (ROE) is constant at 33.3%. If the expected price of the stock in one year is $25, the expected 1-year holding period return on this stock is:
   A. 24.00%.
   B. 28.50%.
   C. 31.25%.

91. Consider the following company data:
   - Earnings retention rate at 40%.
   - Required rate of return of 13%.
   - ROE of 15%, expected to remain constant.

   Using the information above, which of the following statements is *incorrect*? If the:
   A. risk-free rate increases, the P/E ratio will decrease.
   B. earnings retention ratio increases, the P/E ratio will increase.
   C. dividend payout increases, the P/E ratio will increase.

92. An analyst gathered the following data about a company:
   - The historical earnings retention rate of 40% is projected to continue into the future.
   - The sustainable ROE is 12%.
   - The stock's beta is 1.2.
   - The nominal risk-free rate is 6%.
   - The expected market return is 11%.

   If the analyst believes next year's earnings will be $4 per share, what value should be placed on this stock?
   A. $22.24.
   B. $33.32.
   C. $45.45.

93. Tamira Scott, CFA, manager of an index fund, believes in the efficient market hypothesis but remembers that there are a few anomalies she can take advantage of to earn higher returns. Scott would be *least likely* to earn excess returns by purchasing stocks in:
   A. companies that announce stock splits.
   B. mid-December, with the intent to sell in early January.
   C. companies with low price/earnings ratios or with high book-to-market ratios.

94. The assertion that investors, analysts, and portfolio managers exhibit psychological tendencies that cause them to make systematic errors is *most* consistent with:
    A. behavioral finance.
    B. weak-form market efficiency.
    C. smart-money technical analysis.

95. An investor purchases 1,000 shares of each of the stocks in a price-weighted index at their closing prices (ignore transactions costs). On a total return basis, if the index stocks remain the same, this portfolio will certainly:
    A. perform exactly like the index over time.
    B. outperform the index over time.
    C. underperform the index over time.

96. Which of the following statements about measures of relative value is *least accurate*? The:
    A. price-to-book-value ratio can be used for firms with negative earnings or cash flows.
    B. price-to-cash-flow ratio should be used in conjunction with the P/E ratio because cash flows are typically more stable than earnings.
    C. price-to-book-value ratio is an appropriate measure for comparing firms with different levels of fixed assets, such as a heavy industrial firm compared to a financial or service firm.

The following 14 questions relate to Fixed Income. (21 minutes)

97. Which of the following statements about the risks associated with investing in bonds is *most accurate*?
    A. Corporate debentures are not subject to prepayment risk.
    B. Liquidity risk is not relevant if the portfolio manager intends to hold the bond to maturity.
    C. Event risk refers to the possibility that the issuer breaches one of its debt covenants and triggers a "credit event."

98. The type of credit risk that is most directly reflected in a bond's rating is:
    A. default risk.
    B. downgrade risk.
    C. credit spread risk.

99. What effects will an increase in yield volatility have on the values of a putable bond and a callable bond?
    A. Both bonds will increase in value.
    B. Both bonds will decrease in value.
    C. One bond will increase in value and the other will decrease.

100. Which of the following statements about debt securities is *least accurate*?
   A. Commercial paper is a short-term (less than nine months) vehicle for corporate borrowing.
   B. An asset-backed security is a security whose cash flows are linked to a pool of underlying loans or financial instruments.
   C. A medium-term note (MTN) differs from a corporate bond in that an MTN is sold to investors on a "firm commitment" basis wherein the investment banker guarantees a price to the issuer.

101. An inverse floating-rate bond:
   A. may, under certain circumstances, require the bondholder to make payments to the issuer.
   B. increases in principal value as market rates decrease and decreases in principal value as market rates increase.
   C. has an implicit cap on the maximum coupon rate and typically includes a floor on the minimum coupon rate.

102. Portfolio duration *most accurately* approximates the sensitivity of the value of a bond portfolio to:
   A. parallel shifts in the yield curve.
   B. increases in the slope of the yield curve.
   C. decreases in the slope of the yield curve.

103. Which of the following *least accurately* describes the price volatility of an option-free bond?
   A. For a given large change in basis points in the required yield, the percentage price increase is smaller than the percentage price decrease.
   B. For large changes in required yield, the percentage price change is not the same for an increase in required yield as it is for a decrease in required yield.
   C. For small changes in the required yield, the percentage price change for a given bond is roughly the same, whether the required yield increases or decreases.

104. An 8%, semiannual pay, option-free corporate bond that is selling at par has ten years to maturity. What is the effective duration of the bond based on a 75 basis point change (up or down) in rates?
   A. 5.6.
   B. 6.8.
   C. 7.2.

105. The current 4-year spot rate is 4% and the current 5-year spot rate is 5.5%. What is the 1-year forward rate in four years?
    A. 9.58%.
    B. 10.14%.
    C. 11.72%.

106. An economic expansion has caused Treasury yields to increase and absolute credit spreads to narrow. Which of the following is *most likely* accurate?
    A. Relative corporate yield spreads to Treasuries will have increased.
    B. Even if absolute credit spreads had remained the same, the yield ratio and relative yield spread of BBB to AAA bonds could have decreased.
    C. Absolute spreads are generally considered a better indicator than relative yield spreads.

107. The face value of a $1,000,000 T-bill with 78 days to maturity is priced at $987,845. What is the bank discount yield (annualized) quote for the T-bill?
    A. 5.61%.
    B. 5.67%.
    C. 5.75%.

108. A decrease in mortgage interest rates will *most likely* have what effects on the prices of interest-only stripped mortgage-backed securities and principal-only stripped mortgage-backed securities?
    A. Both will increase.
    B. Both will decrease.
    C. One will increase and one will decrease.

109. For which of the following securities is estimating the future cash flows *least* difficult?
    A. 5-year, 6% bond with two years of call protection.
    B. 3-year note with a coupon of Libor + 100 basis points.
    C. 8% preferred stock with mandatory redemption in five years.

110. Which of the following yields *least likely* represents a spot rate?
    A. 91-day Treasury bill holding period yield.
    B. 2-year Treasury inflation protected security yield.
    C. 7-year Treasury coupon strip yield.

The following 6 questions relate to Derivatives. (9 minutes)

111. An investor writes a covered call with a strike price of $44 on a stock selling at $40 for a $3 premium. The range of possible payoffs to the writer of this covered call on the combined position is:
    A. −$40 to $47.
    B. −$37 to $7.
    C. $7 to infinity.

112. The payoff diagram of portfolio insurance (owning a stock and a put) has the same shape as the payoff diagram for:
    A. writing a put option.
    B. buying a call option.
    C. writing a call option.

113. Which of the following statements about interest rate swaps is *least accurate*?
    A. A plain vanilla interest rate swap is a fixed rate for a variable rate swap.
    B. The parties agreeing to a swap typically make no margin deposit.
    C. The counterparties exchange the notional principal at initiation and termination while only net interest rate payments are exchanged on the settlement dates.

114. An investor is following the real-time changes in the price of options on a particular asset. She notices that both a European call and a European put on the same underlying asset each have an exercise price of $45. The two options have six months to expiration and are both selling for $4. She also observes that the underlying asset is selling for $43 and that the rate of return on a 1-year Treasury bill is 6%. According to put-call parity, what series of transactions would be necessary to take advantage of any mispricing in this case?
    A. Sell the call, sell a T-bill equal to the present value of $45, buy the put, and buy the underlying asset.
    B. Buy the call, buy a T-bill equal to the present value of $45, sell the put, and sell the underlying asset.
    C. Buy the call, sell a T-bill equal to the present value of $45, sell the put, and buy the underlying asset.

115. A CFO of a major corporation wants to hedge against a possible interest rate increase by entering into a forward rate agreement. The following quotes are obtained from a dealer for 30-day FRAs:

Dealer Quotes
60-Day LIBOR = 0.0480
90-Day LIBOR = 0.0500
180-Day LIBOR = 0.0525

The contract covers a notional principal of $50 million. The company hedges its risk of an increase in 60-day LIBOR with an FRA, and 30 days later when the contract expires, the 60-day LIBOR rate is 5%. What does the company collect from, or pay to, the dealer? The company:
A. collects $16,529.
B. pays $29,691.
C. neither collects nor pays since the rate on 60-day LIBOR at expiration is the same as the rate on 90-day LIBOR initially.

116. An investor holds a short position in four September gold futures contracts. Each gold futures contract is for delivery of 100 ounces of gold. When the contract was entered into on day zero, the futures price was $350 per ounce. The initial margin is $1,750 per contract, and the maintenance margin is $1,312.50 per contract. The following table gives information on the price of gold for September delivery over a 4-day period:

Day	Closing Futures Price ($)
1	345.50
2	348.75
3	355.50
4	356.25

What will the variation margin be on the first day a margin call is received?
A. $1,800.
B. $2,200.
C. $2,500.

The following 4 questions relate to Alternative Investments. (6 minutes)

117. Which of the following statements with respect to hedge fund investing is *least accurate*?
    A. Hedge funds only publicly disclose performance information on a voluntary basis.
    B. Hedge funds are not typically registered with the SEC in the United States.
    C. Survivorship bias in hedge fund data causes risk to be overstated because funds that take on more risk tend to have higher returns.

118. Which of the following is *least likely* a valuation method for closely held companies?
    A. Cost approach.
    B. Comparables approach.
    C. Discount/premium approach.

119. Michelle Arthur, CFA, is explaining the characteristics of venture capital investments. She states, (1) Direct venture capital investing requires a long time horizon because the payoff typically depends on an eventual initial public offering or private sale of the firm.
    (2) A successful venture capital manager should focus on selecting promising ventures but should not expect to influence their operations.
    Are Arthur's statements accurate?
    A. Both of these statements are accurate.
    B. Neither of these statements is accurate.
    C. Only one of these statements is accurate.

120. A building has the following characteristics:
    - The building generates $100,000 per year in gross rental income.
    - Property taxes are $20,000 per year.
    - Other expenses are 20% of gross rental income.
    - The market capitalization rate is 15%.

    Using the income approach, the value of the building is:
    A. $400,000.
    B. $500,000.
    C. $600,000.

Exam 3
Afternoon Session

Calculating Your Score

Topic	Maximum Score	Your Score
Ethical and Professional Standards	18	
Quantitative Methods	14	
Economics	12	
Financial Reporting and Analysis	24	
Corporate Finance	10	
Portfolio Management	6	
Equity Investments	12	
Fixed Income	14	
Derivatives	6	
Alternative Investments	4	
Total	120	

The morning and afternoon exams are identically weighted over the topics and readings. You can therefore treat the morning and afternoon exams as independent exams.

If you took more than three hours (180 minutes) to complete this portion of the exam, you should adjust your score downward by one point for each minute you ran over.

Remember: the real exam *will be more difficult* than these practice exams. The main reason for this is the general anxiety and stress that you will be feeling on exam day, coupled with the time pressure you will be under. Many of the questions on this practice exam and the real exam are not individually difficult, so if you take extra time to answer the questions on this practice exam, your score will go up significantly. However, if you want an accurate measure of your potential performance on the exam, adhere to the 3-hour time limit.

After you have finished grading your practice exam, you may find it useful to use the exam questions and recommended solutions for review. Many of these questions were specifically written for your use as study tools. Once again, I feel I should remind you not to rely on memorizing these questions; you are not likely to see them on the actual exam. What you will see on the exam, though, are the concepts, terms, and procedures presented in these questions.

Your actual exam will most likely look different than what you see in this book. Please remember, no study provider knows the content of the actual exam. These practice exams are our best guess as to the structure, content, and difficulty of an actual exam.

Test Answers

1. Ⓐ Ⓑ Ⓒ	41. Ⓐ Ⓑ Ⓒ	81. Ⓐ Ⓑ Ⓒ
2. Ⓐ Ⓑ Ⓒ	42. Ⓐ Ⓑ Ⓒ	82. Ⓐ Ⓑ Ⓒ
3. Ⓐ Ⓑ Ⓒ	43. Ⓐ Ⓑ Ⓒ	83. Ⓐ Ⓑ Ⓒ
4. Ⓐ Ⓑ Ⓒ	44. Ⓐ Ⓑ Ⓒ	84. Ⓐ Ⓑ Ⓒ
5. Ⓐ Ⓑ Ⓒ	45. Ⓐ Ⓑ Ⓒ	85. Ⓐ Ⓑ Ⓒ
6. Ⓐ Ⓑ Ⓒ	46. Ⓐ Ⓑ Ⓒ	86. Ⓐ Ⓑ Ⓒ
7. Ⓐ Ⓑ Ⓒ	47. Ⓐ Ⓑ Ⓒ	87. Ⓐ Ⓑ Ⓒ
8. Ⓐ Ⓑ Ⓒ	48. Ⓐ Ⓑ Ⓒ	88. Ⓐ Ⓑ Ⓒ
9. Ⓐ Ⓑ Ⓒ	49. Ⓐ Ⓑ Ⓒ	89. Ⓐ Ⓑ Ⓒ
10. Ⓐ Ⓑ Ⓒ	50. Ⓐ Ⓑ Ⓒ	90. Ⓐ Ⓑ Ⓒ
11. Ⓐ Ⓑ Ⓒ	51. Ⓐ Ⓑ Ⓒ	91. Ⓐ Ⓑ Ⓒ
12. Ⓐ Ⓑ Ⓒ	52. Ⓐ Ⓑ Ⓒ	92. Ⓐ Ⓑ Ⓒ
13. Ⓐ Ⓑ Ⓒ	53. Ⓐ Ⓑ Ⓒ	93. Ⓐ Ⓑ Ⓒ
14. Ⓐ Ⓑ Ⓒ	54. Ⓐ Ⓑ Ⓒ	94. Ⓐ Ⓑ Ⓒ
15. Ⓐ Ⓑ Ⓒ	55. Ⓐ Ⓑ Ⓒ	95. Ⓐ Ⓑ Ⓒ
16. Ⓐ Ⓑ Ⓒ	56. Ⓐ Ⓑ Ⓒ	96. Ⓐ Ⓑ Ⓒ
17. Ⓐ Ⓑ Ⓒ	57. Ⓐ Ⓑ Ⓒ	97. Ⓐ Ⓑ Ⓒ
18. Ⓐ Ⓑ Ⓒ	58. Ⓐ Ⓑ Ⓒ	98. Ⓐ Ⓑ Ⓒ
19. Ⓐ Ⓑ Ⓒ	59. Ⓐ Ⓑ Ⓒ	99. Ⓐ Ⓑ Ⓒ
20. Ⓐ Ⓑ Ⓒ	60. Ⓐ Ⓑ Ⓒ	100. Ⓐ Ⓑ Ⓒ
21. Ⓐ Ⓑ Ⓒ	61. Ⓐ Ⓑ Ⓒ	101. Ⓐ Ⓑ Ⓒ
22. Ⓐ Ⓑ Ⓒ	62. Ⓐ Ⓑ Ⓒ	102. Ⓐ Ⓑ Ⓒ
23. Ⓐ Ⓑ Ⓒ	63. Ⓐ Ⓑ Ⓒ	103. Ⓐ Ⓑ Ⓒ
24. Ⓐ Ⓑ Ⓒ	64. Ⓐ Ⓑ Ⓒ	104. Ⓐ Ⓑ Ⓒ
25. Ⓐ Ⓑ Ⓒ	65. Ⓐ Ⓑ Ⓒ	105. Ⓐ Ⓑ Ⓒ
26. Ⓐ Ⓑ Ⓒ	66. Ⓐ Ⓑ Ⓒ	106. Ⓐ Ⓑ Ⓒ
27. Ⓐ Ⓑ Ⓒ	67. Ⓐ Ⓑ Ⓒ	107. Ⓐ Ⓑ Ⓒ
28. Ⓐ Ⓑ Ⓒ	68. Ⓐ Ⓑ Ⓒ	108. Ⓐ Ⓑ Ⓒ
29. Ⓐ Ⓑ Ⓒ	69. Ⓐ Ⓑ Ⓒ	109. Ⓐ Ⓑ Ⓒ
30. Ⓐ Ⓑ Ⓒ	70. Ⓐ Ⓑ Ⓒ	110. Ⓐ Ⓑ Ⓒ
31. Ⓐ Ⓑ Ⓒ	71. Ⓐ Ⓑ Ⓒ	111. Ⓐ Ⓑ Ⓒ
32. Ⓐ Ⓑ Ⓒ	72. Ⓐ Ⓑ Ⓒ	112. Ⓐ Ⓑ Ⓒ
33. Ⓐ Ⓑ Ⓒ	73. Ⓐ Ⓑ Ⓒ	113. Ⓐ Ⓑ Ⓒ
34. Ⓐ Ⓑ Ⓒ	74. Ⓐ Ⓑ Ⓒ	114. Ⓐ Ⓑ Ⓒ
35. Ⓐ Ⓑ Ⓒ	75. Ⓐ Ⓑ Ⓒ	115. Ⓐ Ⓑ Ⓒ
36. Ⓐ Ⓑ Ⓒ	76. Ⓐ Ⓑ Ⓒ	116. Ⓐ Ⓑ Ⓒ
37. Ⓐ Ⓑ Ⓒ	77. Ⓐ Ⓑ Ⓒ	117. Ⓐ Ⓑ Ⓒ
38. Ⓐ Ⓑ Ⓒ	78. Ⓐ Ⓑ Ⓒ	118. Ⓐ Ⓑ Ⓒ
39. Ⓐ Ⓑ Ⓒ	79. Ⓐ Ⓑ Ⓒ	119. Ⓐ Ⓑ Ⓒ
40. Ⓐ Ⓑ Ⓒ	80. Ⓐ Ⓑ Ⓒ	120. Ⓐ Ⓑ Ⓒ

Exam 3
Afternoon Session

The following 18 questions relate to Ethical and Professional Standards. (27 minutes)

1. Recommended procedures to comply with Standard VI(B) Priority of Transactions are *least likely* to include:
   A. blackout periods.
   B. limited front-running by employees.
   C. disclosure to clients of the firm's policies in regard to personal investing.

2. Juan Perez, CFA, is a research analyst for a large Wall Street brokerage firm where he follows the pharmaceuticals industry. While a large pharmaceuticals convention is in town, Perez happens to be in a restaurant where several analysts he has never met before are discussing their investment recommendations. Perez overhears the analysts agree that PharmCo, Inc. is a strong "Buy," but cannot hear the details of why they are recommending purchasing stock in the company. The next day, Perez changes his "Sell" recommendation on PharmCo to "Buy," based solely on the conversation he overheard between the analysts the night before. Which standard did Perez violate?
   A. Standard V(A) Diligence and Reasonable Basis.
   B. Standard III(E) Preservation of Confidentiality.
   C. Standard II(A) Material Nonpublic Information.

3. Allen Winkler, CFA, an equity analyst, recently had lunch with his former professor, Kim Thompson. Thompson told him about a new theoretical stock valuation model she designed. Upon returning to his office, Winkler recreated Thompson's model and revised it slightly. He then tested the revised model using Standard & Poor's (S&P) equity databases. The results were so impressive that his supervisors decided to create a small new fund called the Technical Fund directed toward their technically oriented clients. In the fund's prospectus, Winkler included a discussion of the model and the results of his tests. According to Standard I(C) Misrepresentation, is Winkler required to credit Thompson for having developed the original model and S&P as the source of the data?
   A. Both of these sources must be cited.
   B. Neither of these sources must be cited.
   C. Only one of these sources must be cited.

4. Donald Smith, CFA, has been assigned by his employer to analyze Braden Corporation. Prior to joining his current firm, Smith worked as an investment banker and received options on 1,000 shares of Braden stock as part of his compensation for assisting the company with a large secondary offering. The options are currently at-the-money and will expire in two years. In addition, Smith has been speaking with Braden about a consulting arrangement in which Smith would be paid to work with Braden's investor relations department to improve the flow of information to the firm's current and prospective shareholders. According to Standard VI(A) Disclosure of Conflicts, if Smith writes a report on Braden Corporation, Smith:

A. must disclose the options to clients, prospects, and his employer, but needs not disclose the consulting agreement because it has not yet been finalized.

B. only needs to disclose the options to clients and prospects and disclose the consulting agreement to his employer.

C. must disclose both the options and the consulting agreement to clients, prospects, and his employer.

5. Jason Socco, a Level 1 candidate for the CFA exam, has severe test anxiety. He is very smart and has a good college grade point average, but he is afraid to take the graduate entrance exam required to get his M.B.A. He has diligently prepared for the exam, but he begins to panic on the night before the exam. He decides to program as much as possible into his handheld computer just in case he needs help on the exam, even though he knows taking this information into the exam room is prohibited and considered cheating. The exam is not as difficult as he expected, however, and he does not actually use any information he stored in his calculator. Socco has:

A. violated both Standard VII(A) conduct as Members and Candidates in the CFA Program and Standard I(D) Misconduct.

B. violated only Standard I(D) Misconduct because it was not the CFA exam.

C. not violated CFA Institute's Standards of Professional Conduct because it was not the CFA exam and was not part of his professional activities for his employer.

6. Diane Harris, a CFA Institute member, is a portfolio manager for Worldwide Investments. Robert Cline, one of her clients, offered her the use of his condominium in Aspen for one week in February if the performance of his portfolio is at least two percentage points above that of the S&P 500 during the next 12 months. Immediately after learning about the offer, Harris informed her manager of all terms of this agreement in writing and received verbal consent to the arrangement. At the end of the year, Harris met the performance criteria set by Cline and accepted the vacation. Did Harris violate Standard IV(B) Additional Compensation Arrangements?
   A. Yes, because written consent from her employer is required.
   B. No, because Harris notified and received consent from her employer to enter the arrangement.
   C. No, because bonuses from clients for doing her job well do not create any conflict of interest.

7. Stan White, CFA, heads the marketing department of a large brokerage firm, American Securities. He reports directly to the president of the firm, who has mandated that beginning this year, the firm must present all past performance results in accordance with the Global Investment Performance Standards. Which of the following statements is an acceptable indication of American Securities' compliance with the Global Investment Performance Standards?
   A. American Securities has prepared and presented this report in compliance with the Global Investment Performance Standards (GIPS®).
   B. American Securities has prepared and presented this report utilizing the calculation methodologies of the Global Investment Performance Standards (GIPS®).
   C. American Securities has presented this report in compliance with the Global Investment Performance Standards (GIPS®). Please reference "Disclosures" for exceptions.

8. Betty Cantor, a CFA Institute member, was about to issue a neutral report on HLC Corporation, a high-tech firm, when she talked to Donald Watson, her former manager and mentor, who is now with another investment firm. Watson is very bullish on HLC and tells Cantor that "everyone knows HLC is going to experience a major stock price increase over the next year." Cantor knows Watson has been an exceptionally insightful analyst in the high-tech sector. According to the CFA Institute Standards of Practice Handbook, is it acceptable for Cantor to change her recommendation to a "Buy" based on the comments of Watson?

    A. Yes, because based on experience, Watson's views are generally correct.

    B. No, because Watson's comments could be considered inside information.

    C. No, because she does not have a reasonable basis for recommending this stock.

9. Six months ago, Tom Hayes, CFA, left his position as a portfolio manager and accepted a position as senior portfolio manager at a smaller boutique firm. One of Hayes's first recommendations at his new job is Selldex. He had researched and recommended the stock six months ago while employed at his old firm, and he still believes it has great investment potential. He recreates his old Selldex research, updates it, and makes the recommendation. According to the CFA Institute Standards of Practice, Hayes's actions:

    A. are not in violation of any Standard.

    B. are in violation of Standard IV(A) Loyalty because his previous employer paid for the original research.

    C. are in violation of Standard I(D) Misconduct because the research he did at his old employer is the employer's property.

10. The CFA Institute Code of Ethics *most likely* requires members and candidates to:

    A. not engage in activity which compromises the integrity of CFA Institute.

    B. stay informed on applicable laws and regulations that pertain to their respective areas of business.

    C. act with competence, integrity, and in ethical manner when dealing with the public, clients, employers, employees, and other market participants.

11. Craig Boone, a Level 1 CFA candidate, is a trader on the fixed income desk at a large Wall Street financial institution. He has observed that one of the salesmen on the desk has been reallocating some trades at the end of the day, giving better execution to a large client at the expense of several smaller clients, a practice he suspects is illegal. A bond trader has also been involved by modifying his books to support the reallocation. Boone was told by the salesman that it is a common practice on Wall Street, that the firm's senior management is aware of it, and that Boone should just do his job, as he is not being asked to do anything illegal or unethical. If Boone makes a personal record of the suspect activity, takes it home for his personal files, and subsequently reveals it to regulatory authorities, he would:
    A. be in violation of the Standards for beaching his duty of loyalty to his employer.
    B. be in violation of the Standards for disclosing confidential information.
    C. not be in violation of any Standards.

12. WEB, an investment-banking firm, is the principal underwriter for MTEX's upcoming debenture issue. Lynn Black, CFA, is an analyst with WEB, and she learned from an employee in MTEX's programming department that a serious problem was recently discovered in the software program of its major new product line. In fact, the problem is so bad that many customers have canceled their orders with MTEX. Black checked the debenture's prospectus and found no mention of this development. The red herring prospectus has already been distributed. According to the CFA Institute Standards of Professional Conduct, Black's *best* course of action is to:
    A. inform her immediate supervisor at WEB of her discovery.
    B. keep quiet because this is material nonpublic information.
    C. notify potential investors of the omission on a fair and equitable basis.

13. Fred Gersey is the compliance officer for Regiment Advisors, a registered investment adviser to retail and institutional mutual funds. Regiment has publicly acknowledged in writing the CFA Institute Code and Standards as part of its internal policies. Regiment is contemplating the use of research and investment decision-making services provided by a third-party in return for commission business on client trading. Gersey has been charged with establishing the review committee for the approval of such services. Which of the following information requests by Regiment personnel would *least likely* be allowable under the CFA Institute Code and Standards, even if they are disclosed to clients?

   A. Research analyst's request for weekly data involving prescriptions, new drug approvals, and patient user rates from a pharmaceutical company.
   B. Marketer's request for daily third-party portfolio analytics for use in client mailings and for print advertising of the firm's investment products.
   C. Portfolio manager's request for proxy information regarding how corporate boards of directors were establishing employee compensation and the vehicles for such compensation.

14. Mary Walters, CFA, is a trust officer at a regional branch of Money Center bank. She has entered into a referral agreement whereby she will refer clients to Bob Sear, a tax attorney who she believes is the best in the business. Sear has told Walters that he will do the tax work on her children's trust, created by their grandparents, in return for such referrals. According to the CFA Institute Code and Standards, Walters should disclose the arrangement to:

   A. her employer only.
   B. prospective clients she refers only.
   C. both her employer and prospective clients she refers.

15. Ronaldo Jenkins, CFA, is chief investment officer of Windwatch Advisors, a discretionary investment advisory firm. With over 15 years experience in various asset classes, Jenkins is head of Windwatch's proxy voting committee. He serves on the boards of several non-profit organizations and public companies and advises local municipal governments. During a recent search for an investment bank for a fixed income offering on behalf of a municipality, Jenkins learns in confidence that an investment bank, which is a large subsidiary of a publicly traded commercial bank owned by Windwatch clients, is experiencing financial difficulties and will be shut down. According to the CFA Institute Standards of Professional Conduct, Jenkins is *least likely* permitted to:
    A. share the information received about the investment bank with his compliance officer.
    B. approach the investment bank about making public disclosure of the financial difficulties and pending closure.
    C. share the information received about the investment bank with Windwatch's head of equity investments for informational purposes as a shareholder of the parent commercial bank.

16. Mary Woods, CFA, is a client services and marketing manager for LAM Asset Management, which has managed domestic equity and fixed income assets for more than 20 years. In an effort to diversify its business, LAM hires two international equity portfolio managers and requires Woods and other employees to take a 2-week course on international equity portfolios, client servicing, and marketing. Subsequently, Woods prepares a marketing presentation regarding LAM's international equity capabilities, citing experienced portfolio managers and a proven track record, and she assures returns above the long-term risk-free rate of return based on 20 years' investment experience in managing client portfolios. Regarding her marketing activities for LAM's international equity product, Woods has:
    A. violated CFA Institute Standards of Professional Conduct by compromising her fiduciary duty to LAM's domestic equity clients.
    B. violated CFA Institute Standards of Professional Conduct by misrepresenting the services that LAM could provide and the firm's qualifications in international equity.
    C. not violated CFA Institute Standards of Professional Conduct since Woods's marketing of the product fulfilled LAM's fiduciary duty to create diversified portfolios for clients, balancing portfolio returns with an appropriate level of risk.

17. While visiting Cassori Company, Mark Ramsey, CFA, overhears management make comments that are not public information but are not really meaningful by themselves. Combining this information with his own analysis and other outside sources, Ramsey decides to change his recommendation on Cassori from "Buy" to "Sell." According to the CFA Institute Standards of Professional Conduct, Ramsey:

    A. must not issue his report until Cassori's management makes their comments public.

    B. may issue his "Sell" report because the facts are nonmaterial, but should maintain a file of the facts and documents leading to this conclusion.

    C. must report these events to his immediate supervisor and legal counsel, since they have become material in combination with his analysis.

18. Compliance with the Global Investment Performance Standards *least likely* requires firms to:

    A. include all fee-paying and non-fee-paying accounts in at least one composite.

    B. document in writing the policies and procedures used to comply with GIPS.

    C. specifically define what constitutes the firm that is claiming compliance.

The following 14 questions relate to Quantitative Methods. (21 minutes)

19. Jim Franklin recently purchased a home for $300,000 on which he made a down payment of $100,000. He obtained a 30-year mortgage to finance the balance on which he pays a fixed annual rate of 6%. If he makes regular, fixed monthly payments, what loan balance will remain just after the 48th payment?

    A. $186,109.

    B. $189,229.

    C. $192,444.

20. An investor purchased a $10,000, 5-year corporate note one year ago for $10,440. The note pays an annual coupon of $600. Over the past year, the note's annual yield-to-maturity has dropped by 1%. What total return did the investor earn over the year?

    A. 8.5%.

    B. 9.0%.

    C. 9.5%.

21.   An investor holds a portfolio consisting of one share of each of the following stocks:

Stock	Price at the Beginning of the Year	Price at the End of the Year	Cash Dividend During the Year
A	$10	$20	$0
B	$50	$60	$1
C	$100	$110	$4

For the 1-year holding period, the portfolio total return is *closest* to:
A. 15.79%.
B. 18.42%.
C. 21.88%.

22.   Which of the following measurement scales provides the *least* information?
A. Ratio.
B. Ordinal.
C. Nominal.

23.   An analyst observes the following four annual returns: $R_1 = +10\%$, $R_2 = -15\%$, $R_3 = 0\%$, and $R_4 = +5\%$. The average compound annual rate over the four years is *closest* to:
A. −5.0%.
B. −0.5%.
C. 0.0%.

24.   Given the observations 45, 20, 30, and 25, the mean absolute deviation is *closest* to:
A. 0.0.
B. 7.5.
C. 13.3.

25. An investor wants to buy a condominium in Florida. The value of her portfolio is currently $1,000,000, and she needs $100,000 in one year for the down payment. She doesn't mind decreasing her capital as long she has $950,000 remaining in her portfolio after the down payment is made. She is considering two new portfolios for her holdings. The details on the two portfolios are:

	Expected Annual Return	Standard Deviation of Returns
Portfolio 1	17%	15%
Portfolio 2	12%	10%
Portfolio 3	8%	6%

According to Roy's Safety-First criterion, the portfolio she would prefer is:
A. Portfolio 1.
B. Portfolio 2.
C. Portfolio 3.

26. Which of the following is *least likely* a perceived advantage of technical analysis?
A. Technical trading techniques do not require subjective judgement.
B. Technical analysis provides signals about when to trade.
C. Technical investors do not depend on accounting information, which can be manipulated.

27. Adam Farman has been asked to estimate the volatility of a technology stock index. He has identified a statistic which has an expected value equal to the population volatility and has determined that increasing his sample size will decrease the sampling error for this statistic. Based only on these properties, his statistic can *best* be described as:
A. unbiased and efficient.
B. unbiased and consistent.
C. efficient and consistent.

28. According to Chebyshev's inequality, the minimum proportion of observations falling within three standard deviations of the mean for a negatively skewed distribution is *closest* to:
A. 68%.
B. 75%.
C. 89%.

©2009 Kaplan, Inc.

29. The following table summarizes the results of a poll taken of CEOs and analysts about the economic impact of a pending piece of legislation:

Group	Predict Positive Impact	Predict Negative Impact
CEOs	40	30
Analysts	70	60

What is the probability that a randomly selected individual from this group will be either an analyst or someone who thinks this legislation will have a positive impact on the economy?
A. 0.75.
B. 0.80.
C. 0.85.

30. A researcher has investigated the returns over the last five years to a long-short strategy based on mean reversion in equity returns volatility. His hypothesis test led to rejection of the hypothesis that abnormal (risk-adjusted) returns to the strategy over the period were less than or equal to zero at the 1% level of significance. He would *most* appropriately decide that:
A. his firm should employ the strategy for client accounts because the abnormal returns are positive and statistically significant.
B. while the abnormal returns are highly significant statistically, they may not be economically meaningful.
C. as long as the estimated statistical returns are greater than the transactions costs of the strategy, his firm should employ the strategy for client accounts.

31. An analyst decides to select 10 stocks for her portfolio by placing the ticker symbols for all the stocks traded on the New York Stock Exchange in a large bowl. She randomly selects 20 stocks and will put every other one chosen into her 10-stock portfolio. The analyst used:
A. cluster sampling.
B. simple random sampling.
C. stratified random sampling.

32. Which of the following tests would generally be considered a nonparametric test?
A. Whether a sample is random or not.
B. Large sample test of the value of a population mean.
C. Value of the variance of a normal population.

The following 12 questions relate to Economics. (18 minutes)

33.   The Zaxon Company produces one product, and labor is the only variable input in the production process. In the short run, Zaxon faces a horizontal demand curve at $20 per unit. The average product of labor in the short run is given in the following table:

Resource Units	Average Product of Labor
1	25.0
2	22.5
3	20.0
4	17.5

If the price of each unit of labor (worker-days) is $350, and only whole units can be employed, how many units of labor will Zaxon employ?
A. 2.
B. 3.
C. 4.

34.   In theory, the supply of a non-renewable resource is:
A. perfectly elastic.
B. fixed over a specific period of time.
C. perfectly inelastic at a price that equals the present value of the expected next-period price.

35.   An analyst gathers the following information about Monument State Bank:
- Demand deposits $400 million
- Loans and securities $260 million
- Reserve requirement   10%
- The bank has a total of $50 million in cash and deposits with the Federal Reserve.

Monument State Bank is in a position to make additional loans of:
A. $5 million.
B. $10 million.
C. $40 million.

36.   The demand for labor will be less elastic:
A. at lower wage rates than at higher wage rates.
B. in the long run than in the short run.
C. the less labor intensive the production process.

37. The quantity theory of money states that in a full employment economy, any increase in the supply of money in excess of the rate of growth of real GDP will lead to a proportional increase in:
    A. the price level.
    B. velocity.
    C. real GDP.

38. The policy variable which the U.S. Federal Reserve *most likely* targets when conducting monetary policy is the:
    A. overnight federal funds rate.
    B. exchange value of the U.S. dollar.
    C. rate of change in the core consumer price index.

39. If the price of Product X increases from $2.00 per unit to $2.25 per unit, the demand will decrease from 7.5 million units to 6.7 million units. The price elasticity of demand for the product is *closest* to:
    A. −0.96.
    B. −1.00.
    C. −1.04.

40. Which of the following statements about a monopolist is *most accurate*? A monopolist will:
    A. maximize the average profit per unit sold.
    B. charge the highest price for which it can sell its product.
    C. produce where marginal revenue equals marginal cost.

41. Assume that the supply of ethanol is relatively more elastic than the demand for ethanol. Compared to an initial competitive equilibrium in the market for ethanol, the imposition of a per-gallon tax on producers of ethanol will *most likely* decrease:
    A. producer surplus by the total amount of tax collected.
    B. producer surplus by less than it reduces consumer surplus.
    C. the sum of consumer and producer surplus by the amount of tax collected.

42. A generational imbalance is *best* described as:
    A. accounting for the taxes owed by and the benefits owed to each generation.
    B. the present value of future government deficits and how future generations deal with this problem.
    C. a difference between the present value of government benefits promised to current taxpayers and the taxes paid by current taxpayers.

43. The short-run supply curve for a firm under perfect competition is the firm's:
    A. marginal cost curve above average total cost.
    B. marginal cost curve above average variable cost.
    C. average variable cost curve above marginal revenue.

44. Long-run aggregate supply is *least likely* to be affected by changes in the:
    A. prices of raw materials inputs.
    B. quantity of labor in the economy.
    C. level of technology.

The following 24 questions relate to Financial Reporting and Analysis. (36 minutes)

45. In accrual accounting, the matching principle states that:
    A. an entity should recognize revenues only when received and expenses only when they are paid.
    B. transactions and events producing cash flows are allocated only to time periods in which the cash flows occur.
    C. expenses incurred to generate revenue are recognized in the same time period as the revenue.

46. Which of the following statements about revenue recognition methods is *most accurate*?
    A. The completed contract method recognizes long-term contract revenue only as each phase of production is complete.
    B. The percentage of completion method recognizes profit corresponding to the costs incurred as a proportion of estimated total costs.
    C. The installment method recognizes sales when cash is received, but no profit is recognized until cash collected exceeds costs.

47. A company changes from an incorrect method of accounting to an acceptable one. Which of the following statements about this change is *most accurate*?
    A. It is treated retrospectively and requires restatement of all prior period results that are presented in the current financial statements.
    B. If the change is voluntary, it is a change in accounting principle and is reported below the line net of taxes.
    C. If the change is mandated by a new accounting standard, it is an unusual or infrequent item and is reported as a separate line item in net income from continuing operations.

48. For which of the following ways of manipulating cash flow would an analyst be *most likely* to reclassify financing cash outflows as operating cash outflows? A firm has:
    A. financed its payables.
    B. securitized receivables.
    C. repurchased stock to offset dilution.

49. An analyst gathers the following information:
    - Net income $100
    - Decrease in accounts receivable 30
    - Depreciation 25
    - Increase in inventory 17
    - Increase in accounts payable 10
    - Decrease in wages payable 5
    - Increase in deferred taxes 17
    - Sale of fixed assets 150
    - Purchase of fixed assets 340
    - Profit from the sale of fixed assets 5
    - Dividends paid out 35
    - Sale of new common stock 120

    Based on the above information, the company's cash flow from operations under U.S. GAAP is:
    A. $155.
    B. $165.
    C. $182.

50. Which of the following statements about cash flow is *least likely* correct? Under U.S. GAAP, cash flow from:
    A. operations includes cash operating expenses and changes in working capital accounts.
    B. financing includes the proceeds of debt issued and from the sale of the company's common stock.
    C. investing includes interest income from investment in debt securities.

51. An analyst gathered the following data about a company:
    - The company had 500,000 shares of common stock outstanding for the entire year.
    - The company's beginning stock price was $40, its ending price was $60, and its average price over the year was $50.
    - The company has 120,000 warrants outstanding for the entire year.
    - Each warrant allows the holder to buy one share of common stock at $45 per share.

    How many shares of common stock should the company use in computing its diluted earnings per share?
    A. 488,000.
    B. 500,000.
    C. 512,000.

52. Books Forever, Inc., uses short-term bank debt to buy inventory. Assuming an initial current ratio that is greater than 1, and an initial quick (or acid test) ratio that is less than 1, what is the effect of these transactions on the current ratio and the quick ratio?
    A. Both ratios will decrease.
    B. Neither ratio will decrease.
    C. Only one ratio will decrease.

53. Costiuk, Inc., is an agricultural firm that has committed to purchasing 10,000 kilograms of fertilizer at specific prices over the next three years. Which part of the financial statements will *most likely* contain information regarding this transaction?
    A. Balance sheet.
    B. Management's discussion and analysis.
    C. Notes to the financial statements.

54. Which of the following statements about expenses and intangible assets is *least likely* accurate?
    A. Advertising fees are generally expensed as incurred.
    B. In most countries, research and development costs are capitalized.
    C. Intangible assets are initially entered on the balance sheet at their purchase prices when they are acquired from an outside entity.

55. Which of the following accounting practices is *most likely* to decrease reported earnings in the current period?
    A. Using the straight-line method of depreciation instead of an accelerated method.
    B. Capitalizing advertising expenses rather than expensing them in the current period.
    C. Using LIFO inventory cost methods during a period of rising prices.

56. Which of the following statements about dilutive securities is *least likely* accurate?
    A. A simple capital structure is one that contains only common stock and antidilutive securities.
    B. A dilutive security is one that will cause earnings per share (EPS) to decrease if it is converted into common stock.
    C. Warrants with exercise prices less than the current stock price can be antidilutive.

57. As of January 1, a company had 22,500 $10 par value common shares outstanding. On July 1, the company repurchased 5,000 shares. The company also has 11,000, 10%, $100 par value preferred shares. If the company's net income is $210,000, its diluted earnings per share is *closest* to:
    A. $5.00.
    B. $7.50.
    C. $10.00.

58. In periods of rising prices and stable or increasing inventory quantities, compared with companies that use LIFO inventory accounting, companies that use the FIFO method will have:
    A. higher COGS and lower taxes.
    B. higher net income and higher taxes.
    C. lower inventory balances and lower working capital.

59. Rowlin Corporation, which reports under IFRS, wrote down its inventory of electronic parts last period from its original cost of €28,000 to net realizable value of €25,000. This period, inventory at net realizable value has increased to €30,000. Rowlin should revalue this inventory to:
    A. €30,000 and report a gain of €5,000 on the income statement.
    B. €28,000 and report a gain of €3,000 on the income statement.
    C. €30,000 but report a gain of only €3,000 on the income statement.

60. Compared with expensing the costs of a long-lived asset, a company that capitalizes these costs will:
    A. show smoother reported net income and higher return on assets in future years.
    B. have higher cash flow from operations and lower cash flow from investing.
    C. have lower profitability ratios in the current year and higher cash flows from operations.

61. In the early years of an asset's life, a firm that chooses an accelerated depreciation method instead of using straight-line depreciation will tend to have:
    A. lower net income and lower equity.
    B. higher return on equity and higher return on assets.
    C. lower depreciation expense and lower turnover ratios.

62. Which of the following definitions used in accounting for income taxes is *least accurate*?
    A. Income tax expense is based on current period pretax income adjusted for any changes in deferred tax assets and liabilities.
    B. A valuation allowance is a reserve against deferred tax assets based on the likelihood that those assets will not be realized.
    C. A deferred tax liability is created when tax expense is less than taxes payable and the difference is expected to reverse in future years.

63. From the extended (5-part) DuPont equation, which of the following components describes the equation EBT / EBIT?
    A. Tax burden.
    B. EBIT margin.
    C. Interest burden.

64. Under U.S. GAAP, which of the following statements about the financial statement effects of issuing bonds is *least likely* accurate?
    A. Issuance of debt has no effect on cash flow from operations.
    B. Periodic interest payments decrease cash flow from operations by the amount of interest paid.
    C. Payment of debt at maturity decreases cash flow from operations by the face value of the debt.

65. When the expected tax rate changes, deferred tax:
    A. expense is calculated using current tax rates with no adjustments.
    B. liability and asset accounts are adjusted to reflect the new expected tax rate.
    C. liability and asset accounts are maintained at historical tax rates until they reverse.

66. In general, as compared to companies with finance leases, companies with operating leases report:
    A. higher working capital and higher asset turnover.
    B. higher cash flow from operations and lower cash flow from financing.
    C. lower expense in the early years of the lease and higher expenses over the life of the lease.

67. An asset is considered impaired if its book value is:
    A. less than its market value.
    B. greater than the present value of its expected future cash flows.
    C. greater than the sum of its undiscounted expected cash flows.

68. Which of the following pairs of general categories are *least likely* to be considered in the formulas used by credit rating agencies to determine the capacity of a borrower to repay a debt?
    A. Operational efficiency; leverage.
    B. Margin stability; availability of collateral.
    C. Leverage; scale and diversification.

The following 10 questions relate to Corporate Finance. (15 minutes)

69. Which of the following statements about the component costs of capital is *least likely* correct?
    A. The cost of common equity is the required rate of return on common stock.
    B. The cost of preferred stock is the preferred dividend divided by the preferred's par value.
    C. The after-tax cost of debt is based on the expected yield to maturity on newly issued debt.

70. Project X has an internal rate of return (IRR) of 14%. Project Y has an IRR of 17%. Both projects have conventional cash flow patterns (all inflows after the initial cash outflow). If the required rate of return is:
    A. 14%, the net present value (NPV) of Project Y will exceed the NPV of Project X.
    B. greater than 17%, Project Y will have a shorter payback period than Project X.
    C. 10%, both projects will have a positive NPV, and the NPV of Project Y will exceed the NPV of Project X.

71. AlcoBanc owns a piece of property that is under consideration for a new bank branch. Which of the following is *least likely* a relevant incremental cash flow in analyzing a capital budgeting project? The:
    A. interest costs of a loan for the property purchase.
    B. business gained at other branches due to new customers at the proposed site.
    C. $150,000 AlcoBanc could get if they sold the property instead of building a new branch.

72. Jay Construction Company is considering whether to accept a new bridge-building project. Jay will use the pure-play method to estimate the cost of capital for the project, using Cass Bridge Builders as a comparable company. To calculate the project beta, Jay should:
    A. estimate Cass's cost of equity capital and apply it to the project.
    B. use the CAPM equation, substituting Cass's equity beta for its own.
    C. adjust Cass's equity beta for any difference in leverage between Cass and Jay.

73. Which of the following would *most likely* indicate deterioration of a firm's working capital management?
    A. An increase in days of payables outstanding.
    B. An increase in days of receivables outstanding.
    C. A decreased amount of cash and cash equivalents.

74. Hanson Aluminum, Inc. is considering whether to build a mill based around a new rolling technology the company has been developing. Management views this project as being riskier than the average project the company undertakes. Based on their analysis of the projected cash flows, management determines that the project's internal rate of return is equal to the company's marginal cost of capital. If the project goes forward, the company will finance it with newly issued debt with an after-tax cost less than the project's IRR. Should management accept or reject this project?
    A. Accept, because the project returns the company's cost of capital.
    B. Accept, because the marginal cost of the new debt is less than the project's internal rate of return.
    C. Reject, because the project reduces the value of the company when its risk is taken into account.

75. Which of the following is *least likely* an important requirement of good corporate governance?
    A. Members of the board should serve staggered, multiple-year terms.
    B. A board should be composed of at least a majority of independent board members.
    C. Board members should have appropriate experience and expertise relevant to the company's business.

76. Pannonia Enterprises, Inc. (PEI) has a target capital structure of 40% debt with 60% equity. PEI's pretax cost of debt will remain at 9% until the firm raises more than $200,000 in new debt capital, at which point its pretax cost of debt will increase to 9.5%. PEI's cost of equity will increase when more than $400,000 in equity capital is raised. PEI's break point for debt capital is *closest* to:
    A. $200,000.
    B. $500,000.
    C. $666,667.

77. Yields on firms' investments in short-term securities for comparison purposes are *best* stated as:

    A. holding period return $\left(\dfrac{360}{\text{days to maturity}} \right)$.

    B. $\dfrac{\text{discount}}{\text{face}} \left(\dfrac{360}{\text{days to maturity}} \right)$.

    C. holding period return $\left(\dfrac{365}{\text{days to maturity}} \right)$.

78. An analyst is forecasting a company's financial performance for the next year and prepares the following pro forma financial statements.

Pro Forma Income Statement

	Actual 20X1	Estimated 20X2
Sales	1,000,000	1,010,000
Cost of goods sold	600,000	606,000
SG&A expenses	300,000	303,000
Interest expense	72,000	72,000
Earnings before tax	28,000	29,000
Income tax	7,000	7,250
Net income	21,000	21,750
Dividends	8,400	8,700
Retained earnings	12,600	13,050

Pro Forma Balance Sheet

	Actual 20X1	Estimated 20X2
Current assets	600,000	606,000
PP&E, net	1,300,000	1,313,000
Total assets	1,900,000	1,919,000
Current liabilities	200,000	202,000
Long-term debt	900,000	900,000
Common stock	300,000	300,000
Retained earnings	500,000	513,050
Total liabilities and equity	1,900,000	1,915,050

The analyst is *most likely* to reconcile these pro forma financial statements by assuming the company:
A. pays out the financial surplus as additional dividends.
B. resolves the financial deficit by issuing long-term debt.
C. eliminates the financial deficit by cutting costs.

The following 6 questions relate to Portfolio Management. (9 minutes)

79. A stock has a beta of 0.9 and an estimated return of 10%. The risk-free rate is 7%, and the expected return on the market is 11%. According to the CAPM, this stock:
    A. is overvalued.
    B. is undervalued.
    C. is properly valued.

80. An analyst gathers the following data about the returns for two stocks.

	Stock A	Stock B
E(R)	0.04	0.09
σ^2	0.0025	0.0064

    $Cov_{A,B} = 0.001$

    The correlation between the returns of Stock A and Stock B ($\rho_{A,B}$) is *closest* to:

    A. 0.25.
    B. 0.50.
    C. 0.63.

81. A portfolio manager would *least* appropriately:
    A. recommend higher-risk investments for a 24-year-old college graduate.
    B. focus on timing and security selection when constructing a client investment strategy.
    C. manage the portfolio of a couple at the midpoint of their careers with a strategy with a long time horizon and moderate risk.

82. Which of the following possible portfolios cannot lie on the efficient frontier?

Portfolio	Expected Return	Standard Deviation
1	8%	6%
2	10%	6%
3	14%	12%
4	14%	16%

   A. Portfolio 3 only.
   B. Portfolios 1 and 4.
   C. Portfolios 2 and 3.

83. Which of the following pairs refer to the same type of risk?
   A. Total risk and the variance of returns.
   B. Systematic risk and firm-specific risk.
   C. Undiversifiable risk and unsystematic risk.

84. Greenbaum, Inc. stock pays no dividend and currently trades at $54. Based on the CAPM and assuming an expected return on the market of 12% and a risk-free rate of 8%, the expected price for Greenbaum one year from now is $62. The beta of Greenbaum shares is *closest* to:
   A. 1.5.
   B. 1.6.
   C. 1.7.

The following 12 questions relate to Equity Investments. (18 minutes)

85. After publishing a "Sell" recommendation on Stardust Inc., Kelly Peterson, CFA, thoroughly reads and saves additional news articles that highlight problems at Stardust and avoids articles that portray Stardust in a more positive light. Peterson is *most likely* exhibiting:
   A. data mining bias.
   B. confirmation bias.
   C. overconfidence bias.

86. The weak form of the efficient market hypothesis (EMH) implies that:
   A. no one can achieve abnormal returns using market information.
   B. insiders, such as specialists and corporate board members, cannot achieve abnormal returns on average.
   C. investors cannot achieve abnormal returns, on average, using technical analysis, after adjusting for transaction costs and taxes.

87.   With regard to the weighting schemes used in the construction of market indexes, which of the following statements is *most likely* correct?
       A. Equal weighting places an upward bias on the index.
       B. Price-weighting produces a downward bias in an index.
       C. Market-weighting places a downward bias on the index relative to price weighting.

88.   Which of the following is *least likely* a component of an investor's required rate of return on a stock?
       A. A growth premium.
       B. The real risk-free rate.
       C. The expected inflation rate.

89.   An analyst is valuing a company's perpetual preferred stock that pays a $6 annual dividend. The company's bonds currently yield 7.5% and preferred shares are selling to yield 75 basis points below the company's bond yield. The value of the preferred stock is *closest* to:
       A. $72.
       B. $80.
       C. $89.

90.   An investor buys a stock at $32 a share and deposits 50% initial margin. Assume that the maintenance margin is 25%, the stock pays no dividends, and transaction costs and interest on the margin loan are zero. The price at which the investor would receive a margin call is *closest* to:
       A. $8.
       B. $21.
       C. $48.

91.   The risk-free rate is 5%, and the expected return on the market index is 15%. A stock has a:
       •   Beta of 1.0.
       •   Dividend payout ratio of 40%.
       •   Return on equity (ROE) of 15%.

       If the stock is expected to pay a $2.50 dividend, its intrinsic value using dividend discount model is *closest* to:
       A. $27.77.
       B. $41.67.
       C. $53.33.

92. All else equal, a stock's price, according to the dividend discount model, will increase when the:
    A. expected dividend decreases.
    B. expected return on equity increases.
    C. difference between the required rate of return and the growth rate increases.

93. Which of the following scenarios is inconsistent with efficient financial markets?
    A. An analyst's buy recommendations have returned 2% more than the broad market index, on average.
    B. Johnson, Inc. reports an increase of 8% in its earnings from a year earlier, and its stock price declines 5% on the news.
    C. Earl Baker, an investor, earns consistently superior risk-adjusted returns by buying stocks when most investment advisors are pessimistic and selling stocks when most investment advisors are optimistic.

94. June Rutherford, CFA, is preparing a research report on Andronicus Fund, an offshore hedge fund that specializes in identifying market pricing inefficiencies and profiting from the arbitrage opportunities they present. Rutherford includes these statements in her report:
    - Statement 1: The rate of return that investors require from Andronicus should reflect the risk that the fund managers will not consistently capture positive abnormal returns from the anomalies they have identified.
    - Statement 2: Arbitrage trading is unlikely to bring about fully efficient prices because Andronicus and other arbitrageurs will not trade if the gains to be captured are less than their transactions costs.

    Are Rutherford's statements accurate?
    A. Both of Rutherford's statements are accurate.
    B. Neither of Rutherford's statements is accurate.
    C. Only one of Rutherford's statements is accurate.

95. Which valuation measure is *most likely* more difficult to interpret when inflation has been high?
    A. Price/sales.
    B. Price/earnings.
    C. Price/book value.

96.   A stock that currently does not pay a dividend is expected to pay its first dividend of $1.00 five years from today. Thereafter, the dividend is expected to grow at an annual rate of 25% for the next three years and then grow at a constant rate of 5% per year thereafter. The required rate of return is 10.3%. The value of the stock today is *closest* to:
       A. $20.65.
       B. $22.72.
       C. $23.87.

The following 14 questions relate to Fixed Income. (21 minutes)

97.   Which of the following statements about bond call features is *least likely* correct? Embedded call options in callable bonds:
       A. expose investors to additional reinvestment rate risk.
       B. create risk because they add uncertainty to the bond's cash flow pattern.
       C. can be valued using the difference between the zero-volatility spread and the nominal spread.

98.   All else equal, which of the following is *least likely* to increase the interest rate risk of a bond?
       A. A longer maturity.
       B. Inclusion of a call feature.
       C. A decrease in the YTM.

99.   One year ago, an investor purchased a 10-year, $1,000 par value, 8% semiannual coupon bond with an 8% yield to maturity. Now, one year later, interest rates remain unchanged at 8%. If the investor sells the bond today (immediately after receiving the second coupon payment, and with no transaction costs), he will have:
       A. a capital gain of $80.
       B. a capital loss of $80.
       C. no capital gain or loss.

100.   Which of the following statements about the risks associated with investing in bonds is *least accurate*?
       A. Credit risk is the likelihood that an investor will be unable to sell the security quickly and at a fair price.
       B. Volatility risk is the risk that the price of a bond with an embedded option will decline when expected yield volatility changes.
       C. Interest rate risk is the risk that a bondholder faces if the price of a bond held in a portfolio will decline due to rising market interest rates.

101. A company has two $1,000 face value bonds outstanding both selling for $701.22. The first issue has an annual coupon of 8% and 20 years to maturity. The second bond has the same yield to maturity as the first bond but has only five years remaining until maturity. The second issue pays interest annually as well. What is the annual interest payment on the second issue?
    A. $18.56.
    B. $27.18.
    C. $37.12.

102. If a bond has a convexity of 60 and a modified duration of 10, the convexity adjustment (to a duration-based approximation) associated with a 25 basis point interest rate decline is *closest* to:
    A. –2.875%.
    B. –2.125%.
    C. +0.0375%.

103. A semiannual-pay bond is callable in five years at $1,080. The bond has an 8% coupon and 15 years to maturity. If an investor pays $895 for the bond today, the yield to call is *closest* to:
    A. 9.3%.
    B. 10.2%.
    C. 12.1%.

104. Recent economic data suggest an increasing likelihood that the economy will soon enter a recessionary phase. What is the *most likely* effect on the yields of lower-quality corporate bonds and on credit spreads of lower-quality versus higher-quality corporate bonds?
    A. Both will increase.
    B. Both will decrease.
    C. One will increase and one will decrease.

105. Which of the following statements regarding provisions for paying off bonds is *least likely* correct?
    A. Nonrefundable bonds can be callable.
    B. "Serial bonds" refers to an issue with several staggered maturity dates.
    C. A sinking fund provision gives the company the option to retire portions of the bond issue prior to maturity.

106. Which of the following statements regarding the risks inherent in bonds is *most likely* correct?
    A. Interest rate risk is the risk that the coupon rate will be adjusted downward if market rates decline.
    B. The reinvestment rate assumption in calculating bond yields is generally not significant to the bond's yield.
    C. Default risk deals with the likelihood that the issuer will fail to meet its obligations as specified in the indenture.

107.   If an investor wants only investment grade bonds in her portfolio, she
       would be *least likely* to purchase a(n):
       A. A-rated municipal bond.
       B. 3-year municipal bond rated BB.
       C. 15-year, semiannual coupon corporate bond rated BBB.

108.   An investor is choosing between a 10% corporate bond and a 6%
       municipal bond with similar risk and similar maturity. What is the
       marginal tax rate that will make the investor indifferent between the
       two bonds?
       A. 0%.
       B. 40%.
       C. 60%.

109.   Changes in a bond's cash flows associated with changes in yield would
       be reflected in the bond's:
       A. effective duration.
       B. modified duration.
       C. Macaulay duration.

110.   Four non-convertible bonds have the indicated yield spreads to
       Treasury securities:

	Maturity	Nominal Spread	Zero-Volatility Spread	Option-Adjusted Spread
Bond W	2 years	156 bp	155 bp	130 bp
Bond X	3 years	173 bp	174 bp	199 bp
Bond Y	5 years	188 bp	189 bp	164 bp
Bond Z	10 years	202 bp	201 bp	226 bp

       Based on these spreads, it is *most likely* that:
       A. Bond X is callable, and Bond Y is putable.
       B. Bond W is callable, and Bond Z is putable.
       C. Bond Z is callable, and the spot yield curve is inverted.

The following 6 questions relate to Derivatives. (9 minutes)

111.   Three months ago, Jen Baker purchased one American put option contract on Mechor Corporation for $4 per option share. Baker also owns 100 shares of Mechor. The following data applies to Baker's position:
   *   Option strike price $60
   *   Stock price on date of option purchase $60
   *   Stock price today $52
   *   Time to option expiry from today   1 month

   Given only the above data, if Baker exercises her option today, the profit/loss (from the date of the option purchase) on Baker's combined stock/put position is:
   A. –$800.
   B. –$400.
   C. $800.

112.   Two Level 1 CFA candidates are discussing futures and make the following statements:

   Candidate 1: Futures are traded using standardized contracts. They require margin and incur interest charges on the margin loan.

   Candidate 2: If the margin balance falls below the maintenance margin amount due to a change in the contract price for the underlying assets, the investor must add funds to bring the margin back up to the initial margin requirement.

   Are the candidates' statements correct or incorrect?
   A. Both statements are correct.
   B. Neither statement is correct.
   C. Only one of the statements is correct.

113.   Which of the following statements for puts at expiration is *least accurate*? The:
   A. put buyer's maximum loss is the put option's premium.
   B. maximum loss to the writer of a put is the strike price less the premium.
   C. put holder will exercise the option whenever the stock's price is greater than the exercise price.

114. Which of the following is *least likely* a way to close a futures position?
   A. Cancellation: canceling the position on the floor of the exchange.
   B. Offset: taking on an opposite position to bring the net position to zero.
   C. Exchange-for-physicals: privately negotiating the terms of the transaction with a trader with an opposite position and delivering the asset and closing the contract off the floor of the exchange.

115. At the expiration of a LIBOR-based forward rate agreement (FRA), the party that holds the short position in the FRA will:
   A. lend money to the party that holds the long position at the rate specified in the FRA.
   B. borrow money from the party that holds the long position at the rate specified in the FRA.
   C. receive a payment if LIBOR is below the rate specified in the FRA.

116. Other things equal, a decrease in the value of a put option on a stock is *most likely* consistent with which of the following changes in the risk-free rate and stock return volatility?

	Risk-free rate	Volatility
A.	Increase	Decrease
B.	Decrease	Increase
C.	Decrease	Decrease

The following 4 questions relate to Alternative Investments. (6 minutes)

117. Which choice below *correctly* specifies both an advantage and a disadvantage of exchange-traded funds (ETFs) relative to other equity investments?

	Advantages of ETFs	Disadvantages of ETFs
A.	Diversification	Large bid-ask spreads for low-volume funds
B.	Trade like traditional equity	Increased capital gains tax
C.	May have better risk management	Composition of fund is not made public

118. Which of the following is *least likely* a type of hedge fund strategy?
   A. Event-driven.
   B. Market-neutral.
   C. Exchange-traded.

119. Compared with purchasing commodities, long positions in commodity derivatives offer the benefit of:
   A. no storage costs.
   B. less volatility.
   C. better correlation with spot prices.

120. A manager establishes a long commodity futures position and deposits Treasury bills to meet the initial margin requirement. If this futures market is in backwardation, the position is *most likely* to have a negative:
     A. roll yield.
     B. price return.
     C. collateral yield.

Exam 1
Morning Session Answer Key

To get valuable feedback on how your score compares to those of other Level 1 candidates, use your Username and Password to gain Online Access at schweser.com and choose the left-hand menu item "Practice Exams Vol. 1."

1. B	31. A	61. C	91. C
2. A	32. C	62. B	92. C
3. A	33. C	63. A	93. C
4. C	34. A	64. B	94. B
5. A	35. C	65. A	95. A
6. A	36. B	66. B	96. A
7. C	37. C	67. A	97. B
8. A	38. A	68. C	98. C
9. A	39. B	69. B	99. C
10. B	40. B	70. A	100. C
11. A	41. B	71. C	101. B
12. A	42. A	72. A	102. C
13. C	43. A	73. A	103. A
14. B	44. A	74. B	104. B
15. A	45. B	75. B	105. C
16. B	46. C	76. B	106. B
17. A	47. A	77. C	107. C
18. B	48. C	78. C	108. A
19. B	49. B	79. A	109. C
20. B	50. C	80. C	110. C
21. B	51. A	81. C	111. A
22. A	52. A	82. A	112. A
23. C	53. A	83. B	113. A
24. B	54. C	84. B	114. A
25. B	55. A	85. C	115. C
26. A	56. C	86. C	116. B
27. A	57. A	87. C	117. C
28. C	58. C	88. C	118. C
29. A	59. A	89. A	119. A
30. B	60. B	90. B	120. B

Exam 1
Morning Session Answers

Answers referencing the Standards of Practice address Study Session 1, LOS 1.b, c and LOS 2.a, b, c, except where noted.

1. **B** Standard I(A) Knowledge of the Law requires candidates and members comply with all applicable rules and regulations, including the CFA Standards of Practice. Further, Standard I(A) requires that members and candidates must not *knowingly* participate in violations of applicable laws and Standards. Even though local law permits purchasing shares for personal accounts before purchasing IPO shares for client accounts, Standard VI(B) Priority of Transactions does not. The analyst *knowingly* violated the Code and Standards and, thus, violated Standard I(A). Since the analyst was unaware of the deceit in the valuation of the IPO stock [a violation of Standard I(D) Misconduct], her participation in publishing the research did not constitute a violation.

2. **A** Ray and the portfolio manager are in violation of Standard VII(B) Reference to CFA Institute, the CFA Designation, and the CFA Program because they have improperly referenced the CFA designation or exaggerated its meaning (e.g., "elite group of the most qualified"). The marketing brochure is only stating factual information regarding the portfolio managers' successful attempts at passing the CFA exams on their first attempts.

3. **A** Standard V(B) Communication with Clients and Prospective Clients requires prompt disclosure of any change that might significantly affect the manager's investment processes. The disclosure need not be in writing.

4. **C** Standard III(C) Suitability requires that members and candidates carefully consider the needs, circumstances, and objectives of clients before taking investment action. However, some members and candidates are merely executing specific instructions for retail clients. In this case, since Wells believes the trade is unsuitable, Wells should confirm that the client is aware the action is unsuitable before executing the trade or refrain from making the trade.

5. **A** James has acted inappropriately in asking Jones to plagiarize the report and has likely violated several Standards, including Standard IV(C) Responsibilities of Supervisors and Standard I(D) Misconduct. However, he has not violated the prohibition against plagiarism in Standard I(C). Jones, on the other hand, even if acting on the request of her supervisor, will violate Standard I(C) Misrepresentation. Making minor changes to a report does not make it your own.

6. **A** According to Standard II(B) Market Manipulation, members and candidates should not engage in any practice that would artificially inflate trading volume or distort prices. However, this Standard does not prohibit transactions done for tax purposes. In this case, there was no intent to mislead market participants as to the stock price of Safety Airlines, and the trades were undertaken to take advantage of a legitimate tax strategy. Thus, there has been no violation of Standard II(B) or any other Standard.

7. **C** Standard I(B) Independence and Objectivity allows investor-paid research but requires that members and candidates limit the type of compensation they accept for writing a research report so that it is not dependent on the conclusions of the research report. Best practice is for analysts to only accept a flat fee for such company-paid research reports. Such research should also include complete disclosure of the nature of the compensation received for writing such a report so that investors will not be misled as to the relationship between the analyst and the company. Paying for one's own transportation and lodging when the analyst is not employed by the subject firm is a recommended procedure for complying with Standard I(B), but it is not a requirement.

8. **A** In the absence of regulatory requirements, Standard V(C) Record Retention recommends maintaining records supporting investment recommendations and actions and records of investment-related communications with clients for at least seven years. Here, there is regulatory guidance and seven years is a recommendation, not a requirement, in any case. Records can be maintained in electronic or hard copy format.

9. **A** Total firm assets must include all accounts whether discretionary or not and whether fee-paying or not. (Study Session 1, LOS 4.a)

10. **B** Under Standard III(B) Fair Dealing, changes from "Buy" to "Sell" should be disseminated, at a minimum, to clients the broker knows have purchased and held the security based on the earlier recommendation and to persons placing orders contrary to the firm's current recommendation.

11. **A** James is not in violation of the Standards. To comply with Standard VI(B) Priority of Transactions, members and candidates must give transactions for clients and employers priority over their personal transactions. In this instance, James did not adversely affect the client's interest because the client's trades were executed before James copied them. He has not acted fraudulently or deceitfully.

12. **A** The circumstances of the bankruptcy did not involve fraudulent or deceitful business conduct; therefore, there is no violation of Standard I(D) Misconduct. Hart's bankruptcy does not compromise his professional reputation.

13. **C** Marshall has an obligation to disclose that she receives special compensation based on the amount of client trading volume. Standard VI(A) Disclosure of Conflicts requires members to disclose to clients and prospects all matters that could potentially impair the member's ability to make investment decisions that are (and to give investment advice that is) objective and unbiased.

14. **B** Lunar can claim compliance as long as it has met the reporting requirements necessary and is held out to clients (advertised) as a distinct business entity. Claiming partial compliance is not allowed. (Study Session 1, LOS 4.b)

15. **A** Under Standard III(E) Preservation of Confidentiality, members and candidates should maintain the confidentiality of information received in the course of their professional service relating to both current and former clients. In the case of illegal activity, however, Reilly may have a legal obligation to report the activity. Ideally, he should consult with his employer first about what actions he may be required to take. Of the choices given, seeking the advice of outside counsel as to whether he has such an obligation under local law and whether the activity is indeed illegal is the one permitted under the Standard.

16. **B**   Standard II(A) Material Nonpublic Information requires that members and candidates who possess material nonpublic information not act or cause others to act on the information. Putting the stock on a restricted list or refusing the trade are violations of this Standard since they involve acting or causing others to act on the nonpublic information he possesses. Dean should seek to have East Street make the information public. If East Street does not do so, Dean is not allowed to act on the information. Refusing to make the trade he was instructed to make would be "acting" on the information in this case. The obligation here is to the integrity of financial markets.

17. **A**   Members and candidates should consider the knowledge and sophistication of those receiving the performance information. If only a brief presentation is given, members and candidates must make detailed information supporting the presentation available upon request. Individual account performance is permitted and no minimum number of years is recommended (these refer to GIPS, with which the Code and Standards do not require compliance). The primary requirement of Standard III(D) Performance Presentation is to not present false or misleading information.

18. **B**   GIPS require that, to claim compliance, firms must present GIPS-compliant performance information for a minimum of five years or since inception if in existence less than five years. (Study Session 1, LOS 3.a)

19. **B**   This problem involves determining the present value of an annuity followed by finding the present value of a lump sum. Enter PMT = 10,000, N = 10, and I = 14. Compute PV = 52,161.16. That is the present value of the 10-year annuity, four years from today. Next, we need to discount that back to present for four years to find the amount of the investment today. Enter FV = –52,161.16, N = 4, I = 14, PMT = 0. Compute PV = 30,883.59. (Study Session 2, LOS 5.e)

20. **B**   The cumulative absolute frequency of the fourth interval is 80, which is the sum of the absolute frequencies from the first to the fourth intervals. (Study Session 2, LOS 7.b)

21. **B**   Rising investor credit balances (uninvested cash) in brokerage accounts indicate that investors are bearish, and, thus, contrarians are bullish. Low mutual fund cash balances indicate that mutual fund managers are bullish, and, as a result, contrarians are bearish. An increasing ratio of over-the-counter volume to NYSE volume indicates an increase in speculative trading, which suggests market sentiment is bullish, in which case contrarians are bearish. (Study Session 3, LOS 12.c)

22. **A**   The average annual compound growth rate is calculated as:

$$[(1 + 0.25)(1 - 0.25)(1 + 0.30)(1 - 0.30)]^{0.25} - 1 = 0.9611 - 1 = -0.0389 \text{ or } -3.89\%$$

(Study Session 2, LOS 7.e)

23. **C**   Mean = 120 / 10 = 12, median = 10, and mode = 10. The distribution is skewed to the right, so the mean is greater than the median and mode. Generally, for positively skewed distributions, the mode is less than the median, which is less than the mean. In this case, the mode and median are equal because the number of observations is small. (Study Session 2, LOS 7.e, j)

24. **B**   The coefficient of variation, CV = standard deviation / arithmetic mean, is a common measure of relative dispersion (risk). CV_X = 0.7 / 0.9 = 0.78; CV_Y = 4.7 / 1.2 = 3.92; and CV_Z = 5.2 / 1.5 = 3.47. Because a higher CV means higher relative risk, Security Y has the highest relative risk. (Study Session 2, LOS 7.i)

25. **B** The median is the midpoint of a distribution, such that 50% of the observations are greater than the median and 50% are less than the median. This is equivalent to the second quartile (4 groups) and the fifth decile (10 groups). If a distribution is divided into quintiles (5 groups), 60% of the observations are less than the third quintile. (Study Session 2, LOS 7.f)

26. **A** *Subjective probability* is based on personal judgement. A *joint probability* is a probability that two or more events happen concurrently. An *a priori probability* is one based on logical analysis rather than on observation or personal judgment. An *empirical probability* is calculated using historical data. A *conditional probability* is the probability of one event happening on the condition that another event is certain to occur. (Study Session 2, LOS 8.a, b, d)

27. **A** Technical analysis assumes that supply and demand are governed by many factors, both rational and irrational. (Study Session 3, LOS 12.a)

28. **C**

	Selected by the Previous Portfolio Manager	Selected by the Current Portfolio Manager	Total
Value stocks	28 (28%)	12 (12%)	40
Growth stocks	48 (48%)	12 (12%)	60
Total	76	24	100

This problem involves the addition rule for probabilities, P(A or B) = P(A) + P(B) − P(AB).

P(A) is the probability that a randomly selected stock is a value stock, which is given as 40%.

P(B) is the probability that a stock was picked by the previous manager. That probability is (0.7)(0.4) + (0.8)(1 − 0.4) = 0.76. The previous manager selected 76% of the stocks in the portfolio.

P(AB) is the probability that a randomly selected stock is a value stock picked by the previous manager. Since the previous manager picked 70% of the 40% of the stocks that are value stocks, the probability that a randomly selected stock is a value stock picked by the previous manager is 40% × 70% = 28%.

From this, we have P(A or B) = 40% + 76% − 28% = 88%. (Study Session 2, LOS 8.f)

29. **A** The *standard* normal distribution has a mean of 0 and a standard deviation of 1. (Study Session 2, LOS 8.g and Study Session 3, LOS 9.i)

30. **B** The 95% confidence interval is 10% ± 1.96(4%) or from 2.16% to 17.84%. The 90% confidence interval is 10% ± 1.65(4%) or from 3.4% to 16.6%. The probability of a return ± 1 standard deviation from the mean, between 6% and 14%, is approximately 68%. (Study Session 3, LOS 9.j)

31. **A** Using the standard normal probability distribution,

$$z = \frac{\text{observation} - \text{mean}}{\text{standard deviation}} = \frac{0 - 10}{5} = -2.0 \text{, the chance of getting zero or less return}$$

(losing money) is $1 - 0.9772 = 0.0228\%$ or 2.28%. An alternative explanation: the expected return is 10%. To lose money means the return must fall below zero. Zero is about two standard deviations to the left of the mean. 50% of the time, a return will be below the mean, and 2.5% of the observations are below two standard deviations down. About 97.5% of the time, the return will be above zero. Thus, only about a 2.5% chance exists of having a value below zero. (Study Session 3, LOS 9.k)

32. **C** According to the central limit theorem, the sample mean for large sample sizes will be distributed normally regardless of the distribution of the underlying population. (Study Session 3, LOS 10.b, c, d)

33. **C** The crowding-out effect refers to a reduction in private borrowing and investment as a result of higher interest rates generated by budget deficits that are financed by borrowing in the private loanable funds market. (Study Session 6, LOS 26.b)

34. **A** Aggregate hours measures the total number of hours worked in a year by all employed people. Aggregate hours takes account of both the level of employment and the average workweek, making it superior to the number of employed as an indicator of total labor performed. Total labor compensation is a measure of real wage rates that includes wages, salaries, and employer-paid benefits. (Study Session 5, LOS 22.b)

35. **C** At competitive equilibrium, the sum of consumer and producer surplus is at its maximum level. Neither consumer nor producer surplus is necessarily at a maximum at the equilibrium output and price. Which surplus is larger or smaller depends on the elasticities of supply and demand. (Study Session 4, LOS 14.d)

36. **B** Open market operations are the U.S. Federal Reserve's most often used tool for changing the money supply. (Study Session 6, LOS 24.d)

37. **C** The demand for labor is a derived demand. When the demand for the final good or service increases, the price of that final good or service increases. That increase in price will lead to the firm employing more of the resources used in production at each resource price, including labor. (Study Session 5, LOS 21.b)

38. **A** In the short run, an increase in the money supply will increase aggregate demand. The new short-run equilibrium will be at a higher price level and a greater level of real output (GDP). (Study Session 5, LOS 23.c and Study Session 6, LOS 24.h)

39. **B** The law of diminishing returns states that at some point, as more of a resource is used in a production process, holding other inputs constant, output increases at a decreasing rate. This accounts for the upward slope of the SRMC curve beyond that point. Returns to scale determine the shape of the long-run cost curves. (Study Session 4, LOS 17.c)

40. **B** Under perfect competition, each firm faces a flat demand curve. This means the price is constant and the marginal revenue line is flat. A company will continue to produce as long as MR > MC, so the competitive company will produce as long as P > MC. It will stop when MC = MR = P. (Study Session 5, LOS 18.b)

41. **B** In the short run, the decision to operate is based on whether price covers average variable costs. In the long run, average fixed costs must be considered as well. The marginal revenue from selling an additional unit of output must be at least as great as its marginal cost of production. (Study Session 4, LOS 17.d)

42. **A** For a process to have the lowest production cost (be economically efficient), it must be technologically efficient. A process is technologically efficient if there is no other process that can produce the same output with less of at least one input and no more of the other inputs. A process that uses no less of any input and more of at least one input cannot be the lowest cost process and is, by definition, not technologically efficient. (Study Session 4, LOS 16.c)

43. **A** The Laffer curve indicates that tax revenues reach a maximum at some tax rate and decrease if tax rates are increased above that rate. (Study Session 6, LOS 26.a)

44. **A** A natural monopoly may exist when economies of scale are great. The large economies of scale mean that a single producer results in the lowest production costs. (Study Session 5, LOS 19.a)

45. **B** Extraordinary items are unusual and infrequent items that are reported separately, net of tax, after net income from continuing operations. (Study Session 8, LOS 32.f)

46. **C**

original shares of common stock	= 1,000,000(12)	= 12,000,000
stock dividend	= 100,000(12)	= 1,200,000
new shares of common stock	= 400,000(3)	= 1,200,000
total shares of common stock	$= \dfrac{14,400,000}{12}$	= 1,200,000

Stock dividends are assumed to have been outstanding since the beginning of the year. (Study Session 8, LOS 32.g)

47. **A** Cash conversion cycle is days in inventory + days in receivables − days in payables. Financing payables reduces accounts payable, decreases days' payables, and lengthens the cash conversion cycle. Stretching out payables increases accounts payable, increases days' payables, and decreases the cash conversion cycle. Securitization of receivables decreases receivables and days' receivables, which decreases the cash conversion cycle. (Study Session 8, LOS 35.d and Study Session 10, LOS 41)

48. **C** A classified balance sheet has accounts grouped by type and presents subtotals for these groups of assets. (Study Session 8, LOS 33.b)

49. **B** When using the direct method of calculating operating cash flows, depreciation and amortization are not "added back" (to net income) because we don't begin with net income under the direct method. Depreciation and amortization are noncash changes and are not used under the direct method. The other statements are true. Interest payments on debt affect cash flow from operations. When using the indirect method, an analyst should add any losses on sales of fixed assets to net income since they are not operating cash flows. (Study Session 8, LOS 34.c, e)

50. **C** In a period of rising prices, LIFO results in higher COGS, lower taxes, lower net income, lower inventory balances, lower working capital, and higher cash flows due to less taxes paid out, as compared to FIFO. In a falling price environment, these effects are the opposite. (Study Session 9, LOS 36.c, e)

51. **A**   ROE 20X6 = (0.7)(0.85)(0.15)(1.5)(1.5) = 0.2008

ROE 20X7 = (0.7)(0.85)(0.10)(1.8)(1.6) = 0.1714

Profit margin fell, and the increase in the total asset turnover ratio and the leverage multiplier were not enough to offset the decline, so ROE decreased.
(Study Session 8, LOS 35.f)

52. **A**   The LIFO inventory method is permitted under U.S. GAAP but is not allowed under IFRS. Proportionate consolidation of joint ventures is permitted under IFRS but not under U.S. GAAP. Unrealized gains and losses from held-for-trading securities are recognized on the income statement under both IFRS and U.S. GAAP.
(Study Session 10, LOS 43.a)

53. **A**   If equity equals 45% of assets and current liabilities equal 20%, long-term debt must be 35%.

$$\text{long-term debt-to-equity ratio} = \frac{\text{long-term debt}}{\text{total equity}} = \frac{0.35}{0.45} = 0.778 = 77.8\%$$

CA = 0.1 + 0.15 + 0.20 = 0.45

$$\text{current ratio} = \frac{\text{CA}}{\text{CL}} = \frac{45}{20} = 2.25\text{x}$$

(Study Session 8, LOS 33.h, 35.d)

54. **C**   Interest expense is shown as a non-operating component of net income for a manufacturing company but would typically be classified as an operating expense for a financial services company. (Study Session 8, LOS 32.e)

55. **A**   The switch from FIFO to LIFO during a period of rising prices reduces the value of the company's inventory and, therefore, inflates COGS. Higher COGS would produce lower earnings. Choice B would tend to reduce annual expenses and increase earnings. Choice C would clearly increase revenue and net income in a fixed period of time if the practice is followed on a regular basis. (Study Session 9, LOS 36.e, 37.b)

56. **C**   With an operating lease, the entire lease payment (rent expense) is subtracted from operating income. With a capital lease, only depreciation is subtracted from operating income, so operating income is higher with a capital lease. Net income in the first year is lower with a capital lease because the sum of depreciation (operating expense) and interest (non-operating expense) is greater than the lease payment.
(Study Session 9, LOS 39.g)

57. **A** The warrants are dilutive because their exercise price is less than the average market price.

~~shares issued to warrant holders = 100~~

warrants generate cash of 100(50) = \$5,000

$$\text{repurchased shares} = \frac{5,000}{60} = 83$$

net new shares created = 100 − 83 = 17

Alternatively, $\frac{60-50}{60} \times 100 \approx 17$

$$\text{diluted EPS} = \frac{\text{NI} - \text{preferred dividends}}{\text{weighted average \# shares} + \text{warrant adjust}}$$

$$\text{diluted EPS} = \frac{5,000 - 500}{1,017} = \$4.42$$

(Study Session 8, LOS 32.g, h)

58. **C** Corporate press releases are written by management and are often viewed as public relations or sales materials because of the great possibility of inherent management bias in such documents. Often, little or none of the material is independently reviewed by outside auditors. Such documents are not mandated by the securities regulators. Form 10-Q (quarterly financial statements) and proxy statements are mandatory SEC filings in the United States, which inherently increases their reliability given the penalties that can be imposed by the SEC if any serious irregularities are subsequently found. (Study Session 7, LOS 29.e)

59. **A** The impairment writedown in 20X3 will reduce depreciation expense in 20X4, which will increase 20X4 EBIT and net income. Operating cash flow and taxes payable are not affected because an impairment cannot be deducted from income for tax reporting purposes until the asset is sold or otherwise disposed of. (Study Session 9, LOS 37.i)

60. **B** There is a 20% reduction in the tax rate [(40% − 50%) / 50% = −0.2]. Hence, the deferred tax asset will be \$800 = \$1,000(1 − 0.2), the deferred tax liability will be \$4,000 = \$5,000(1 − 0.2), and the income tax expense will fall by the net amount of the decline in the asset and liability balances (\$1,000 − \$200 = \$800). (Study Session 9, LOS 38.d)

61. **C** Under U.S. GAAP, costs incurred to establish technological feasibility of software for sale are expensed, but software development costs incurred after technological feasibility has been established must be capitalized. Under IFRS, research costs are expensed as incurred and development costs are capitalized. Thus, both East and West will capitalize \$90,000 of development costs. (Study Session 9, LOS 37.c)

62. **B** Capitalizing costs tends to smooth earnings and reduces investment cash flows. It will also increase cash flows from operations and increase profitability in the early years. (Study Session 9, LOS 37.b)

63. **A** Gains or losses from changes in the market value of outstanding debt are not recognized. U.S. GAAP requires disclosures about the fair value of outstanding debt based on year-end or quarter-end prices. These disclosures are made in the notes to the financial statements. (Study Session 9, LOS 39.d)

64. **B**   Based on the data given, use the basic DuPont equation and solve for expected net income.

ROE = (net income / revenues) × (revenues / total assets) × (total assets / total equity)

0.15 = (net income / $3 billion) × ($3 billion / $5 billion) × 2.5

net income / $3 billion = 0.1

net income = $300 million

Alternatively, A/E = 2.5 and assets = $5 billion, so equity = $2 billion.

net income / equity = 15%, so net income = 0.15($2 Billion) = $300 million
(Study Session 10, LOS 42.b)

65. **A**   PMT = 800,000; FV = 10,000,000; N = 5; I/Y = 8.25; CPT → PV = $9,900,837

interest expense = 9,900,836.51 × 0.0825 = $816,819.01

year-end adjustment = 816,819.01 − 800,000 = $16,819.01

year-end debt = $9,900,836.51 + $16,819.01 = $9,917,655.52

Note: Since this is a discount bond, we know the initial liability will be less than the face value, so we really didn't have to do any calculations to answer this question.
(Study Session 9, LOS 39.a)

66. **B**   Unrealized gains and losses from trading securities are reflected in the income statement and affect owners' equity. However, unrealized gains and losses from available-for-sale securities are included in other comprehensive income. Transactions included in other comprehensive income affect equity but not net income. Dividends paid to shareholders reduce owners' equity but not net income. (Study Session 8, LOS 32.j)

67. **A**   Conversion of bonds into common stock is a non-cash transaction, but the conversion should be disclosed in a footnote to the statement of cash flows.
(Study Session 8, LOS 34.e)

68. **C**   Liabilities for debt guarantees should be added to balance sheet liabilities. Finance (capital) lease obligations are already included in both liabilities and assets. To reverse the receivables sale, CFO should be reduced. (Study Session 9, LOS 37.i)

69. **B**

Year	0	1	2	3	4
Net cash flow	−$5,000.00	$1,900.00	$1,900.00	$2,500.00	$2,000.00
Net cash flow discounted at 12%	−$5,000.00	$1,696.43	$1,514.67	$1,779.45	$1,271.04
Cumulative discounted net cash flows	−$5,000.00	−$3,303.57	−$1,788.90	−$9.45	$1,261.59

discounted payback period $= 3 + \dfrac{9.45}{1,271.04} = 3.01$ years.

(Study Session 11, LOS 44.d)

70. **A**   To compare these short-term securities, state the return on each as a bond-equivalent yield. For the commercial paper, the BEY is given as 5.10%. The BEY for the certificate of deposit is 2.5% × 365 / 180 = 5.07%. For the Treasury bill, the BEY is [(100 − 97.5) / 97.5] × 365 / 180 = 5.20%. Miller should purchase the Treasury bill. (Study Session 11, LOS 46.e)

71. **C**   Current market yields, not the coupon rate, should be used to estimate the cost of debt capital. (Study Session 11, LOS 45.f)

72. **A**   Surveys indicate that European companies and private companies tend to use the payback period criterion more than other types of companies. (Study Session 11, LOS 44.f)

73. **A**   Investors should take steps to discourage the use of the corporate funds to pay "greenmail." (Study Session 11, LOS 48.g)

74. **B** $$K_e = \frac{0.93(1.07)}{16} + 0.07 = 13.2\%$$

(Study Session 11, LOS 45.h)

75. **B**   Good corporate governance practices will discourage or prohibit both the payment of finder's fees to board members for identifying attractive merger or acquisition targets and the use of corporate assets by board members or their families. (Study Session 11, LOS 48.e)

76. **B**   IRR and NPV lead to the same decision when choosing independent projects but may lead to different decisions when choosing between projects. (Study Session 11, LOS 44.e)

77. **C**   Break points in the marginal cost of capital structure occur at the levels where the cost of one of the components of the company's capital structure increases, increasing its weighted average cost of capital. (Study Session 11, LOS 45.k)

78. **C**   Provisions that require a supermajority can even make changes strongly supported by shareowners more difficult to enact. (Study Session 11, LOS 48.g)

79. **A**   As the correlation between two assets *decreases*, the benefits of diversification increase. Combining assets that are not perfectly correlated reduces the risk of the portfolio, as measured by standard deviation. (Study Session 12, LOS 50.e)

80. **C**   The capital market line plots expected return against standard deviation of returns for efficient portfolios. The efficient frontier plots expected return against the standard deviation of return, a measure of total risk. (Study Session 12, LOS 51.b, c, d)

81. **C**   As randomly selected securities are added to a portfolio, the diversifiable (unsystematic) risk decreases, and the expected level of nondiversifiable (systematic) risk remains the same. (Study Session 12, LOS 51.c)

82. **A**   Based on the CAPM, the portfolio should earn: E(R) = 0.05 + 1.5(0.15 − 0.05) = 0.20 or 20%. On a risk-adjusted basis, this portfolio lies on the SML and is, thus, properly valued. (Study Session 12, LOS 51.e)

83. **B**   These ethical issues fall under the heading of unique needs and preferences. Some investors would exclude these types of investments due to their own personal preferences. Legal restrictions and regulatory factors have to do with the type of account and its supporting legal documents. (Study Session 12, LOS 49.d)

84. **B** Points on the CML do not represent individual securities, but rather portfolios that contain a well diversified portfolio (the tangency portfolio) combined with either lending or borrowing at the risk-free rate. The other statements are correct. (Study Session 12, LOS 51.a, d, e)

85. **C** A *stop buy order* is a conditional market order by which an investor directs the purchase of a stock if it rises to a certain price. Stop buys are placed above the current market price. Limit orders can have market price as the limit, used when lack of liquidity is a concern. (Study Session 13, LOS 52.e)

86. **C** There is no maximum time for which a security can be borrowed. It must be returned whenever the lender requires it to be. (Study Session 13, LOS 52.f)

87. **C** The expected growth rate in dividends is an input into the dividend discount model, but the real risk-free rate, the expected inflation rate, and the risk premium are the components of the required rate of return. (Study Session 14, LOS 56.g)

88. **C** Brokerage fees and transactions costs are not considered in assessing the risk premium. The risk premium consists of business risk, financial risk, liquidity risk, exchange-rate risk, and country risk (potential unexpected economic and political events). (Study Session 14, LOS 56.e)

89. **A** If capital markets are weak-form efficient and semistrong-form efficient, no publicly available information can be used to earn abnormal (risk-adjusted) returns. (Study Session 13, LOS 54.c)

90. **B** Time line = $0 now; $0 in year 1; $0 in year 2; $1 in year 3.

$$P_2 = \frac{D_3}{(k-g)} = \frac{1}{(0.17-0.07)} = \$10$$

Note that the price is always one year before the dividend date. Solve for the PV of $10 to be received in two years.

FV = 10; N = 2; I = 17; CPT $\rightarrow$ PV = $7.31. (Study Session 14, LOS 56.c)

91. **C** The forecast year-end price, *P*, is:

$$P = EPS \times \left(\frac{P}{E}\right) = 10(12) = 120$$

$$\text{expected return} = \frac{\text{dividend} + (\text{ending price} - \text{beginning price})}{\text{beginning price}} = \frac{\$5 + \$120 - \$100}{\$100} = 0.25 \text{ or } 25\%$$

(Study Session 14, LOS 58.b, 59.b)

92. **C** $$P/E = \frac{\text{dividend payout ratio}}{k-g}$$

dividend payout ratio = 1 − retention ratio = 1 − 0.4 = 0.6

growth rate (g) = retention rate × ROE = 0.4 × 15% = 6%

$$P/E = \frac{0.6}{0.14 - 0.06} = 7.5$$

(Study Session 14, LOS 56.d)

93. **C** Low correlations among global markets imply that both bond and stock portfolios composed of 100% U.S. securities can benefit from diversifying into international securities. (Study Session 13, LOS 53.c)

94. **B** The top-down, 3-step approach to security valuation starts with an economic forecast. (Study Session 14, LOS 56.a)

95. **A** $P = \dfrac{D_1}{k-g}$, so price is positively related to the growth rate and the dividend and negatively related to the required return. The growth rate is positively related to ROE and the retention ratio (g = RR × ROE).
(Study Session 14, LOS 56.c)

 Professor's Note: Start with the pricing equation and hold all variables constant except prices and the one you are interested in.

96. **A** When constructing samples, researchers must be very careful not to include just surviving companies, mutual funds, or investment newsletters. Since survivors tend to be those that have done well (by skill or chance), samples of mutual funds that have 10-year track records, for example, will exhibit performance histories with upward bias. Mutual fund companies regularly discontinue funds with poor performance histories or roll their assets into better performing funds. (Study Session 13, LOS 55.c)

97. **B** Long-term, low-coupon bonds are more sensitive than short-term and high-coupon bonds. Prices are more sensitive to rate decreases than to rate increases (duration rises as yields fall). (Study Session 15, LOS 61.c)

98. **C** The friend is incorrect about TIPS (the coupon rate is fixed, the par value is adjusted for inflation) and is correct about the bid-ask spread for on-the-run issues (on-the-run issues are more liquid and, thus, have a narrower bid-ask spread). (Study Session 15, LOS 62.b)

99. **C** $\text{taxable-equivalent yield} = \dfrac{\text{tax-exempt yield}}{1 - \text{marginal tax rate}} = \dfrac{0.04}{1 - 0.28} = 0.0556 \text{ or } 5.56\%$

(Study Session 15, LOS 63.i)

100. **C** *Prefunded municipal bonds* are bonds collateralized by an escrow of securities guaranteed by the U.S. government. *Revenue bonds* are supported through revenues generated from projects that are funded with the proceeds of the original bond issue.
(Study Session 15, LOS 62.b, f, g)

101. **B** A BEY of 8% is equivalent to a 6-month discount rate of 8 / 2 = 4%.

$$1,025 = \frac{50}{1.04} + \frac{1,050}{(1+r)^2}$$

$$1,025 - 48.08 = \frac{1,050}{(1+r)^2}$$

$$(1+r)^2 = \frac{1,050}{976.92} = 1.0748$$

$$r = (1.0748)^{0.50} - 1$$

$$r = 0.0367 \text{ or } 7.34\% \text{ on a bond equivalent basis}$$

(Study Session 16, LOS 65.e)

102. **C** $\quad _4r_1 = \dfrac{(1+R_5)^5}{(1+R_4)^4} - 1 = \dfrac{(1.08)^5}{(1.075)^4} - 1 = \dfrac{1.47}{1.335} - 1 = 0.10 \text{ or } 10\%$

Note: $(5 \times 8) - (4 \times 7.5) = 10$

(Study Session 16, LOS 65.h)

103. **A** $\quad \dfrac{\Delta P}{P} = -D_{mod}\Delta i + C(\Delta i)^2$

$\dfrac{\Delta P}{P} = (-)(8)(-0.005) + (50)(-0.005)^2 = +0.0400 + 0.00125 = +0.04125, \text{ or up } 4.125\%$

The price would thus be $\$1,000 \times 1.04125 = \$1,041.25$. (Study Session 16, LOS 66.g)

104. **B** Creating a CMO can redistribute the prepayment risk among the tranches, but it does not alter the overall prepayment risk of a mortgage passthrough security. CMOs are created from MBS. The prepayment option benefits the issuer, or homeowner, not the investor. (Study Session 15, LOS 62.e, f)

105. **C** A put option may be exercised by the holder, not the issuer. The other statements are true. Interest rate floors benefit the holder by providing a lower limit (or minimum) on the interest rate the bondholder will receive. To understand why the prepayment right granted to a mortgage holder benefits the issuer, remember that the issuer here is the homeowner. The bank acts as a passthrough from the homeowner to the owner of a bond collateralized by the loan. The right to prepay if interest rates decrease is a benefit to the homeowner. If the homeowner prepays, the holder of the bond has reinvestment risk. (Study Session 15, LOS 60.e)

106. **B** The clean price of the bond is the quoted price, 89.14% of par value, which is $891.40. (Study Session 15, LOS 60.c)

107. **C** Resetting interest rates makes the bond less, not more, susceptible to interest rate changes. (Study Session 15, LOS 61.e)

108. **A** When the foreign currency appreciates, each foreign currency-denominated cash flow buys more domestic currency units—increasing the domestic currency return from the investment. The appreciation of the foreign asset benefits the investor as well. (Study Session 15, LOS 61.l)

109. **C** Reinvestment risk becomes more problematic when the current coupons being reinvested are relatively large. (Study Session 15, LOS 61.i)

110. **C** The zero-volatility spread is the constant spread that is added to each Treasury spot rate to equate the present value of a bond's cash flows to its actual market price. (Study Session 16, LOS 65.f, g)

111. **A** Call options represent an obligation to perform in the case of the seller. The owner of the option (buy) has the right, but not an obligation, to purchase an underlying good at a specified price for a specified time from the seller. (Study Session 17, LOS 70.a)

112. **A** Forward contracts are with a specific counterparty, so renegotiation is always an option, but it may not come to the desired result. Entering into an offsetting forward would not eliminate the existing contract obligation but would eliminate price risk. Forward contracts do not typically offer an option to terminate the contract early for a cash payment equal to the current difference between the contract price and the price of the underlying security. (Study Session 17, LOS 68.b)

113. **A** In a foreign currency swap, both parties exchange full interest payments. The New Zealand company pays 6% variable on USD (USD 60,000). The U.S. company pays 7% fixed on NZD (NZD 140,000). (Study Session 17, LOS 71.b)

114. **A** The dealer pays the fixed rate for 91 days. Dealer payment = (5.50%)(91 / 365)($50M) = $685,616.44.

The fund pays the return on the Midcap Index: $\left(\dfrac{1,052.5}{1,038.4} - 1\right)\$50M = \$678,929.12$

The dealer is the net payer: $685,616.44 − $678,929.12 = $6,687.32

(Study Session 17, LOS 71.b)

115. **C** *Forwards* are subject to default risk, but *futures* are not. *Forwards* are individualized contracts, but *futures* are standardized. (Study Session 17, LOS 69.b)

116. **B** A futures exchanges sets the minimum price fluctuation, or "tick size," for the contracts that trade on that exchange. Speculators enter the futures market in pursuit of profit, accepting risk in the endeavor. Hedgers trade futures to reduce some pre-existing risk exposure. The clearinghouse takes no active position in the market but interposes itself between both parties to every transaction. Thus, the clearinghouse guarantees that traders in the future market will honor their obligations. (Study Session 17, LOS 69.a)

117. **C** Loan payments (N = 20; I = 10%; FV = 0; PV = 2 million) are $234,919.

First-year interest is 10% × $2 million = $200,000.

First-year principal payment is $234,919 − $200,000 = $34,919.

After-tax cash flow is (300,000 − 200,000 − 60,000 − 35,000)(1 − 0.35) − 34,919 + 60,000 = 28,331. (Study Session 18, LOS 73.f)

118. **C** The fee may actually be substantial since, in addition to paying the manager of the FOF, a fee must be paid to each hedge fund within the FOF.
(Study Session 18, LOS 73.j)

119. **A** Open-end funds redeem existing shares or issue new shares in accordance with investor demand. Closed-end fund shares are fixed in number and trade on exchanges as though they were common stock. (Study Session 18, LOS 73.a)

120. **B** Long commodities positions would tend to hedge the risk that bonds would decline in value because of increases in inflation or because of higher interest rates due to an increase in the overall level of economic activity. Selling bond futures would hedge against rising rates. Interest rate puts increase in value as rates fall and would not provide a hedge. (Study Session 17, LOS 69.f, 70.f, and Study Session 18, LOS 73.r)

Exam 1
Afternoon Session Answer Key

To get valuable feedback on how your score compares to those of other Level 1 candidates, use your Username and Password to gain Online Access at schweser.com and choose the left-hand menu item "Practice Exams Vol. 1."

1. B	31. C	61. B	91. B
2. C	32. B	62. C	92. B
3. C	33. A	63. C	93. C
4. A	34. C	64. B	94. B
5. A	35. A	65. A	95. B
6. B	36. B	66. A	96. C
7. A	37. A	67. C	97. B
8. A	38. B	68. B	98. B
9. B	39. C	69. B	99. C
10. B	40. B	70. C	100. B
11. B	41. B	71. A	101. A
12. A	42. A	72. C	102. C
13. A	43. C	73. C	103. C
14. C	44. B	74. C	104. B
15. A	45. A	75. B	105. B
16. C	46. C	76. B	106. C
17. C	47. C	77. A	107. B
18. A	48. B	78. C	108. A
19. C	49. C	79. C	109. A
20. B	50. C	80. B	110. A
21. C	51. B	81. A	111. A
22. A	52. C	82. B	112. A
23. B	53. A	83. C	113. C
24. A	54. A	84. A	114. A
25. C	55. A	85. B	115. B
26. C	56. B	86. A	116. A
27. C	57. B	87. C	117. B
28. C	58. B	88. A	118. C
29. B	59. B	89. A	119. A
30. B	60. A	90. C	120. C

Exam 1
Afternoon Session Answers

Answers referencing the Standards of Practice address Study Session 1, LOS 1.b, c and LOS 2.a, b, c, except where noted.

1. **B** According to Standard VII(B) Reference to the CFA Institute, the CFA Designation, and CFA Program, the CFA® and Chartered Financial Analyst® designations must always be used as adjectives, never as nouns or common names. The appropriate description would be "Roger Langley is one of three CFA charterholders in the company."

2. **C** All investment personnel in this example are subject to the CFA Institute Code and Standards as part of the firm's established policies. The candidate's reference to her Level 3 status and the inclusion of such information in her biographical information is not in violation of the CFA Institute Code and Standards. Candidates may clearly reference their participation in the CFA program, provided such reference does not imply the achievement of any type of partial designation. The analyst is considered a candidate since she is registered to take the next scheduled examination. Choice A is incorrect since the Code and Standards prohibit using material nonpublic information. Since the Code and Standards are *stricter* than the local law, they must be followed by the analyst. Choice B is incorrect since the analyst failed to exercise diligence and thoroughness in making investment recommendations and failed to have a reasonable and adequate basis for such recommendations.

3. **C** Under Standard VI(B) Priority of Transactions, since the family account is a client account, it should be treated as any other client account and trades should be entered prior to trades for the employer's account. A firm may put a stock on its recommended list without ever making its change in recommendation public, since there is no requirement that they do.

4. **A** To comply with Standard IV(B) Additional Compensation Arrangements, Bryant must obtain written consent from her employer before undertaking the independent consulting project. Bryant must also provide a description of the types of services being provided, the length of time the arrangement will last, and the compensation she expects to receive for her services.

5. **A** Standard V(C) Record Retention requires members to maintain records of the data and analysis they use to develop their research recommendations. Recommendations may be brief, in capsule form, or simply a list of buy/sell recommendations. A list of recommendations may be sent without regard to suitability, including both safe income stocks and aggressive growth stocks, for example.

6. **B** Standard IV(C) Responsibilities of Supervisors indicates that a member should decline supervisory responsibility in writing until the firm adopts reasonable compliance procedures. Otherwise, Brooks cannot adequately exercise her responsibility.

7. **A** Standard VI(C) Referral Fees indicates that members shall disclose to clients and prospects any consideration or benefits received for the recommendation of services. Investment managers in the Macrovest program pay a portion of their management fees earned from client assets to Rogers as compensation for his recommendation of their services. Rogers' recommendations may be predicated on the potential increase in compensation he will receive for recommending an investment manager rather than the manager's ability to provide good investment returns for the client. Therefore, in accordance with the Standard, Rogers is required to disclose the referral fee arrangement to clients and prospects before agreeing to perform any services covered by the arrangement. The disclosure must describe the nature of the consideration and the estimated dollar value of the consideration.

8. **A** Standard V(B) Communication with Clients and Prospective Clients requires that Toma separate opinion from fact. Toma's statement that excess demand will persist into the foreseeable future is an opinion, not a fact.

9. **B** Under Standard III(A) Loyalty, Prudence, and Care, the fiduciary duty in this case is to plan participants and beneficiaries, not shareholders or plan trustees.

10. **B** According to Standard III(B) Fair Dealing, if a client places an order that goes against the firm's recommendation for that security, members and candidates should inform the client of the discrepancy between the order and the firm's recommendation before accepting the order.

11. **B** Private equity is one of the eight major sections of the GIPS standards; the others are not. (Study Session 1, LOS 4.d)

12. **A** Standard V(A) Diligence and Reasonable Basis. When a member or candidate relies on others within the firm to determine whether a model is sound, it can be used in good faith unless the member or candidate has reason to question its validity. In this case, Wilcox is simply unfamiliar with the model but has no reason to believe it is unreliable.

13. **A** Hoffman has violated both Standard I(B) Independence and Objectivity, which specifically addresses the requirement of disclosure of the nature of any compensation from the subject company, and Standard VI(C) Conflicts of Interest, which, more generally, requires disclosure of any potential conflict of interest in research reports and investment recommendations.

14. **C** Both market-making activities by her firm and the directorship held by a principal in the firm must be disclosed according to Standard VI(A) Disclosure of Conflicts.

15. **A** According to Standard II(A) Material Nonpublic Information, Farr is free to act under the mosaic theory because nonmaterial nonpublic information does not fall within the prohibition on trading based on material nonpublic information. He should keep detailed documentation of his analysis to prove that he did not advise or act based upon material nonpublic information.

16. **C** In order to initially claim compliance with GIPS, a firm must have a minimum of five years (or since firm inception) of GIPS-compliant data. After the first compliant presentation, another year of compliant performance must be added each year until the compliant performance history reaches at least ten years. (Study Session 1, LOS 3.c, 4.b)

17. **C** Standard VI(C) Referral Fees states that members and candidates must disclose to employers and to affected clients, before entering into any formal agreement for services, any benefits received for the recommendation of services provided by the member.

18. **A** Michaelson's recommendation regarding the purchase of Network is in violation of Standard II(A) Material Nonpublic Information. Members who possess material nonpublic information are prohibited from trading, or causing others to trade in, based on that information. Since the information Michaelson received during her flight involved Collective's proposed tender offer for the shares of Network, she was in possession of material nonpublic information and should not have recommended purchase of Network based on the information. Therefore, Michaelson's actions violate Standard V(A) and, potentially, federal securities laws, which would also cause a violation of Standard I(A) Knowledge of the Law.

19. **C** If p is the probability that an event occurs, then the odds for the event occurring are expressed as p / (1 – p), or the probability that the event occurs divided by the probability that the event does not occur. The odds against the event are expressed as the reciprocal of the odds for the event. (Study Session 2, LOS 8.c)

20. **B** The investor has to ensure that the amount deposited now will grow into the amount needed to fund the perpetuity. With semiannual compounding, the effective annual rate (EAR) earned on funds in the account is:

$$EAR = \left(1 + \frac{\text{annual rate}}{2}\right)^2 - 1 = \left(1 + \frac{0.04}{2}\right)^2 - 1 = 0.0404 = 4.04\%$$

The present value of the perpetuity = $25,000/0.0404 = $618,811.88.

Note that since the first scholarship award is paid out in four years, the present value of the perpetuity represents the amount that must be in the account at time t = 3. We can find the required deposit from:

FV = –618,811.88; N = 3; I = 4.04; CPT → PV = $549,487.24 or $\dfrac{618,811.88}{1.0404^3}$

(Study Session 2, LOS 5.c, d, e)

21. **C** If a return distribution has positive excess kurtosis and the analyst uses statistical models that do not account for the fatter tails, the analyst will *underestimate* the likelihood of very bad or very good outcomes. The fatter the tails associated with the positive kurtosis, the higher the probabilities of very high and very low returns as compared to the normal distribution with kurtosis = 3.0. (Study Session 2, LOS 7.j, k)

22. **A** We cannot assume that the distribution is normal, so we cannot rely on the *z*-table. We must use Chebyshev's inequality, which states that for any distribution, the proportion of observations that lie within k standard deviations of the mean is *at least* $1 - 1 / k^2$, we calculate $1 - 1 / 2.4^2 = 1 - 0.17361 = 0.82639$, or 82.6%. (Study Session 2, LOS 7.h)

23. **B** Dividing the covariance between returns of two assets by the individual *standard deviations* of returns of the two assets yields the correlation coefficient. (Study Session 2, LOS 8.k)

24. **A** The data are cross-sectional, which means that it is a sample of observations taken at a single point in time. Time-series data are observations taken at specific and equally spaced points in time (for example, the monthly returns on a specific stock for the period January 1 through December 31 of a given year. The other choices are accurate statements. The sampling error is the difference between a sample statistic (here, the mean) and the corresponding population parameter, or 10.5 – 9.7 = 0.80. The sample statistic (here, the mean) is itself a random variable and has its own probability distribution. (Study Session 3, LOS 10.c)

25. **C**   Many factors, both rational and irrational, govern supply and demand. (Study Session 3, LOS 12.a)

26. **C**   The standard deviation of two stocks that are perfectly positively correlated is the weighted average of the standard deviations: 0.5(18.9) + 0.5(14.73) = 16.82%. This relationship is true only when the correlation is one. Otherwise, you must use the formula:

$$\sigma_p = \sqrt{w_1^2\sigma_1^2 + w_2^2\sigma_2^2 + 2w_1w_2\sigma_1\sigma_2\rho_{1,2}}$$

(Study Session 2, LOS 8.l)

27. **C**   The Sharpe measure for a portfolio is calculated as the (mean portfolio return – mean return on the risk-free asset)/portfolio standard deviation. The Sharpe measures for the three mutual funds are:

mutual fund P = (13 – 5) / 18 = 0.44
mutual fund Q = (15 – 5) / 20 = 0.50
mutual fund R = (18 – 5) / 24 = 0.54

Assuming that investors prefer return and dislike risk, they should prefer portfolios with large Sharpe ratios to those with smaller ratios. Thus, the investor should prefer mutual fund R. (Study Session 2, LOS 7.i)

28. **C**   When order of selection matters, as it does here, use the permutation formula:

$$_nP_r = \frac{n!}{(n-r)!}$$

$_nP_r$ = 6! / (6 – 3)! = (6 × 5 × 4 × 3 × 2 × 1) / (3 × 2 × 1) = (6 × 5 × 4) = 120

(Study Session 2, LOS 8.o)

29. **B**   The standard error of the sample mean can be estimated by dividing the population standard deviation by $\sqrt{n}$. (Study Session 3, LOS 10.d, e)

30. **B**   Given that the population variance is unknown and the sample size is large, the 95% confidence interval for the population mean is:

$$\bar{x} \pm z_{\alpha/2}\frac{s}{\sqrt{n}}$$

The confidence interval is:

$$1.7 \pm 1.96\left(\frac{0.4}{\sqrt{100}}\right) = 1.7 \pm 1.96(0.04) = 1.7 \pm 0.0784 = 1.622 \text{ to } 1.778.$$

(Study Session 3, LOS 10.j)

31. **C**   This is a test of the value of a single variance and is based on a test statistic with a performed via the chi-square distribution. (Study Session 3, LOS 11.i)

32. **B**   Analysis based on accounting information is fundamental analysis. Technical analysis relies on price. (Study Session 3, LOS 12.a)

33. **A** Price discrimination involves a single product, not two alternatives. As long as the company faces a downward-sloping demand curve, can identify at least two groups of customers with different price elasticities of demand, and can prevent reselling between groups, the company can profit from price discrimination. (Study Session 5, LOS 19.c)

34. **C** Automatic stabilizers are built-in features that tend to automatically promote a budget deficit during a recession and a budget surplus during an inflationary boom, without a change in policy. (Study Session 6, LOS 26.e)

35. **A** The extra revenue that product innovation produces must be weighted against its costs. A firm is considered to be spending the optimal amount on innovation when the marginal cost of additional innovation just equals the marginal revenue from additional innovation. (Study Session 5, LOS 20.c)

36. **B** A firm will increase production if its marginal revenue is greater than its marginal cost, until it reaches the profit-maximizing output level at which marginal revenue equals marginal cost. Under perfect competition, marginal revenue equals price.
(Study Session 5, LOS 18.b)

37. **A** Utilitarianism refers to the idea that the greatest good occurs to the greatest number of people when wealth is transferred from the rich to the poor in order to make everyone's wealth equal. (Study Session 4, LOS 14.f)

38. **B** $\text{percentage change in quantity demanded} = \dfrac{180-200}{\left(200+180\right)\big/2} = -0.1053 = -10.53\%$

$\text{percentage change in price} = \dfrac{1.15-1.0}{\left(1.15+1.0\right)\big/2} = 0.1395 = 13.95\%$

$\text{price elasticity of demand} = \dfrac{-0.1053}{0.1395} = -0.7548$

The absolute value of price elasticity determines whether demand is elastic or inelastic. Here, the absolute value is less than 1, and demand is inelastic. When demand is inelastic, a price increase will lead to an increase in total expenditure on the good. The slope of the demand curve is not the same as the elasticity of demand. Elasticity is measured from a specific point.

 Professor's Note: You can also get this by directly multiplying P × Q to see if expenditure goes up. (Study Session 4, LOS 13.a, b)

39. **C** In a competitive price-searcher market, companies face downward-sloping demand curves. (Study Session 5, LOS 20.a)

40. **B** A subsidy will increase supply and decrease the price to consumers. A new law imposing penalties for consuming the product will decrease demand and decrease the equilibrium price. A new law imposing high penalties for selling the product will decrease supply, leading to a higher equilibrium price. (Study Session 4, LOS 15.d)

41. **B** Falling money wages would cause businesses to increase (profit-maximizing) output levels at each price level for final goods and services. Changes in the price level of goods and services are represented by a movement along a short-run aggregate supply curve, not a shift in the curve. A rise in resource prices will decrease aggregate supply. An increase in government spending will shift the aggregate demand curve but not the aggregate supply curve. (Study Session 5, LOS 23.a)

42. **A** The monetary base is comprised of currency in circulation, bank reserve deposits, and coins (issued by the Treasury). (Study Session 6, LOS 24.f)

43. **C** Farm land is a renewable resource and is modeled with inelastic supply per time period so that the equilibrium price is determined by demand. The other choices are most appropriately treated as non-renewable resources with perfectly elastic supply at a point in time so that changes in current demand do not affect the equilibrium price. (Study Session 5, LOS 21.g)

44. **B** In the short run, the average product of labor curve is first increasing and then decreasing as diminishing marginal returns to that factor take effect. In the short run, the marginal product of labor is first increasing and then decreasing when diminishing marginal returns take effect. The marginal product of labor curve will be above the average product of labor curve initially, and, at some point, will intersect the average product curve at its maximum. When the total product of labor begins to increase at a decreasing rate, the average product of labor will be decreasing. (Study Session 4, LOS 17.b)

45. **A** The $478,000 is unearned revenue, a liability. The $2.3 million owed to the government but not yet paid is income tax payable, also a liability. Deferred tax accounts arise from temporary differences between tax reporting and financial reporting. (Study Session 7, LOS 30.a, d)

46. **C** The installment method should be used when future cash collection *cannot* be reasonably estimated. (Study Session 8, LOS 32.b)

47. **C** Use the direct method.

Collections from customers	$5,000
Cash expenses	−$2,000
Cash flow from operations	$3,000

Cash expenses are given. If you had been given COGS, you would need to adjust that for inventory changes to get cash expenses for inputs. Depreciation is a non-cash change.

Changes in depreciation are used with the indirect method. Net change in cash will reflect CFI and CFF, not just CFO. (Study Session 8, LOS 34.e)

48. **B** Using the indirect method requires adjusting for change in working capital accounts such as accounts receivable, inventory, and accounts payable. (Study Session 8, LOS 34.e)

49. **C** The original debt-to-equity ratio = 35 / 70 = 0.5. An analyst should add the present value of the commitment to both assets and liabilities. Equity is unchanged. Therefore, the company's new debt-to-equity ratio is (35 + 12) / 70 = 0.671. (Study Session 9, LOS 39.i)

50. **C**   In periods of declining prices, LIFO inventory values will be higher, leading to higher asset and equity values and *lower* debt-to-equity ratios. FIFO inventory values are preferred because they better approximate replacement cost. FIFO COGS = LIFO COGS – change in LIFO reserve. (Study Session 9, LOS 36.c, f)

51. **B**   Operating profit margin can be read directly from a common-size income statement. Asset turnover and return on equity mix balance sheet and income statement items. (Study Session 8, LOS 35.a, c)

52. **C**   Use the Treasury stock method:

   Step 1:   Determine the number of common shares created if the warrants are exercised = 100,000.

   Step 2:   Calculate the cash inflow if the warrants are exercised: (100,000)($50 per share) = $5,000,000.

   Step 3:   Calculate the number of shares that can be purchased with these funds using the average market price ($60 per share): 5,000,000 / 60 = 83,333 shares.

   Step 4:   Calculate the net increase in common shares outstanding from the exercise of the warrants: 100,000 – 83,333 = 16,667.

   Step 5:   Add the net increase in common shares from the exercise of the warrants to the number of common shares outstanding for the entire year: 1,000,000 + 16,667 = 1,016,667.

   (Study Session 8, LOS 32.g)

53. **A**   Unless impairment has been recognized, land is reported at historical cost and is not subject to depreciation. Increases in value are not reflected in balance sheet values under U.S. GAAP. (Study Session 8, LOS 33.e)

54. **A**   The income statement reports the amounts for each of the major line items within the general categories of revenues and expenses. The various accruals, adjustments, and management assumptions are implicit in the reported amounts but are not specifically explained in the income statement. Much of the detail contained in various accruals, adjustments, and management assumptions that go into the financial statements can be found in the footnotes to the statements and Management's Discussion and Analysis. Supplementary schedules contain additional information, including a more detailed breakdown of certain large account balances. (Study Session 7, LOS 29.c)

55. **A**   The income statement shows an extraordinary item, which is permitted under U.S. GAAP but not under IFRS. From this we can conclude that the firm reports under U.S. GAAP. U.S. GAAP requires dividends received to be classified as CFO, while IFRS allows them to be classified as either CFO or CFI. A firm reporting under U.S. GAAP may not revalue assets upward but may use LIFO. (Study Session 10, LOS 43.b, c)

56. **B**   The installment sales method of revenue recognition does not result in permanent differences between pretax and taxable income. Premium payments on life insurance of key employees is an expense on the financial statements, but is not deducted on tax returns. Tax exempt interest is recognized as revenue on the financial statements. These items result in permanent differences between pretax income and taxable income. (Study Session 9, LOS 38.f)

57. **B**   Cash flows from operations, financing, and investing are affected by the capitalization/expensing choice. Total cash flows are the same, but expensing results in lower early-year and higher later-year profitability ratios, lower operating cash flow, and greater investing cash flow compared to capitalizing expenses.
(Study Session 9, LOS 37.b)

58. **B**   Depreciation methods do not affect sales or cost of goods sold, but assets are higher with straight-line versus accelerated depreciation. Using straight-line depreciation results in lower turnover ratios compared with accelerated depreciation.
(Study Session 9, LOS 37.d)

59. **B**   Operating leases are not recognized as liabilities and therefore the debt-to-equity ratio will be lower than a similar finance lease. Capitalizing a lease will increase the asset base and decrease asset turnover. Lease capitalization decreases the operating cash outflow and therefore increases operating cash flows (all else equal). (Study Session 9, LOS 39.g)

60. **A**   "Pretax income" denotes earnings before taxes for financial reporting. "Taxable income" is earnings before taxes for computing taxes payable, where taxes payable refers to the actual tax liability to the government. (The difference between the two is due to accounting for inventories and depreciation.) Since taxable income is $80,000, the difference in taxes payable is ($80,000)(0.5) – ($80,000)(0.4) = $8,000.
(Study Session 9, LOS 38.d)

61. **B**   A mindset that allows rationalization or justification of the fraud is the third important condition underlying accounting fraud. Poor financial controls are an example of opportunity for fraud and pressure to meet earnings expectations is a possible motive.
(Study Session 10, LOS 40.d)

62. **C**   For a financial services company, interest income, interest expense, and financing expenses are likely considered operating activities. For both financial and nonfinancial companies, income tax expense is a non-operating item that is reported within "income from continuing operations" as opposed to "operating profit" as with the other answer choices. Therefore, of the three choices, income tax expense is least likely to be considered an operating item. (Study Session 8, LOS 32.e)

63. **C**   When stated on a per-share basis, different companies' financial data cannot be compared meaningfully because these ratios depend on the number of shares outstanding, which is unrelated to the companies' operating performance or profitability. A company with a $200 share price should have much higher valuation measures than a company with a $2 share price. (Study Session 8, LOS 35.g)

64. **B**   When an asset is permanently impaired, it must be written down to the present value of its future cash flows in the period in which the impairment is recognized.
(Study Session 9, LOS 37.i)

65. **A**   This is a discount bond since the market interest rate at issuance exceeds the coupon rate. The initial liability is equal to the proceeds received when the bond was issued. We can find this amount from the following calculation: FV = 50,000,000; N = 10; I = 3.5; PMT = 1,500,000; CPT → PV = $47,920,848.67. Change N to 8 and calculate PV to get liability value at the beginning of the second year of the bond's life, 48,281,511. Interest expense for the next semiannual period is 48,281,511(0.035) = $1,689,853. The subsequent change in the market rate has no effect on the amortization of the discount.
(Study Session 9, LOS 39.a)

66. **A** The idea here is to "undo" the transaction and treat it like a loan. The sale of receivables would have increased cash and decreased accounts receivable, leaving equity unchanged. (Study Session 9, LOS 39.i)

67. **C** LIFO, under rising prices, results in lower net income for both accounting and tax purposes, so income taxes are lower using LIFO than using FIFO. Cash flows are higher using LIFO because taxes are lower. (Study Session 9, LOS 36.e)

68. **B** Reducing the numerator and denominator by the same amount will increase a ratio that is greater than one and decrease a ratio that is less than one. (Study Session 8, LOS 35.d)

69. **B** Selecting an external auditor (subject to shareholder approval) is a responsibility of the Board's audit committee. (Study Session 11, LOS 48.f)

70. **C** $k_{ce} = D_1/P_0 + g = (3)(1.05)/(31.50) + 0.05 = 0.15$ or 15%

    $k_d(1 - t) = 10\%(1 - 0.4) = 6\%$

    If the company has a debt-to-equity ratio of 0.5, it will have $0.50 in debt for each $1.00 in equity. V = debt + equity = 0.5 + 1 = 1.5. Therefore, the weight is 33.3% (0.5 / 1.5) for the debt component and 66.7% (1.0 / 1.5) for the equity component.

    $$\text{WACC} = \frac{D}{V}\left(k_{debt}\right)\left(1-t\right)+\left(\frac{E}{V}\right)k_s = 0.333\left(6.0\%\right)+0.677\left(15\%\right) = 2\% + 10\% = 12\%.$$

    (Study Session 11, LOS 45.h)

71. **A** The 19th space is neither an incremental cost, nor an opportunity cost or a type of cannibalization. It is a sunk cost since the firm has already committed to parking for 20 taxis. The cost of the 19th parking space is not directly relevant to the capital budgeting decision. (Study Session 11, LOS 44.b)

72. **C** Risky projects will seem relatively more attractive than they actually are, causing them to be undertaken a disproportionately high percentage of the times they are considered. (Study Session 11, LOS 45.a)

73. **C** When companies that require shareholder attendance to vote hold their meetings on the same day but in different locations, it prevents shareholders from attending all the meetings and therefore exercising their full voting rights. (Study Session 11, LOS 48.g)

74. **C** The firm should reject both projects.

	0	1	2	3	4	5	6
Project A	−$12,000	$4,000	$5,000	$6,000			
Project B	−$20,000	$3,000	$3,000	$3,000	$5,000	$8,000	$8,000

Project A: I/Y = 12; CF_0 = (12,000); CF_1 = 4,000; CF_2 = 5,000; CF_3 = 6,000; CPT → NPV = −172.

Project B: same process. NPV = −1,025. (Study Session 11, LOS 44.d).

75. **B** The recommended method is to treat flotation costs as a cash outflow at project initiation rather than as a component of the cost of equity. (Study Session 11, LOS 45.l)

76. **B** Given that they have the same amount of sales and Acme's receivables turnover (sales/average accounts receivable) is higher, Acme must have lower average accounts receivable than Butler. Given that they have equal quick ratios, subtracting accounts receivable from the numerators of the quick ratios of both firms will produce a cash ratio for Butler that is lower than the cash ratio for Acme. (Study Session 11, LOS 46.b)

77. **A** The crossover rate is the rate at which the NPV for two projects is the same. That is, it is the rate at which the two NPV profiles cross. At a discount rate of 9%, the NPV of Project A is: $CF_0 = -4$; $CF_1 = 3$; $CF_2 = 5$; $CF_3 = 2$; $I = 9\%$; CPT → NPV = $4.51. Now perform the same calculations except that we need to set the unknown $CF_0 = 0$. The remaining entries are: $CF_1 = 1.7$; $CF_2 = 3.2$; $CF_3 = 5.8$; $I = 9\%$; CPT → NPV = $8.73. Since by definition the crossover rate produces the same NPV for both projects, we know that both projects should have an NPV = $4.51. Since the NPV of Project B (with $CF_0 = 0$) is $8.73, the unknown cash flow must be a large enough negative amount to reduce the NPV for Project B from $8.73 to $4.51. Thus the unknown initial cash flow for Project B is determined as $4.51 = $8.73 + CF_0, or $CF_0 = -\$4.22$. (Study Session 11, LOS 44.e)

78. **C** The firm would not want to exhaust its capital budget on "bad" projects, (i.e., projects with IRR < cost of capital [NPV < 0]). They should continue to invest as long as the project's return is greater than the marginal cost of capital of the firm. When the project's IRR = cost of capital, the NPV = 0. This project will only make the firm larger; it will add nothing to the stock price. The investment opportunity schedule plots expected project returns from highest to lowest IRR. (Study Session 11, LOS 45.d)

79. **C** This is the formula for the variance. The formula for the standard deviation is:

$$\sigma_P = \sqrt{w_1^2\sigma_1^2 + w_2^2\sigma_2^2 + 2w_1w_2\sigma_1\sigma_2\rho_{1,2}}$$

(Study Session 12, LOS 50.c)

80. **B** Risk aversion implies that investors require a higher return to induce them to accept greater risk. Triple A-rated bonds are less risky than single A-rated bonds and, therefore, have lower yields. (Study Session 12, LOS 50.a and Study Session 15, LOS 61.j)

81. **A** Portfolio X has a lower expected return and a higher standard deviation than Portfolio Y. X must be inefficient. (Study Session 12, LOS 50.f)

82. **B** $E(R_1) = 0.5(25) + 0.3(10) + 0.2(-25) = 10.5\%$

$E(R_2) = 0.5(1) + 0.3(-5) + 0.2(35) = 6.0\%$

$E(R_p) = w_1R_1 + w_2R_2 = 0.6(10.5) + 0.4(6.0) = 8.7\%$

(Study Session 12, LOS 50.c, e)

83. **C** With positive transactions costs, there will be rates of return on both sides of the SML for which the cost of trading will be greater than the expected gains from trading. This means there is a band of expected returns for each level of systematic risk that is consistent with efficient pricing, once transactions costs are considered. (Study Session 12, LOS 51.d)

84. **A**   Stock A: k_A = 8% + 1.5(7%) = 18.5%. Because the estimated return of 18.1% is less than the required return of 18.5%, Stock A is *overvalued*.

Stock B: k_B = 8% + 1.1(7%) = 15.7%. Because the estimated return of 15.7% equals the required return of 15.7%, Stock B is *properly valued*.

Stock C: k_C = 8% + 0.6(7%) = 12.2%. Because the estimated return of 12.5% is greater than the required return of 12.2%, Stock C is *undervalued*.

(Study Session 12, LOS 51.e)

85. **B**   New share issues from firms whose shares are already trading are called seasoned or secondary issues. They are, however, primary market issues since they are sold directly to investors. After their initial offering in the primary market, securities trade in the secondary market. Origination, risk bearing, and distribution are the three functions performed by an underwriter. In call markets, all trades, bids, and asks are declared over some period of time, and then one negotiated price is set that clears the market for the security. (Study Session 13, LOS 52.b)

86. **A**   P/S ratios do not capture differences in cost structures across companies because they are based only on sales and share price, not income. Inflation and technological change may cause the book and market value of assets to differ significantly. This makes book value difficult to interpret as an accurate measure of an investor's value and would reduce the usefulness of P/BV ratios when comparing different companies.
(Study Session 14, LOS 59.a)

87. **C**   Event studies on exchange listings provide some evidence of short-run profit opportunities from public information about an upcoming listing on a national exchange. This evidence favors rejection of the semi-strong-form EMH.
(Study Session 13, LOS 54.b)

88. **A**   A potential drawback to using price-to-sales ratios is that increases in sales are not necessarily linked to increases in earnings or increases in the value of the firm. The others are all typically advantages of using P/S ratios in valuation.
(Study Session 14, LOS 59.a, b)

89. **A**   dividend payout = 1 − earnings retention rate = 1 − 0.6 = 0.4

$$R_S = R_f + \beta\left(R_{mkt} - RFR\right) = 0.05 + 1.0\left(0.10 - 0.05\right) = 0.10$$

g = (retention rate)(ROE) = (0.6)(0.10) = 0.06

$$P/E = \frac{\text{dividend payout}}{k - g} = \frac{0.4}{0.10 - 0.06} = 10$$

price = (E)(P/E) = (2)(10) = $20

Alternatively, dividend will be 40% of $2 earnings or $\dfrac{0.80}{0.10 - 0.06} = \$20$

(Study Session 14, LOS 56.d, g)

90. **C** g = (retention rate)(ROE); retention rate = 1 − payout ratio = 1 − 0.55 = 0.45

$$P/E = \frac{\text{dividend payout}}{k-g} = \frac{0.55}{0.12-(0.45)(0.15)} = \frac{0.55}{0.12-0.0675} = 10.48$$

price = (E)(P/E) = $4.00(10.48) = $41.92

(Study Session 14, LOS 56.d)

91. **B** The three steps in the top-down approach to security selection are economic analysis, industry analysis, and firm analysis. Determining a security's suitability for a specific investor is not directly related to the security selection process itself. (Study Session 14, LOS 56.a and 57)

92. **B** Arbitrage is frequently not riskless. Just because fundamentals indicate that one stock is overpriced relative to another, or absolutely over- or underpriced, does not mean that trading based on this information will be immediately profitable. Choice A is incorrect because arbitrageurs are not in short supply. Choice C is incorrect because there are limits, such as transactions costs, on the ability of the process of arbitrage to bring about efficient prices. (Study Session 13, LOS 55.b, d)

93. **C** The short seller loses if the stock price increases. The other choices are accurate statements. (Study Session 13, LOS 52.f)

94. **B** Bond indexes are more difficult to build and maintain than stock indexes for several reasons. Bonds in an index have to be replaced as they mature, so turnover is likely to be greater in a bond index than in a stock index. Many bonds lack the continuous trade data that exists for exchange-traded equities. (Study Session 13, LOS 53.b)

95. **B** You can select the correct answer without calculating the share values. Royal is using a shorter period of supernormal growth and a higher required rate of return on the stock. Both of these factors will contribute to a lower value using the multistage DDM.

$$\text{Knight: } \frac{\$1(1.10)}{1.09} + \frac{\$1(1.10)^2}{1.09^2} + \frac{\$1(1.10)^3/(0.09-0.04)}{1.09^2} = \$24.43$$

$$\text{Royal: } \frac{\$1(1.10)}{1.10} + \frac{\$1(1.10)^2/(0.10-0.04)}{1.10} = \$19.33$$

Royal's valuation is $5.10 less that Knight's valuation. (Study Session 14, LOS 56.c)

96. **C** If growth opportunities are already incorporated into the price of the stock, then the stock will earn risk-adjusted market-based (average) returns. (Study Session 14, LOS 58.a)

97. **B** The market value of the Treasury note is the present value of the remaining coupons plus the present value of the principal, discounted at the semiannual rates available from dividing each annual spot rate in the table by two.

$$\text{value of T-note} = \frac{\$25}{(1.015)} + \frac{\$25}{(1.0175)^2} + \frac{\$25}{(1.02)^3} + \frac{\$1,025}{(1.0225)^4} = \$1,010.05$$

At $1,008, the T-note is priced below the present value of its cash flows ($1,010) and is therefore underpriced. (Study Session 16, LOS 64.f)

98. **B** An issuer of a callable bond must compensate the bondholder when the issue is sold by offering a higher coupon rate or accepting a lower price than if the call feature was not included. Convexity will typically be much less than for an option-free bond, and reinvestment risk is greater for callable bonds. (Study Session 15, LOS 61.h)

99. **C** The bond equivalent yield rate on the par bond (Z) is 6% or a 3% semiannual rate. The equivalent quarterly rate, $1.03^{1/2} - 1 = 0.014889$. Security X makes 20 quarterly payments of \$15 and 20 quarterly payments of \$20. We need to use the cash flow function as follows: $CF_0 = 0$; $CF_1 = 15$; $F_1 = 20$; $CF_2 = 20$; $F_2 = 19$; $CF_3 = 1,020$; $F_3 = 1$; $I = 1.4889$; $CPT \rightarrow NPV = \$1,067.27$. Note that CF_3 contains the final quarterly payment of \$20 along with the \$1,000 face value payment. (Study Session 16, LOS 64.c)

100. **B** A 25 basis point increase in rates will result in an approximate price decrease of (0.25×7.41) or 1.85%. (Study Session 16, LOS 66.g)

101. **A** The full price is clean price plus accrued interest. (Study Session 15, LOS 60.c)

102. **C** Companies would retire through the delivery of securities if rates have gone up, not down. (Study Session 15, LOS 60.d, e)

103. **C** The annualized discount is $\left(\dfrac{1,000 - 983.10}{1,000}\right)\left(\dfrac{360}{160}\right) = 3.8025\%$.

(Study Session 2, LOS 6.d)

104. **B** Calculate the new bond prices at the 50 basis point change in rates both up or down and then plug into the effective duration equation:

current price: N = 50; FV = 1,000; PMT = (0.075/2)1,000 = 37.50; I/Y = 4.625; CPT $\rightarrow$ PV = \$830.54

+50 basis pts: N = 50; FV = 1,000; PMT = (0.075/2)1,000 = 37.50; I/Y = 4.875; CPT $\rightarrow$ PV = \$790.59

−50 basis pts: N = 50; FV = 1,000; PMT = (0.075/2)1,000 = 37.50; I/Y = 4.375; CPT $\rightarrow$ PV = \$873.93.

$$D_{effective} = \frac{V_- - V_+}{2V_0 \Delta y} = \frac{\$873.93 - \$790.59}{2(830.54)(0.005)} = 10.03$$

(Study Session 16, LOS 66.d)

105. **B** $[1 + 7.48 (0.0075)]\ 1,018 = \$1,075$ (Study Session 15, LOS 61.f)

106. **C** With YTM = 10.45% (I/Y = 5.225), PMT = 40, N = 24, FV = 1,000, PV = \$834.61. With YTM = 10.07% (I/Y = 5.035), PV = \$857.67, an increase of \$23.06. (Study Session 15, LOS 61.f)

107. **B** Inflation adjustments to principal are made semiannually. The coupon rate is fixed. Inflation adjustments make the yields on TIPS good estimates of their real returns. (Study Session 15, LOS 62.b)

108. **A** If we want the 3-year forward rate in three years, the appropriate formula is:

$$_3f_3 = \left[\frac{(1+z_6)^6}{(1+z_3)^3}\right]^{1/3} - 1$$

z_6 = 6-year spot rate and z_3= 3-year spot rate. (Study Session 16, LOS 65.h)

109. **A** The call benefits the issuer, so a bondholder will require a higher yield on a callable bond, while the put option has value to the bondholder. Therefore a callable bond will have a higher yield spread to Treasuries than an otherwise identical putable bond. Other things equal, a bond with less liquidity will have a higher spread to Treasuries than a bond with more liquidity. Smaller issue size is associated with less liquidity. (Study Session 15, LOS 63.g, h)

110. **A** This question does not require calculations. Because the return on reinvested coupon interest is less than the note's yield to maturity, the investor's realized yield on the note must be less than the YTM. Only Choice A can be correct. (Study Session 16, LOS 65.c)

111. **A** Powers is betting that the stock's price will not rise above $50. If she's right, she will pocket the $3.50 and lose nothing. If the stock rises above the strike price, she is losing all of the upside potential. Once the stock price rises above $53.50, the benefit of the strategy (i.e., the income generated by the option premium) is offset by the gain she has foregone on the stock. (Study Session 17, LOS 72.b)

112. **A** The forward contract price is $\left[1-\left(0.0185\times\frac{80}{360}\right)\right] \times \$20,000,000 = \$19,917,777.78.$

The market price at settlement is $\left[1-\left(0.0195\times\frac{80}{360}\right)\right] \times \$20,000,000 = \$19,913,333.33.$

The long will pay $19,917,777.78 – $19,913,333.33 = $4,444.45.

Alternatively, $0.001\left(\frac{80}{360}\right)\times\$20,000,000 = \$4,444.44.$

(Study Session 17, LOS 68.d)

113. **C** For most options with values greater than zero, a longer time to expiration makes an option more valuable than an otherwise identical option with a shorter time to expiration. One exception is an in-the-money European style put, which under certain conditions (low volatility, high interest rate) can have a lower value than an otherwise identical put with a shorter time to expiration. For both American and European style options, a call with a lower exercise price will be more valuable than an otherwise identical call with a higher exercise price, and a put with a higher exercise price will have more value than a put with a lower exercise price. (Study Session 17, LOS 70.j)

114. **A** If the no-arbitrage condition is met, a riskless portfolio (a portfolio with zero standard deviation of returns) will yield the risk-free rate of return. (Study Session 17, LOS 67.e)

115. **B** The price (or premium) of an option is its intrinsic value plus its time value. An out-of-the-money option has an intrinsic value of zero, so its entire premium consists of time value. Time value is zero at an option's expiration date. Time value is the amount by which an option's premium exceeds its intrinsic value. (Study Session 17, LOS 70.g)

116. **A** While Treasury securities are never at risk to default, forward contracts have default risk because the counterparty may default. The short has delivery options with T-bond futures, not a T-bill forward contract. The forward contract locks in a purchase price, which will not change regardless of the bill's performance. (Study Session 17, LOS 68.a)

117. **B** Distressed security investing and venture capital investing generally have long, not short, investment horizons. (Study Session 18, LOS 73.o)

118. **C** Net asset value

$10,000,000	(500,000 @ 20)
1,000,000	(100,000 @ 10)
3,000,000	(200,000 @ 15)
1,000,000	(cash)

$15,000,000 / 1,000,000 = $15 per share.

(Study Session 18, LOS 73.a)

119. **A** A collateralized commodity futures position is made up of a position in commodity futures *and* a position in government securities equal to the underlying value of the futures contracts involved. In this case, the initial underlying value of two gold futures contracts is 2(5,000)($350) = $3,500,000. To collateralize the position, $3,500,000 worth of Treasury bills must be purchased. At a yield of 3%, the price of the T-bills is: N = 2; I/Y = 3 / 12 = 0.25; FV = 3,500,000; CPT → PV = 3,482,630. Interest income from the T-bills = $3,500,000 − $3,482,630 = $17,370. The long futures position will lose: 2 × 5,000 × ($350 − $347.40) = $26,000.

The net loss is $26,000 − $17,370 = $8,630. (Study Session 18, LOS 73.r)

120. **C** Highly risk-averse investors would typically avoid hedge funds. Real estate offers a hedge against unexpected inflation, which long-term corporate bonds do not. (Study Session 18, LOS 73.d)

Exam 2
Morning Session Answer Key

To get valuable feedback on how your score compares to those of other Level 1 candidates, use your Username and Password to gain Online Access at schweser.com and choose the left-hand menu item "Practice Exams Vol. 1."

1. B	31. B	61. C	91. C
2. C	32. A	62. C	92. B
3. B	33. A	63. C	93. C
4. C	34. C	64. B	94. C
5. B	35. C	65. B	95. C
6. B	36. C	66. A	96. A
7. A	37. A	67. A	97. B
8. A	38. C	68. B	98. C
9. A	39. A	69. C	99. B
10. A	40. B	70. A	100. C
11. B	41. C	71. B	101. B
12. B	42. C	72. B	102. C
13. C	43. C	73. A	103. C
14. A	44. A	74. C	104. B
15. A	45. B	75. C	105. A
16. A	46. C	76. A	106. C
17. C	47. A	77. B	107. B
18. A	48. B	78. B	108. C
19. A	49. B	79. A	109. A
20. A	50. A	80. C	110. B
21. B	51. C	81. C	111. C
22. B	52. B	82. A	112. B
23. C	53. B	83. C	113. A
24. A	54. C	84. B	114. C
25. C	55. B	85. C	115. A
26. C	56. A	86. A	116. B
27. A	57. A	87. A	117. C
28. B	58. C	88. B	118. C
29. A	59. A	89. C	119. C
30. A	60. A	90. C	120. B

Exam 2
Morning Session Answers

Answers referencing the Standards of Practice address Study Session 1, LOS 1.b, c and LOS 2.a, b, c, except where noted.

1. **B** Schute has violated the Standard by not taking steps to ensure that the nonpublic information he has received as part of his investment banking work was not shared with others in the firm.

2. **C** Under Standard VII(B) Reference to CFA Institute, the CFA Designation, and the CFA Program, candidates in the CFA Program may appropriately reference their participation in the CFA Program. However, to be considered a candidate, individuals must be registered to take the next scheduled CFA examination. Therefore, Wellington, who completed Level 2 of the CFA examination two years ago, does not appear to be a candidate in the CFA Program. Therefore, his reference to his status as a CFA candidate in client presentation materials violates Standard VII(B). Wellington may indicate that he passed Level 2 of the CFA Program and the year in which he passed.

3. **B** Global Investment Performance Standards represent ethical reporting standards, but compliance with GIPS is not a requirement of CFA Institute membership or to sit for the CFA examination. (Study Session 1, LOS 3.a)

4. **C** Michaels has violated Standard IV(C) Responsibilities of Supervisors, which requires him to make reasonable efforts to detect and prevent violations of compliance procedures. Simply making employees aware of the rules is not enough. Monitoring of employee trades, duplicate confirms, establishing blackout periods, or pre-clearance of employee trades are all methods that would have revealed the problem prior to the external audit.

5. **B** According to Standard IV(A) Loyalty, members and candidates may undertake an independent practice that could result in compensation or other benefits in competition with their employer, provided they disclose to their employer in writing the types of services that will be provided, the duration of services, and the compensation. Members and candidates must also obtain consent from their employer before engaging in independent practice. The other preparations that he has made to begin his own business need not be disclosed and are not violations as long as they are done on his own time and he doesn't actually begin soliciting new clients for the business until he leaves his current employment.

6. **B** To comply with Standard IV(B) Additional Compensation Arrangements, Nelson must disclose outside compensation or benefits to employers, in writing, which includes e-mail and any form of communication that can be documented. Nelson must also receive written consent. Note that the additional compensation is contingent on future performance and not simply a gift for past good work.

7. **A** To comply with Standard I(C) Misrepresentation, all sources used in an analyst's report should be referenced as to the source, author, and publisher—the only exception being factual information published by recognized financial and statistical reporting services.

8. **A**   Because the itinerary required charter flights due to a lack of commercial transportation, River Casino can appropriately provide them. While Standard I(B) Independence and Objectivity recommends that members pay their own room costs, it is not required and it is not unusual for members to accept accommodations.

9. **A**   Portfolios must be assigned to composites before the returns are known; assigning them at the end of the year is not acceptable. The composite return must be asset weighted, not a simple average (equal-weighted). Asset weighting will ensure that the performance reported will be representative of (if not exactly equal to) the performance of all the accounts assigned to a single composite over the reporting period. (Study Session 1, LOS 3.b, 4.a)

10. **A**   Smart violated both Standards. Smart violated Standard III(B) Fair Dealing because she not deal fairly and objectively with all clients and prospects when disseminating investment recommendations, giving priority to some of the firm's clients by trading for her clients first before issuing the report. She also sold her own shares before issuing the report, which violated Standard VI(B) Priority of Transactions. Smart did not give clients an opportunity to react to and benefit from her recommendation before she personally benefited from her research.

11. **B**   Whatever his motivation, Jacobs' attempt to manipulate the market price of Timeco shares with the intent to deceive market participants (in this case his own client) constitutes a violation of Standard II(B) Market Manipulation.

12. **B**   Under Standard III(D) Performance Presentation, members and candidates must make reasonable efforts to make sure that investment performance information is fair, accurate, and complete. Rex has misled his potential clients by not disclosing that the first four years of his performance record were achieved at another firm. There is no prohibition on presenting simulated results as long as the fact that the results are simulated is disclosed.

13. **C**   Standard I(A) Knowledge of the Law. If Roberts suspects someone is engaging in activities that are illegal or violate the Code and Standards, he must dissociate from the activities if he cannot remedy the situation. In this situation, the colleague is acting within the applicable laws but is violating CFA Institute Standards of Professional Conduct. When the Code and Standards are more strict than applicable law, the Code and Standards apply. However, Roberts is not required by the Code and Standards to report violations of laws or the Code and Standards to CFA Institute or to governmental regulators, although it may be prudent or even required by law that he do so.

14. **A**   Government bonds are default risk free but are subject to price risk. Thus, Blush misrepresented the expected performance of the fund and therefore violated Standard I(C) Misrepresentation.

15. **A**   Standard VII(A) Conduct as Members and Candidates in the CFA Program does not prohibit members and candidates from expressing negative opinions about CFA Institute or the CFA program. Disclosing confidential information such as specific exam questions and misrepresenting information on the annual PCS are violations of Standard VII(A).

16. **A**   To comply with Standard III(C) Suitability, a member or candidate should establish a written investment policy statement for a client. Because Marlow depends on the portfolio for income and she has only moderate risk tolerance, risky currency derivatives are not appropriate for her account, and thus Pate has violated Standard III(C).

17. C Firms may include performance figures for periods prior to January 1, 2006, that were compliant with their applicable CVG, together with GIPS-compliant performance figures for periods after that date, and claim GIPS compliance. (Study Session 1, LOS 4.c)

18. A Standard III(E) Preservation of Confidentiality states that candidates and members can disclose confidential client information to authorized fellow employees who are also working for the client. Acting in the client's interest requires that her investment manager be aware of her circumstances and needs.

19. A First we need to find the proper rate to use in the problem. The relevant interest rate must consider the effect of quarterly compounding. We can find this effective annual rate (EAR) with quarterly compounding by solving:

$$\text{EAR} = \left(1 + \frac{\text{stated rate}}{\text{comp. periods/yr.}}\right)^{\text{comp. periods/yr.}} - 1 = \left(1 + \frac{0.05}{4}\right)^4 - 1 = 5.0945\%$$

The amount needed in the account at retirement is the present value of the desired withdrawals.

This amount is determined from N = 20; I = 5.0945; PMT = −20,000; FV = 0; CPT → PV = $247,259.14. The annual contribution must grow into $247,259.14. The required payment can be found from PV = 0; N = 15; I = 5.0945; FV = 247,259.14; CPT → PMT = $11,377.30. Subtracting the $2,000 annual employer contribution gives us the client's required contribution of $9,377.30. (Study Session 2, LOS 5.f)

20. A geometric mean = $[(1.10)(1.14)(1.12)(1.10)(0.90)(1.12)]^{1/6} - 1 = 0.0766$, or 7.66% (Study Session 2, LOS 7.e)

21. B There are 415 members of the group in favor of the continuing education requirement. 180 of these are candidates, so the probability is 180 / 415 = 43.37%. Note that this question is quite similar to those where we apply Bayes' Theorem. The priors here are the probabilities that a member of the group is a charterholder or is a candidate. Both of these are 1,000 / 2,000 = 50%. Given the information that the member of the group favors continuing education, we can update the probability that that group member is a candidate to 43.37%. (Study Session 2, LOS 8.d)

22. B Smart-money technicians believe that in periods of confidence about the future direction of the economy, fixed income investors try to increase yields by selling higher quality bonds and buying lower quality bonds, which tends to narrow the yield spread between lower quality and higher quality bonds. The Confidence Index is high-quality bond yields divided by average bond yields. If average bond yields increase relative to high-quality bond yields (that is, if credit spreads are widening), the Confidence Index will decrease. (Study Session 3, LOS 12.c)

23. C A normal distribution is a *continuous* symmetric probability distribution. (Study Session 3, LOS 9.a, e, i)

24. A A binomial random variable has an expected value or mean equal to *np*.
Mean = 12(0.4) = 4.8. (Study Session 3, LOS 9.f)

25. C The standard normal random variable, denoted Z, has mean equal to 0 and variance equal to 1. (Study Session 3, LOS 9.j, k)

26. **C** To generate $60,000 in income, the portfolio must achieve a minimum threshold return of ($60,000 / $1,200,000) = 5%.

$$\text{portfolio X: SFRatio} = \frac{12-5}{14} = 0.50$$

$$\text{portfolio Y: SFRatio} = \frac{17-5}{20} = 0.60$$

$$\text{portfolio Z: SFRatio} = \frac{22-5}{25} = 0.68$$

According to the safety-first criterion, Portfolio Z, with the largest ratio (0.68), is the best alternative. (Study Session 3, LOS 9.l)

Professor's Note: The intuition here is that the portfolio for which the minimum/target return is the greatest number of standard deviations below its mean has the greatest probability of achieving the minimum/target return. 5% is 0.68 standard deviations below the expected return for Portfolio Z.

27. **A** The appropriate test is an *F*-test, where the larger sample variance (Index A) is placed in the numerator. (Study Session 3, LOS 11.i)

28. **B** When testing hypotheses about the population mean, the sample standard deviation must be used in the denominator of the test statistic when the population standard deviation is unknown, the population is normal, and/or the sample is large. The statistic is a *t*-stat with n − 1 degrees of freedom. The numerator is the sampling error for the population mean if the true mean is μ_0 and the denominator is the standard error of the sample mean around the true mean. (Study Session 3, LOS 11.f)

29. **A** The 20 quarters he has used are a sample of all the possible outcomes for the quarterly returns on the index. The difference between the true population parameter (mean index return) he is trying to estimate and the sample statistic he has calculated is called the sampling error. (Study Session 3, LOS 10.a)

30. **A** The significance level of a test is the probability that a true null hypothesis will be rejected by chance because the test statistic is from a sample and may take on a value that is outside the range of critical values because of sampling error. Choice B is incorrect because the probability of making a correct decision also must account for the probability of failing to reject a false null hypothesis. (Study Session 3, LOS 11.b)

31. **B** The lognormal distribution is most appropriate for modeling asset prices because the values cannot be less than zero and are not bounded on the upside. A binomial distribution allows only two possible outcomes over a period. (Study Session 3, LOS 9.m)

32. **A** Calculate the NPV as in any other project. Discount the cash flows back at a rate of 10%. CF_0 = −200,000; CF_1 = 50,000; CF_2 = 60,000; CF_3 = 70,000; CF_4 = 80,000; CF_5 = −20,000; I/Y = 10; CPT → NPV = −$10,144. (Study Session 2, LOS 6.a)

33. **A** Increases in expected future incomes will decrease savings, which will decrease the supply of financial capital and increase the equilibrium interest rate. If the demand for financial capital rises, interest rates also rise; so both changes tend to increase the equilibrium interest rate. (Study Session 5, LOS 21.f)

34. C   Potential expansion multiplier $= \dfrac{1}{\text{reserve requirement}} = \dfrac{1}{0.2} = 5$

~~(100)(5) – 500~~

(Study Session 6, LOS 24.e)

35. C   At a minimum wage above the equilibrium wage, there will be an excess supply of workers, since firms will not employ all the workers who want to work at the minimum wage. Firms will substitute other productive inputs for labor and use more than the economically efficient amount of capital. The result is increased unemployment because even though there are workers willing to work for less than the minimum wage, firms cannot legally hire them. (Study Session 4, LOS 15.b)

36. C   Firms will employ additional labor until the marginal revenue product of labor equals the wage rate. The marginal revenue product falls as the firm increases the use of the resource. The relationship between quantity of labor demanded and wage rate is identical to this negative relationship between quantity employed and marginal revenue product. (Study Session 5, LOS 21.a, b)

37. A   The only item listed that is not an automatic stabilizer is property taxes. When the economy enters a recession, unemployment compensation increases, which tends to increase (reduce the decrease in) consumption and aggregate demand. Induced taxes, personal income taxes, and corporate taxes decrease during a recession, which tends to increase (reduce the decrease in) aggregate demand by allowing more funds for both consumption by individuals and investment by corporations. (Study Session 6, LOS 26.e)

38. C   Average cost pricing is meant to force a natural monopolist to reduce price to where the firm's average total cost intersects the market demand curve. This results in higher output and a lower price than would prevail for an unregulated natural monopoly. (Study Session 5, LOS 19.e)

39. A   A partnership can continue after the death of a partner, and all partners are jointly and severally liable for the debts of the partnership. A sole proprietor has unlimited liability but there is no separate business entity to survive the proprietor. (Study Session 4, LOS 16.e)

40. B   Colluding restricts output and puts upward pressure on price, but cheating actually increases output and ultimately, if enough cheating occurs, puts downward pressure on the price. Colluders cheat to increase their share of the profits. (Study Session 5, LOS 20.d)

41. C   The nominal rate is approximately equal to the real rate plus a premium for expected inflation. An increase in inflation increases the inflation premium, and the nominal rate as a result, but not the real rate of interest. (Study Session 6, LOS 25.d)

42. C   Since some of the societal costs of copper production are not considered by the copper producers, the marginal social cost curve lies above the industry supply curve, and equilibrium copper production is greater than the efficient level of output. This results in a deadweight loss from overproduction. The "free rider" problem arises when consumers can enjoy the benefit of public goods without paying anything towards their production. (Study Session 4, LOS 14.e)

43. C   An inferior good is one that experiences a decline in demand when income rises. (Study Session 4, LOS 13.a)

44. **A** According to the Keynesians, policymakers can use the budget to diminish aggregate demand through restrictive fiscal policy. Reducing government expenditures and/or increasing tax rates should lead to a decline in the expected size of the budget deficit or an increase in the budget surplus. (Study Session 5, LOS 23.d)

45. **B** Firms usually support the idea of having a single set of reporting standards because having one set of standards would reduce the cost and the time spent on reporting. Disagreement among different standard-setting bodies and regulatory authorities does hamper agreement on a single set of standards, as does political pressure from business groups and others who would be affected by changes in reporting standards. (Study Session 7, LOS 31.c)

46. **C** Foreign currency translation gains and losses are not reported on the income statement as a component of net income, but affect owners' equity because they are included as other comprehensive income. The other items are included on the income statement so they affect both net income and owners' equity. (Study Session 8, LOS 32.j)

47. **A**

Sale of common stock	45
Issuance of bonds	25
Financing cash flows	$70

(Study Session 8, LOS 34.e)

48. **B** Since the value of newly released DVDs will typically fall most rapidly in the first year after their release, some form of accelerated depreciation is appropriate. The declining balance method is the only accelerated depreciation method among the answer choices. Straight-line depreciation is appropriate when the decrease in value is uniform over an asset's life. Units-of-production depreciation assumes that there is a given amount of service that an asset will provide. (Study Session 8, LOS 32.d)

49. **B** When a firm has a controlling interest in (>50%), but less than 100% ownership of, a subsidiary, it includes (consolidates) the assets and liabilities of that firm on its own balance sheet. Minority interest in the equity section of the balance sheet represents the portion of the subsidiary that is not owned by the reporting firm. (Study Session 8, LOS 33.d)

50. **A** FCFF = Cash flow from operations + interest expense net of tax − net capital expenditures

    FCFF = $800 + 80(1 − 0.35) − 40 + 30 = $842

    Depreciation and amortization do not have to be added when calculating FCFF from CFO. They are added when calculating FCFF from net income. (Study Session 8, LOS 34.h)

51. **C** Securities held with the intent to profit over the short term are classified as trading securities, and changes in their market values are reflected in their balance sheet values and also reported on the income statement. Debt securities issued by the firm, and debt securities that the firm intends to hold until maturity, are both reported at amortized cost, not market value. Debt and equity securities that the firm does not expect to hold to maturity or to sell in the near term are marked to market on the balance sheet, but unrealized gains and losses do not affect the income statement. (Study Session 8, LOS 33.f)

52. **B** IFRS and U.S. GAAP both require discontinued operations to be reported on the income statement separately from continuing operations and net of tax. U.S. GAAP permits unusual and infrequent items to be treated as extraordinary items, but IFRS does not permit extraordinary items. Fixed assets can be ~~revalued upward under IFRS~~ but not under U.S. GAAP. (Study Session 10, LOS 43.a,b)

53. **B** COGS FIFO = COGS LIFO – (ending LIFO reserve – beginning LIFO reserve)

    COGS FIFO = 27,000 – (1,400 – 1,200) = \$26,800. (Study Session 9, LOS 36.g)

54. **C** The listing of all the journal entries in order of their dates is called the general journal. The general ledger sorts the entries in the general journal by account. "Trial ledger" is not part of an accounting system. (Study Session 7, LOS 30.f)

55. **B** When the capital structure contains options or warrants, the treasury stock method uses the average price. In this situation, the warrants are antidilutive because the exercise price of the warrant (\$25) is higher than the market price of the stock (\$20). Thus, warrants are excluded. Otherwise, common shares would be reduced.

    $$\text{original shares of common stock} = 1,000,000 \left(\frac{12}{12} \right)$$

    Then add the impact of the bond conversion:

    $(10,000)(20) \times (6/12) = 100,000$

    Thus, the adjusted denominator for fully diluted EPS is:

    1,000,000 + 100,000 = 1,100,000 (Study Session 8, LOS 32.g, h)

56. **A** During periods of rising prices, the last units purchased are more expensive than the existing units. Under LIFO, the cost of the last units purchased is assigned to cost of goods sold. This higher cost of goods sold results in lower income, as compared to the FIFO method. As the name suggests, the weighted average method is based on mathematical averages rather than timing of purchase/use. Thus, cost of goods sold using this method falls between that of LIFO and FIFO. (Study Session 9, LOS 36.c)

57. **A** If convertible bonds are dilutive, interest expense multiplied by (1 – tax rate) must be added back to the numerator to calculate diluted EPS. (Study Session 8, LOS 32.g, h)

58. **C** Inventory turnover, defined as COGS / average inventory, is often meaningless for LIFO companies due to the mismatching of costs. The numerator represents current costs, whereas the denominator reports outdated historical costs. Thus, the turnover ratio under LIFO will, when prices increase, trend higher because of larger COGS and smaller inventory. Net profit margin, defined as EAT / sales, is lower during periods of rising profits for LIFO companies. LIFO leads to a larger COGS, which reduces EAT without affecting sales. (Study Session 9, LOS 36.f)

59. **A** The three-part DuPont approach is as follows: net profit margin × asset turnover × leverage ratio, where the leverage ratio is assets-to-equity. (Study Session 8, LOS 35.f)

60. **A** Impairment writedowns are reported losses "above the line" and are included in income from continuing operations. (Study Session 8, LOS 32.f and Study Session 9, LOS 37.i)

61. **C** Compared to expensing (in the current period), capitalizing expenses will increase reported net income, assets, equity, ROE, and ROA. The capitalizing company will show greater CFO and lower CFI since the capitalized expenses will be treated as a (negative) investing cash flow. Total cash flows and debt are unaffected. (Study Session 9, LOS 37.b)

62. **C** Deferred tax assets and liabilities are adjusted for changes in expected tax rates under the liability method. (Study Session 9, LOS 38.e)

63. **C** $\text{average useful life} = \dfrac{\text{ending gross investment}}{\text{depreciation expense}} = \dfrac{\$480,000}{\$25,000} = 19.2 \text{ years}$

    (Study Session 9, LOS 37.e)

64. **B** Since retained earnings increased by 245,000 − 215,000 = 30,000 and net income less dividends paid was 20,000 − 10,000 = 10,000, the difference, 30,000 − 10,000 = 20,000, must have been other comprehensive income. Dividends received and interest paid are both included in net income. (Study Session 8, LOS 32.i)

65. **B** The company that capitalizes its leases will have a *lower* current ratio because the current portion of the principal repayment component will be added to current liabilities. (Study Session 9, LOS 39.g)

66. **A** Sensitivity analysis is based on hypothetical ("what if") questions about a single variable, such as "what if sales decline by 10%?" Simulation is a technique in which probability distributions for key variables are assumed and a computer is used to generate a distribution of outcomes based on repeated random selection of values for the key variables. Scenario analysis is based on one or more specific scenarios (a specific set of outcomes for key variables), which include changes in multiple variables. (Study Session 8, LOS 35.h)

67. **A** The balance sheet reports the company's financial position at a point in time. In contrast, the income statement reports on financial performance over a period of time and the cash flow statement reports a company's cash receipts and payments over a period of time. (Study Session 7, LOS 29.b)

68. **B** The issuance of debt, regardless of the attachment of warrants, is reported on the balance sheet. (Study Session 9, LOS 39.i)

69. **C** CAPM: $k_s = RFR + B_s \left(R_{mkt} - RFR \right)$

    $k = 6\% + \left(14\% - 6\% \right) 1.125 = 15.0\%$

    $$WACC = \left(\frac{D}{D+E} \right)\left(k_{Debt}\right)\left(1-t\right) + \left(\frac{E}{D+E} \right)k_s = \left(\frac{\$100}{\$300} \right)\left(9\%\right)\left(1-0.3\right) + \left(\frac{\$200}{\$300} \right)15\% = 12.1\%$$

    (Study Session 11, LOS 45.a, h)

70. **A** $\text{WACC} = \left(w_d\right)\left(k_d\right)\left(1-t\right)+\left(w_{ce}\right)\left(k_{ce}\right)$

     WACC = (0.5)(6%)(1 − 0.33) + (0.5)(12%) = 8.0%

     The increase in after-tax cash flows for each year is 3,000 × (1 − 0.33) = $2,010.

     I = 8; N = 8; PMT = $2,010; CPT → PV = $11,550.74

     NPV = PV income − cost = $11,550.74 − $10,000 = $1,550.74

     (Study Session 11, LOS 44.d, 45.a)

71. **B**   For a board to be independent, it should not have a majority of members who are firm executives. Board members should not be closely aligned with customers, suppliers, or pension advisors since their interests may conflict with those of shareholders. The board should meet regularly *outside* the presence of management. (Study Session 11, LOS 48.c)

72. **B**   The investment opportunity schedule is a downward sloping curve of the internal rates of return (expected returns) of potential projects ranked from highest to lowest. This curve intersects the company's upward sloping marginal cost of capital curve at an amount of capital where the marginal project's IRR just equals the firm's cost of capital. The firm should accept projects with IRRs that exceed the marginal cost of capital (lie to the left of the intersection) and reject projects with IRRs less than the marginal cost of capital (lie to the right of the intersection). (Study Session 11, LOS 45.d)

73. **A**   An increase in the weighted average collection period indicates that customers are taking longer to pay their outstanding accounts. This represents a drag on the company's liquidity. A vendor that changes its payment terms from "net 30" to "net 60" is allowing the company 60 days to pay instead of 30. This extension of trade credit is a source of liquidity for the company. An inventory turnover ratio that is increasing relative to the industry average is a sign of good inventory management, which can also be a source of liquidity for a company. (Study Session 11, LOS 46.a,f)

74. **C**   The break points in its marginal cost of capital schedule at 1.5 / 0.3 = $5 million to reflect the increase in the cost of debt past $1.5 million and at 1.6 / 0.4 = $4 million to reflect the fact that an equity investment greater than $1.6 million will require the issuance of new common stock and increase the cost of equity capital above the opportunity cost of retained earnings. (Study Session 11, LOS 45.k)

75. **C**   Using the CAPM approach, the estimated cost of common equity = 3% + 0.89(12% − 3%) = 11%. Using the dividend discount model approach, the growth rate = (0.3)(0.2) = 6% and the estimated cost of common equity = $3/$50 + 6% = 12%. To get a cost of common equity of 14%, Harlan most likely added a risk premium to Cyrene's bond yield. (Study Session 11, LOS 45.h)

76. **A**   The cash conversion cycle is equal to the operating cycle minus the number of days of payables. If Quixote is extending the time it takes to pay its suppliers, its number of days of payables will increase, and its cash conversion cycle will decrease. Its operating cycle (days of inventory plus days of receivables) is unaffected by the increase in days of payables. Changes in inventory or receivables management would affect both the operating cycle and the cash conversion cycle. (Study Session 11, LOS 46.c)

77. **B**   If the total undiscounted cash flows from two projects are equal, their NPV profiles intersect the vertical axis at the same value. The NPV profile will have a steeper slope for Project Smith, which has more of its cash inflows occurring later in its life, and therefore the IRR of Project Smith (its intersection with the horizontal axis) must be less than the IRR of Project Jones. The NPV for Project Jones will be greater at any rate of discount, and Project Jones will be preferred over the entire range. However, if the discount rate applied to the cash flows is greater than the IRR of Project Jones, both projects will have negative NPVs and the company should reject both of them. (Study Session 11, LOS 44.e)

78. **B**   Other Board experience can be beneficial. Choice A is incorrect because this may present the board member with a conflict of interest. Choice C is incorrect because a substantial stock position in the firm aligns the board member's interests closely with those of other shareholders. (Study Session 11, LOS 48.d)

79. **A**   The SML equation, $E(R_i) = RFR + \beta_i \left[E(R_{mkt}) - RFR \right]$ yields the following expected (required) rates of return for these three stocks.

$R_X = 0.05 + 0.6(0.12 - 0.05) = 0.092$ or 9.2%
$R_Y = 0.05 + 1.2(0.12 - 0.05) = 0.134$ or 13.4%
$R_Z = 0.05 + 1.8(0.12 - 0.05) = 0.176$ or 17.6%

Stock	Estimated Return	Required Return	Estimated Return – Required Return	Evaluation
X	8.0%	9.2%	–1.2%	Overvalued
Y	18.0%	13.4%	4.6%	Undervalued
Z	22.5%	17.6%	4.9%	Undervalued

The analyst would not recommend buying the overvalued Stock X. (Study Session 12, LOS 51.e)

80. **C**   The investment policy statement provides a clear articulation of the risk a client will accept and addresses risk in the context of the client's return requirement or expectations. The other answers are benefits of other steps in the portfolio management process after developing the investment policy statement. (Study Session 12, LOS 49.a)

81. **C**   Capital preservation is the objective of earning a return on an investment that is at least equal to the inflation rate. The concern is the maintenance of purchasing power, which means that the real rate of return must equal the inflation rate. (Study Session 12, LOS 49.c)

82. **A**   Of the five categories of investment constraints, the four matters listed are related to Pope's time horizon (years to retirement), liquidity needs (available cash), legal and regulatory factors (required copies of account statements to Pope's compliance officer), and unique needs and preferences (no investments in Lower Pannonia). None of these constraints address Pope's tax situation or the taxable status of the investment account. (Study Session 12, LOS 49.d)

83. **C**   This statement is not correct; the standard deviation of returns for the resulting portfolio is a weighted average of the returns standard deviation of the risk-free asset (zero) and the returns standard deviation of the risky-asset portfolio. (Study Session 12, LOS 51.a)

84. **B** One of the key assumptions of the CAPM is the ability of investors to lend and borrow at the risk-free rate. This assumption is necessary to produce a straight line CML. Investors can lend all they want by buying investments at the risk-free rate, but investors must pay a premium over the risk-free rate to borrow. Unequal borrowing and lending rates put a kink in the CML. The other choices result in an SML that is a band rather than a line. (Study Session 12, LOS 51.d)

85. **C** Characteristics of a well-functioning market include timely and accurate (not complete) information on the price and volume of past transactions; liquidity, which includes marketability (the ability to buy or sell quickly) and price continuity (minimal changes in price from one transaction to the next in the absence of new information); internal efficiency, or low transactions costs; and external or informational efficiency, which means prices reflect all information available about the asset and adjust quickly to new information. (Study Session 13, LOS 52.a)

86. **A** Value-weighted indexes do not need to be adjusted for stock splits because the market capitalization of the company remains the same. (Study Session 13, LOS 53.a)

87. **A** The numerator of the formula for the P/E is the payout ratio, which is unchanged (both expected earnings and dividends increase by the same percentage). The denominator $(k - g)$ doubles from 3% to 6%, which will decrease the P/E by half. (Study Session 14, LOS 56.d)

88. **B** $k = RFR + \beta(R_M - RFR) = 0.08 + 1.2(0.13 - 0.08) = 0.08 + 0.06 = 0.14$

$$P_0 = \frac{P_1 + D_1}{1 + k} = \frac{25 + 1.10}{1.14} = \$22.89$$

(Study Session 14, LOS 56.c)

89. **C** The strong form reflects security market, nonmarket, and inside or private information. The weak form states that stock prices fully reflect all currently available security market information and that investors cannot achieve excess returns using technical analysis. The semistrong form reflects that security prices rapidly adjust to the arrival of all new public information (market and fundamental) and that investors cannot achieve abnormal returns using fundamental analysis. Event studies are one of the tests used to test the semistrong form of the EMH. (Study Session 13, LOS 54.a)

90. **C** Arbitrageurs do not have unlimited funds. Given the limited funds for exploiting mispricings, along with limitations the suppliers of capital may place on the positions the arbitrageurs can take, only the more significant mispricings may be exploited while others are allowed to persist. Buying an underpriced security and selling an overpriced security is not riskless to the arbitrageur if the securities do not have exactly the same risk characteristics, and this risk may make exploiting some mispricings unattractive. Arbitrageurs may be correct about a mispriced security, but there is no guarantee that mispricings will be corrected in a short time frame. (Study Session 13, LOS 55.b)

91. **C** Value @ t = 2 = $\dfrac{D_3}{k - g} = \dfrac{D_0(1+g)^3}{k - g} = \dfrac{\$6.25(1.07)^3}{0.12 - 0.07} = \$153.13$

(Study Session 14, LOS 56.c)

92. **B** The superior historical performance of exchange specialists and corporate insiders is inconsistent with the strong form of the EMH but consistent with the semi-strong form since exchange specialists and corporate insiders have private (non-public) information. The other statements are correct. (Study Session 13, LOS 54.b)

93. **C** Differences in use of fixed assets and profit margins among different industries make the use of P/BV and P/S ratios inappropriate for assessing relative values of firms in different industries. (Study Session 14, LOS 59.b)

94. **C** $P_2 = \dfrac{D_3}{k-g} = \dfrac{2.25(1.2)^2}{0.15-0.05} = 32.40$

    $P_0 = \dfrac{\$2.25}{1.15} + \dfrac{2.70}{(1.15)^2} + \dfrac{32.40}{(1.15)^2} = \$28.50$

    (Study Session 14, LOS 56.c)

95. **C** Given: The earnings multiplier (P/E ratio) = dividend payout ratio / (k − g)
    - If g increases, then k − g decreases, and the earnings multiplier *increases*.
    - If the payout ratio increases, then the earnings multiplier *increases*.
    - If k increases, then k − g increases, and the earnings multiplier *decreases*.

    (Study Session 14, LOS 56.d)

96. **A** The internal or sustainable growth rate is the retention ratio multiplied by the return on equity. (Study Session 14, LOS 56.f)

97. **B** CMOs redistribute prepayment risk and/or the expected repayment term of the underlying MBS among the CMO tranches. If some tranches have less prepayment risk, others must have more. (Study Session 15, LOS 62.f)

98. **C** This question can be answered without calculations. Since the spot rates are less than the coupon rate, the price must be greater than par value, so C is the only possible correct choice.

    This is a four-period bond with $50 cash flows each period. Divide each spot rate by two to get the semiannual rate.

    PV_1: N = 1; I/Y = 3.00; FV = $50; CPT → PV = $48.54
    PV_2: N = 2; I/Y = 3.25; FV = $50; CPT → PV = $46.90
    PV_3: N = 3; I/Y = 3.50; FV = $50; CPT → PV = $45.10
    PV_4: N = 4; I/Y = 3.75; FV = $1,050; CPT → PV = $906.23

    or $\dfrac{50}{1.03} + \dfrac{50}{1.0325^2} + \dfrac{50}{1.035^3} + \dfrac{50}{1.0375^4} = \$1,046.77$

    Sum to get $1,046.77. (Study Session 16, LOS 65.e)

99. **B** The change in price due to a change in yield is only approximate because the calculation of effective duration does not reflect all of the curvature of the price-yield curve (convexity). It is a linear approximation of a non-linear relation. (Study Session 15, LOS 61.f)

100. **C** Issuing asset-backed securities allows a corporation to dedicate the assets' cash flows to specific debt issues. This enables the issue to receive a higher credit rating than that of the corporation. (Study Session 15, LOS 62.i)

101. **B** absolute yield spread = yield on Bond A − yield on Bond B = 7.5% − 7.0% = 0.5%

    yield ratio $= \dfrac{\text{Bond A yield}}{\text{Bond B yield}} = \dfrac{7.5\%}{7.0\%} = 1.071$.

    (Study Session 15, LOS 63.e)

102. **C** The duration/convexity approach provides an approximation of the interest rate sensitivity of a bond/bond portfolio. This approach estimates the risk for a parallel shift in the yield curve and allows the analyst to express interest rate risk with the summary measures of duration and convexity. The full valuation approach is more precise and can be used to evaluate the risk from more complex interest rate change scenarios than a parallel shift in the yield curve. Both approaches account for the curvature of the price-yield relation. (Study Session 16, LOS 66.a)

103. **C** $\sqrt{\dfrac{(1.07)^4}{(1.05)^2}} - 1 = 0.0904$, or $\dfrac{(4 \times 7) - (2 \times 5)}{2} = 9$ as an approximation.

(Study Session 16, LOS 65.h)

104. **B** $\text{current yield} = \dfrac{\text{annual dollar coupon interest}}{\text{bond price}} = \dfrac{\$100}{\$1,100} = 0.0909$, or 9.1%

(Study Session 16, LOS 65.b)

105. **A** When the yield curve is flat, all spot interest rates are equal, and the spot rates will equal the YTM of the bond. The static spread and the YTM spread will diverge when the yield curve gains shape (upward-sloping, humped, or downward-sloping). The option-adjusted spread is the spread *without* the option. Hence, to compare the relative valuation of these two securities, we would compare their OAS and buy the bond with the biggest OAS (Bond B). (Study Session 16, LOS 65.f)

106. **C** A company may refund the debt as long as they do not issue cheaper debt to do so. The firm could not refund the bonds by issuing zero-coupon bonds. (Study Session 15, LOS 60.d)

107. **B** This bond has no cash flows for the first five years. It then has a $100 cash flow for years 6 through 10. Additionally, the accrued interest ($500) that wasn't paid in the first five years would have to be paid at the end, along with the principal. A financial calculator using the CF/NPV worksheet can handle this type of problem. The required inputs are $CF_0 = 0$, $CF_1 = 0$, $F_1 = 5$, $CF_2 = 100$, $F_2 = 4$, $CF_3 = 1,600$, $F_3 = 1$, NPV, I = 10%, CPT = 813.69. Note that CF_3 is made up of the principal ($1,000) plus the remaining $100 coupon plus the accrued interest ($500) that was not paid during the first five years of the bond's life. (Study Session 16, LOS 64.c)

108. **C** The market segmentation theory states that the shape of the yield curve is determined by the supply and demand for bonds within certain market segments. If the demand for long-term bonds exceeds supply, prices will be forced up and yields down. Hence, a large demand for long bonds could force a downward-sloping yield curve. (Study Session 15, LOS 63.c)

109. **A** Floating-rate securities are subject to interest rate risk because their coupon rates are not reset continuously. The longer the time until the security's next reset date, the greater its potential price fluctuation away from par value (to a discount or premium). Other reasons that the price can differ from par include caps and floors on the floating rate, changes in the issuer's credit risk that are not reflected in the coupon's margin over LIBOR, and changes in the market's required yield premium for the firm's level of credit risk. A decrease in the yield premium for credit risk would be likely to cause the security to trade at a premium rather than a discount. Liquidity risk is much less likely to change than default risk and market interest rates. (Study Session 15, LOS 61.e)

110. **B** PVBP represents the change in the price of the bond when its yield changes by one basis point, or 0.01%. PVBP = duration × 0.0001 × bond value. This calculation ignores convexity because for a small change in yield, the curvature of the price-yield relationship typically has no material effect on the PVBP. (Study Session 16, LOS 66.i)

111. **C** In a currency swap, the *full* notional principal is exchanged at the beginning and termination of the swap. (Study Session 17, LOS 71.b)

112. **B** Interest rate caps are designed to protect floating-rate borrowers from higher interest rates by paying the borrowers when rates reach a certain level. The combination of a long cap and a short floor is called a collar and offers downside protection at the cost of a sacrifice of upside. A bond call option will gain if interest rates decrease, not if they increase. (Study Session 17, LOS 70.e)

113. **A** When the stock's price (S) – the strike price (X) is positive, a call option is in the money. 35 – X = 3, so X = 32. (Study Session 17, LOS 72.a)

114. **C** The word "hedge" means to reduce risk. Since the investor is short the portfolio, he will have gains as stock prices fall and will have losses as stock prices rise. Hence, hedging requires a position that provides gains as prices rise and losses as prices fall. If the investor buys calls and writes puts in the correct proportions, he will have offset the market risk of his short portfolio. (Study Session 17, LOS 72.b)

115. **A** Writer of put's maximum loss = $50 – $4 = $46 (Study Session 17, LOS 72.a)

116. **B** In the first year, the net payment for the fixed-rate payer will be (0.06 – 0.05) × $10,000,000 = $100,000. In the second year, the net payment will be zero if the interest rate is indeed 6%. (Study Session 17, LOS 71.b)

117. **C** The description relates best to the early stage wherein the capital that is supplied helps speed up product development and also helps pay for the beginning of a marketing campaign. The seed stage involves funding research and development to develop and test product ideas. (Study Session 18, LOS 73.g)

118. **C** $$\text{market value} = \frac{\text{annual net operating income}}{\text{market capitalization rate}}$$

    NOI = $2,000,000 – (0.10)($2,000,000) – $200,000 = $1,600,000 (NOI is before financing and personal taxes)

    $$\text{market value} = \frac{\$1,600,000}{0.10} = \$16,000,000$$

    (Study Session 18, LOS 73.f)

119. **C** A unique feature of ETFs is their use of "in-kind" shares to create or redeem shares. This is done to ensure an efficient and orderly market in the shares and to prevent the fund shares from trading at (much of) a premium or discount, thereby avoiding one of the pitfalls of closed-end funds. (Study Session 18, LOS 73.b, c)

120. **B** One potential drawback of the cost approach is that there could be a significant difference between the construction cost and the market value of an existing property. (Study Session 18, LOS 73.e)

Exam 2
Afternoon Session Answer Key

To get valuable feedback on how your score compares to those of other Level 1 candidates, use your Username and Password to gain Online Access at schweser.com and choose the left-hand menu item "Practice Exams Vol. 1."

1. C	31. B	61. B	91. C
2. A	32. B	62. C	92. C
3. A	33. C	63. B	93. A
4. C	34. B	64. B	94. A
5. A	35. B	65. C	95. B
6. B	36. C	66. A	96. C
7. B	37. A	67. B	97. C
8. A	38. C	68. B	98. A
9. B	39. B	69. A	99. A
10. B	40. C	70. B	100. B
11. A	41. A	71. B	101. B
12. A	42. C	72. C	102. B
13. C	43. C	73. A	103. C
14. C	44. B	74. A	104. C
15. C	45. C	75. A	105. C
16. B	46. C	76. A	106. B
17. C	47. B	77. C	107. B
18. B	48. C	78. C	108. C
19. B	49. C	79. C	109. B
20. C	50. B	80. C	110. B
21. B	51. A	81. A	111. B
22. A	52. C	82. B	112. A
23. A	53. B	83. B	113. C
24. B	54. A	84. C	114. B
25. A	55. B	85. B	115. C
26. A	56. C	86. A	116. C
27. B	57. B	87. C	117. B
28. C	58. A	88. A	118. A
29. C	59. A	89. A	119. C
30. A	60. C	90. B	120. C

Exam 2
Afternoon Session Answers

Answers referencing the Standards of Practice address Study Session 1, LOS 1.b, c and LOS 2.a, b, c, except where noted.

1. **C** Standard VI(C) Referral Fees. Members and candidates shall disclose to clients and prospects any consideration or benefit received by the member or delivered to others for the recommendation of any service to the client or prospect. This allows the client to evaluate possible bias in referrals.

2. **A** Standard IV(C) Responsibilities of Supervisors explicitly states that speaking to the employee to determine the extent of the violations and receiving assurances that it will not be repeated is not enough. Finley must take positive steps to insure that the violation will not be repeated, including promptly launching an investigation and limiting the employee's activities and/or increasing supervision of the employee until the results of the investigation are known.

3. **A** Stein violated Standard I(C) Misrepresentation by presenting material developed by another without proper acknowledgment.

4. **C** Standard V(A) Diligence and Reasonable Basis. The recommendation reflects the consensus of the group and not necessarily the opinion of the member or candidate. If the consensus opinion has a reasonable basis, the member does not have to dissociate from the report but should document the difference of opinion.

5. **A** Under Standard IV(C) Responsibilities of Supervisors, if Klein clearly cannot discharge supervisory responsibilities because of an inadequate compliance system, he should decline in writing to accept the supervisory responsibility until the firm adopts reasonable procedures to allow him to adequately exercise such responsibility.

6. **B** Standard III(A) Loyalty, Prudence, and Care. Crocker is essentially using a soft-dollar arrangement to pay for research used in managing her clients' accounts. Crocker may pay higher fees without violating her fiduciary duty as long as (1) the commission paid is reasonable in relation to the research and execution of services received and (2) the research benefits the firm's clients.

7. **B** Standard IV(A) Loyalty does not prohibit former employees from contacting clients of their pervious firm so long as the contact information does not come from the records of the previous employer or violate a non-compete agreement.

8. **A** Chambers resides in and does business in Botwari and is bound by the stricter of local law, U.S. law, and the Standards. The Standards permit referral fees that are properly disclosed to clients and do not prohibit gifts to clients in return for their business.

9. **B** To comply with Standard VI(A) Disclosure of Conflicts, members and candidates must make full disclosure of all matters that could impair their independence. Sell-side members and candidates should disclose to their clients any ownership in a security that they are recommending.

10. **B** According to Standard IV(B) Additional Compensation Arrangements, members and candidates must obtain written permission from their employer before accepting an offer of compensation (for the performance of work done for their employer) in addition to what they receive from their employer and that is contingent on future performance. Payment to investment bankers to complete an underwriting is standard business practice.

11. **A** Compliance requires that the firm follow local law and disclose the conflict between local law and GIPS. (Study Session 1, LOS 4.c)

12. **A** Standard III(D) Performance Presentation requires that statements about performance be not only accurate but also fair and complete. While Vance's statement may be accurate in a technical sense, it is neither fair nor complete, and it seems intended to mislead prospects about Vance's track record in managing equities accounts and/or selecting equity securities. While compliance with GIPS and its methods of composite construction are recommended, they are not required by the Standards.

13. **C** Drake is in violation of Standard V(B) Communication with Clients and Prospective Clients. Brief communications must be supported by background reports or data that can be made available to the client if requested. Drake should have given the client a more detailed analysis of the investment when the client called to request such information. Drake did not violate Standard III(C) Suitability because he thoroughly read and evaluated the analysis and determined that the structured product was in line with his client's objectives before recommending the product to his client.

14. **C** Farley is in violation of Standard VI(B) Priority of Transactions. Client transactions must take precedence over members' or candidates' trades. He should have submitted his personal trade order only after trading for his client. Standard III(B) Fair Dealing requires that Farley deal fairly with all clients when recommending securities or taking investment action. Since the endowment fund is Farley's only account, he has not disadvantaged any other client by only taking action on the behalf of the endowment.

15. **C** Under Standard III(A) Loyalty, Prudence, and Care, members and candidates must comply with their fiduciary duty to those persons and interests by whom the duty is owed. Specifically, members must always act for the benefit of their clients and place clients' interests before their own. Murphy's actions in directing trades to Casanova violate the fiduciary duty owed to Wellington & Worrel's clients, as he appears to be selecting Casanova for the discounts received on personal securities transactions. Casanova charges higher commission rates and delivers poorer execution than other brokers used by the firm. By using Casanova, Murphy violates his fiduciary duty by failing to act in the clients' best interest. Alternatively, the arrangement with Cedrock appears to comply with Murphy's fiduciary duty, as the firm receives investment research used in managing client portfolios (a soft-dollar arrangement) and achieves better execution for client trades. Because the trading arrangement with Cedrock benefits clients, it does not violate Standard III(A).

16. **B** Dodd has most likely violated Standard III(B) Fair Dealing by giving Phillips an overgenerous allocation of the oversubscribed ("hot") new issue. The issue is not that he is offering compensation to a client to resolve a dispute, but that by overallocating the IPO shares to Phillips he is not treating his other clients fairly. Standard III(B) Fair Dealing requires that candidates and members not use shares of "hot issues" as an incentive to achieve a reward or benefit. The benefit in this case is that the dispute will "go away."

17. **C** The eight major sections of the CFA Institute Global Investment Performance Standards are Fundamentals of Compliance, Input Data, Calculation Methodology, Composite Construction, Disclosures, Presentation and Reporting, Real Estate, and Private Equity. (Study Session 1, LOS 4.d)

18. **B** Standard III(C) Suitability requires that the client portfolio fit the client risk and return objectives as stated in the investment policy statement, and that seems to be the case here. The proper focus of risk analysis is on the entire portfolio and need not be applied on an issue-by-issue basis. There appears to be no violation of V(A) Diligence and Reasonable Basis since his previous analysis indicated the portfolio was suitable and his records supported that conclusion.

19. **B** With no interest paid on the original $5,000 loan, at 6% in five years the loan balance will be:

    New loan balance = $5,000(1.06)^5 = $6,691.13 or PV = 5,000; I/Y = 6; N = 5; PMT = 0; CPT → FV = −$6,691.13.

    $6,691.13 is the loan that has to be retired over the next five years. The financial calculator solution is:

    PV = 6,691.13; I/Y = 6; N = 5; FV = 0; CPT → PMT. You obtain PMT = −1,588.45. (Study Session 2, LOS 5.e)

20. **C** N = 4; PMT = 0; PV = −4,000; FV = 6,520; CPT → I/Y = 12.99%,

    or $\left(\dfrac{6,520}{4,000}\right)^{1/4} - 1 = 12.99\%$.

    The question asks for the *effective* annual rate and gives the beginning and ending values. That the ending value was arrived at by monthly compounding is not relevant. (Study Session 2, LOS 5.c)

21. **B** Choice A describes a histogram, and Choice C describes a frequency polygon. (Study Session 2, LOS 7.d)

22. **A** holding period return (HPR) = $\dfrac{\text{ending value} + \text{dividends}}{\text{beginning value}} - 1$

    $HPR = \dfrac{10 + 50 + 105 + 2 + 4}{20 + 40 + 100} - 1 = 0.06875 = 6.875\%$

    (Study Session 2, LOS 6.b, 7.e)

23. **A**   Calculate the mean: $\frac{25+15+35+45+55}{5} = 35$. To get the mean absolute deviation, sum the deviations around the mean (ignoring the sign), and divide by the number of observations $= \frac{10+20+0+10+20}{5} = 12$. (Study Session 2, LOS 7.g)

24. **B**   mean $= \frac{5+10+15}{3} = 10$

   population standard deviation $= \sqrt{\frac{(5-10)^2 + (10-10)^2 + (15-10)^2}{3}} = 4.0825$

   $CV = \frac{\text{standard deviation}}{\text{mean}} = \frac{4.0825}{10} = 0.408$

   (Study Session 2, LOS 7.i)

25. **A**   For the positively skewed distribution, the mode is less than the median, which is less than the mean. (Study Session 2, LOS 7.j)

26. **A**   The probability of surviving to the end of the fifth year is the product of the probabilities of surviving in each year, or one minus the probability of failure. Therefore, the 5-year survival probability is $(1 - 0.25)(1 - 0.20)(1 - 0.20)(1 - 0.15)(1 - 0.10) = 0.3672$.

   The present value of the expected payoff is $\frac{\$20,000(0.3672)}{1.25^5} = \$2,407$.

   (Study Session 2, LOS 8.i)

27. **B**   The first year account return was $\frac{55}{42} - 1 = 31\%$. The second year return was $\frac{54}{55} - 1 = -1.8\%$. The geometric mean is $(1.31 \times 0.982)^{1/2} - 1 = 13.4\%$, which is the time-weighted return. Since only one asset was involved, $\left(\frac{54}{42}\right)^{1/2} - 1 = 13.4\%$ also gives the time-weighted return. To calculate the money-weighted return, use the cash flow function with Cf0 = –42,000, Cf1 = –55,000, and Cf2 = 54,000 × 2 = 108,000, and compute IRR, which is 7.73%. The money-weighted return is lower because the amount in the account was greater in the second period, when the return was poor. (Study Session 2, LOS 6.c)

28. **C**   The binomial distribution is a discrete distribution, while the normal distribution is an example of a continuous distribution. Univariate distributions can be discrete or continuous. (Study Session 3, LOS 9.a)

29. **C**   About 68% of all observations fall within ±1 standard deviation of the mean. Thus, about 68% of the values fall between 5 and 25. (Study Session 3, LOS 9.k)

30. **A**   The central limit theorem holds for any distribution as long as the sample size is large (i.e., n > 30). (Study Session 3, LOS 10.d)

31. **B**   The population variance is known (in this case 100), so the standard error of the sample mean is $\sigma/\sqrt{n} = \sqrt{100}/\sqrt{225} = 10/15 = 0.67$. (Study Session 3, LOS 10.e)

32. **B** The *t*-test must be used when the sample size is small, the population is normal, and the population variance is unknown. If the population is non-normal and the variance is unknown, there is no valid test statistic when the sample is small. (Study Session 3, LOS 11.c, e, f)

33. **C** Increased government borrowing would decrease, not increase, the profitability of corporate investment projects since it will tend to increase interest rates and required rates of return in general. (Study Session 6, LOS 26.b)

34. **B** The money multiplier is a function of the reserve ratio, *r*, and the currency drain, *c*.

$$\text{money multiplier} = \frac{1+c}{r+c} = \frac{1.05}{0.2 + 0.05} = 4.2$$

(Study Session 6, LOS 24.f)

35. **B** External benefits result in a demand curve that does not represent the marginal societal benefit of the good or service, so that the equilibrium quantity produced and consumed is less than the efficient quantity. (Study Session 4, LOS 14.e)

36. **C** An individual is technically unemployed when he is actively seeking employment or is waiting to return to a job from which he was just laid off. Not all people who are not working are considered unemployed. Examples include household workers, students, retirees, and discouraged workers. (Study Session 5, LOS 22.c)

37. **A** The long-run production decision differs from the short-run production decision in that fixed costs can be changed in the long run but not the short run. Thus, short-run cost curves apply for a given size of a plant, and long-run cost curves can show costs for different size plants. (Study Session 4, LOS 17.d)

38. **C** One brand of flour likely has many good substitutes, and elasticity of demand is likely high. The other statements are true. Demand elasticity is greater in the long run than in the short run. The demand for gasoline is likely inelastic. Thus, when the price increases, the percentage change in quantity demanded is less than the percentage change in price. There are few substitutes for gasoline, especially in the short run. For goods that are complements, cross elasticity is negative. (Study Session 4, LOS 13.a)

39. **B** In some cases, a monopolist may be unable to sell for a profit. Price may be insufficient to cover the per-unit cost of the monopolist, even when operating at the MR = MC rate of output. The monopolist faces a downward-sloping demand curve. (Study Session 5, LOS 19.a, b)

40. **C** These conditions characterize *monopolistic competition*. By contrast, monopolies and oligopolies have high barriers to entry and involve either a single seller (monopoly) or a small number of interdependent sellers (oligopoly). Similar to monopolistic competition, pure competition involves a large number of independent sellers. With pure competition, products are homogeneous (not differentiated), no barriers to entry exist (not low barriers to entry), and the demand schedule is horizontal (not downward sloping) and perfectly elastic (not highly elastic). (Study Session 5, LOS 18.a, 20.a)

41. **A**   The demand-pull inflation process originates with an increase in aggregate demand from either expansion of the money supply or an increase in the federal deficit when the economy is already at its full-employment level. Persistent increases in the price level (inflation) will only result if policy makers repeatedly attempt to increase real GDP above the full-employment level through monetary or fiscal expansion. Although cost-push inflation originates with an increase in the price of an important productive resource, it only results in inflation if the monetary authorities repeatedly increase the money supply to counteract the (short-term) reductions in real GDP that result from further increases in the price of the productive input. (Study Session 6, LOS 25.b)

42. **C**   Accounting profit is often an unsatisfactory performance measure from an economic point of view because accounting costs generally do not include the opportunity costs of equity capital. Accounting costs do reflect the cost of depreciation. (Study Session 4, LOS 16.a)

43. **C**   The Taylor rule places emphasis on both price level stability and business cycle stability (i.e., reducing deviations of real GDP from potential real GDP). The rule increases the federal funds target rate as inflation (and inflation indicators) increase, as well as when real GDP rises above potential GDP. The Taylor rule uses the federal funds target rate as its policy variable, whereas the McCallum rule uses the growth rate of the monetary base. Inflation targeting emphasizes price level stability at every stage of the business cycle. (Study Session 6, LOS 27.b, d)

44. **B**   At a minimum wage above the equilibrium wage, there will be an excess supply of workers. Firms substitute other productive resources for labor and use more than the economically efficient amount of capital. The result is increased unemployment and a decrease in economic efficiency. Firms may decrease the quality or quantity of the non-monetary benefits they previously offered to workers. (Study Session 4, LOS 15.b)

45. **C**   Paying off accounts payable from cash lowers current assets and current liabilities by the same amount. Because the current ratio started off above 1, the current ratio will increase. Because the quick ratio started off less than 1, it will decrease further. The other choices are incorrect. Buying fixed assets on credit decreases both ratios because the denominator increases, with no change to the numerator. Using cash to purchase inventory would result in no change in the current ratio but would decrease the quick ratio by decreasing the numerator. (Study Session 8, LOS 33.h, 35.d)

46. **C**   cash conversion cycle (CCC) = days of sales outstanding + days of inventory on hand – number of days of payables

$$\text{number of days of payables} = \frac{365}{\text{payables turnover}} = \frac{365}{11} = 33.18 \text{ days}; \ \frac{365}{10} = 36.5 \text{ days}$$

Since the payables payment period increases by 3.32 days and receivables days increases by 5, CCC increases by 1.68 days. (Study Session 8, LOS 35.d)

47. **B** The income statement reports on the financial performance of the firm over a period of time. Revenues, expenses, gains, and losses are taken together to arrive at a figure (net income) that is often used to assess a company's performance. The balance sheet reports the company's financial position at a point in time and does not illustrate performance. The cash flow statement reports the company's cash receipts and payments. Although it provides information about one aspect of firm performance (the generation of operating cash flow), the income statement is the best source of information about firm performance. The statement of changes in owners' equity reports the amounts and sources of changes in equity investors' investment in the company over a period of time and does not provide information about firm performance. (Study Session 7, LOS 29.b)

48. **C** The three objectives of financial market regulation according to IOSCO are to (1) protect investors; (2) ensure the fairness, efficiency, and transparency of markets; and (3) reduce systemic risk. Because of the increasing globalization of securities markets, IOSCO seeks to attain uniform financial regulations across countries. (Study Session 7, LOS 31.b)

49. **C** Sales revenue for which the product or service has yet to be delivered gives rise to a liability account, unearned revenue. This liability will be reduced as the product or service is actually delivered. (Study Session 8, LOS 33.c)

50. **B**

Sales	+$4,000	
Cash received from customers		+$4,000 (since no change in AR)
Cost of goods sold	–2,000	
Increase in inventory	–100	
Increase in accounts payable	+300	
Other cash input expenses	–500	
Cash paid for inputs		–2,300
Cash paid for taxes		–200
Cash flow from operations		+1,500

(Study Session 8, LOS 34.e)

51. **A** The analyst should add the U.S. GAAP firm's LIFO reserve to its balance sheet inventory and subtract the change in the LIFO reserve from its cost of goods sold. This adjustment will increase the firm's total assets and change its pretax income, income taxes, net income, and retained earnings (increasing them if the LIFO reserve increased, or decreasing them if the LIFO reserve decreased). These adjustments will change the firm's debt-to-equity ratio by changing total equity, and change the cash conversion cycle by changing inventories. The adjustments do not change current liabilities or current assets other than inventories, so the quick ratio is not affected. (Study Session 10, LOS 43.d)

52. **C** Capitalization smooths net income by spreading costs over time. This also makes profitability ratios such as ROA less volatile. A capitalizing company classifies the costs of long-lived assets as CFI outflows, while a company that expenses these costs classifies them as CFO outflows. So Alfred's CFO will be higher and CFI lower. Asset and equity levels will be higher for a firm that capitalizes, so given identical debt levels, the capitalizing firm will show less financial leverage (lower debt/equity and debt/assets ratios) than the expensing firm. (Study Session 9, LOS 37.b)

53. **B** $\text{ROE} = \dfrac{\text{net income}}{\text{equity}} = \dfrac{0.16(1,500)}{(1-0.40)(2,000)} = 0.20$, or 20%

       If the debt ratio (TD/TA) is equal to 40% and the firm has no preferred stock, the percentage of equity is 1 – 0.40, or 60%. (Study Session 10, LOS 35.d)

54. **A**   Shares issued post-split need not be adjusted for the split as they are already "new" shares. Options with an exercise price greater than the average share price do not affect diluted EPS. (Study Session 8, LOS 32.g)

55. **B**   Diluted EPS uses average price. Since the average price is greater than the exercise price, the warrants are dilutive.

       $\dfrac{60-50}{60} \times 1,000,000 = 166,667$

       (Study Session 8, LOS 32.g, h)

56. **C**   The cash conversion cycle is (365/6) + (365/9) – (365/12) = 60.8 + 40.6 – 30.4 = 71 days. ROA is lower than ROE when net income is positive and debt is present. Just the fact that a company has a high gross profit margin does not necessarily mean it will have a high net profit margin. For example, the company could have very high operating expenses and end up with a low net profit margin. (Study Session 10, LOS 35.d)

57. **B**   During periods of rising prices and stable or increasing inventory quantities, FIFO, compared to LIFO, results in higher inventory, and therefore working capital, and lower cost of goods sold. Net income will be higher with FIFO. (Study Session 9, LOS 36.e)

58. **A**   FIFO COGS:
         100 @ $210   = $21,000
          70 @ $225   = $15,750
                          $36,750

       LIFO ending inventory:
       Purchases   190
       Sales   170
       Balance   20 @ $210 = $4,200 (Study Session 9, LOS 36.c)

59. **A**   Straight-line depreciation: $14 million / 7 = $2.0 million

       Accelerated depreciation: $14 million × 0.333 = $4.662 million

       Difference in depreciation: $4.662 million – $2.0 million = $2.662 million
                              × Tax rate   0.35
                              Increase in deferred tax liability $931,700

       (Study Session 9, LOS 38.d)

60. **C**   FIFO ending inventory = LIFO ending inventory + LIFO reserve = 22,000 + 4,000 = $26,000

       FIFO after-tax profit = LIFO after-tax profit + (change in LIFO reserve)(1 – t)
       = $2,000 + ($4,000 – $3,000)(1 – 0.4) = $2,000 + $600 = $2,600

       (Study Session 8, LOS 32.e, and Study Session 9, LOS 36.c, e)

61. **B** The total cash flows are equal, but the expensing firm will see lower early-year profitability rather than higher early-year profitability. (Study Session 9, LOS 37.a)

62. **C** This transaction results in a reduction of debt and an increase in equity. However, since no cash is involved, it is not reported as a financing activity in the cash flow statement, but will be disclosed in the notes to the cash flow statement. (Study Session 8, LOS 34.b)

63. **B** $\text{average depreciable life} = \dfrac{\text{ending gross investment}}{\text{annual depreciation expense}} = \dfrac{750}{150} = 5$

$\text{average life of the plant and equipment} = \dfrac{300}{150} = 2 \text{ years}$

(Study Session 9, LOS 37.e)

64. **B** Cash flows are no different under the percentage-of-completion method compared with the completed-contract method. Income statement and balance sheet accounts will differ between the two firms. (Study Session 8, LOS 32.b)

65. **C** A specific explanatory paragraph that makes reference to (questions) the going concern assumption may be a signal of serious problems and call for close examination by the analyst. Therefore, in the absence of such a paragraph, there is no need for a close examination of the going concern assumption by the analyst. The objective of an audit is to enable the auditor to provide an opinion on the fairness and reliability of the financial statements. This is not the same as numerical accuracy. The auditor generally only provides reasonable assurance that there are no material errors in the financial statements, not an opinion about their numerical accuracy. An independent certified public accounting firm must be appointed by the audit committee of the company's board of directors, not by its management. Appointment of the auditors by management would reduce the level of perceived independence. (Study Session 7, LOS 29.d)

66. **A** A firm's issuance of discount bonds will lead to an understatement of cash flows from financing over the life of the debt and an overstatement of cash flows from operations, but it will have no effect on cash flows from investing. Increasing interest rates have no bearing on whether operating and financing cash flows are overstated or understated. Instead, they would simply decrease the market value of outstanding debt. (Study Session 9, LOS 39.a)

67. **B** A take or pay agreement obligates a buyer to pay the seller of a product or service a minimum amount, regardless of whether the product or service is delivered. An analyst should add the discounted value of the commitment to the company's assets and liabilities. (Study Session 9, LOS 39.i)

68. **B** When the PV of the lease payments is greater than the carrying value of an asset, the lessor records an immediate gross profit on sale equal to the excess of the PV over the carrying value, and the lease is termed a sales-type lease, not a direct financing lease. (Study Session 9, LOS 39.h)

69. **A** After-tax cost of debt:

N = 20; FV = 1000; PV = –894; PMT = 60; CPT → I/Y = 7%
$k_d = (7\%)(1 - 0.4) = 4.2\%$

(Study Session 11, LOS 45.h)

70. **B**   The weights used to calculate WACC should be based on the firm's target capital structure. If the company does not provide information about its target capital structure, an analyst can use the company's current capital structure or the average capital structure weights for the industry. Similar size is not enough for the average weights for other companies to be relevant if those companies are not in the same industry. (Study Session 11, LOS 45.c)

71. **B**   Information is typically not available to compare the aging of receivables between companies, among groups of companies, or within an industry. Receivables turnover can be calculated from the balance sheet. An aging schedule shows either the absolute or percentage amount of accounts receivable that are current and that are past due by various lengths of time. (Study Session 11, LOS 46.f)

72. **C**   Klepp is incorrect about both consulting contracts for Board members and Board members' use of company assets. Either practice is likely to compromise the independence of Board members and their incentive to act in shareholders' best interests. A strong corporate code of ethics should discourage such forms of compensation to Board members. (Study Session 11, LOS 48.e)

73. **A**   CF0 = −$25,000; annual cash flow = $5,000 for 10 years; I/Y = 12. NPV = 3,251.12. The machine has a positive net present value, so the club should purchase it. (Study Session 11, LOS 44.d)

74. **A**   Since the net present value of the five projects is the expected increase in firm value from undertaking the projects, maximizing the NPV of the projects chosen will result in the selection of the optimal group of five projects. Since the profitability index is the ratio of the present value of the expected after-tax cash flows to the initial outlay, choosing the five projects with the greatest profitability indexes will identify the five projects with the greatest total present values and the projects with the greatest total net present values. (Study Session 11, LOS 44.c)

75. **A**   The policy statement is inappropriate because it is too restrictive. A policy statement should focus on meeting the specific safety and liquidity needs of the firm but should also allow the flexibility to increase yield within these constraints. There are many other securities potentially suitable for cash management that would provide equivalent or better liquidity and safety of principal at least equivalent to that of the securities issued by A+ rated banks. (Study Session 11, LOS 46.d, e)

76. **A**   Sunk costs are not to be included in investment analysis. Opportunity costs and the project's impact on taxes are relevant variables in determining project cash flow for a capital investment. (Study Session 11, LOS 44.b)

77. **C**   An increase in the number of days of payables suggests a company is taking longer to pay its vendors. This reduces the cash conversion cycle and represents effective working capital management, a source of liquidity for a company. A decrease in days of payables would be a drag on liquidity because the company is paying its vendors more quickly, which uses cash. (Study Session 11, LOS 46.a,c)

78. **C**   Regularly reviewing performance, independence, skills, and experience of existing board members is a responsibility of the Remunerations/Compensation Committee, not the Audit Committee. The other choices are positive characteristics of the Audit Committee. (Study Session 11, LOS 48.f)

79. **C** The introduction of a zero-beta (no systematic risk) portfolio with a return that is higher than the risk-free rate can result in a straight CML, even with the assumption that borrowing and lending rates are different. Margin accounts represent borrowing, so unless the margin lending rate is the same as the risk-free rate, this does not solve the problem (a kinked CML) that results from unequal borrowing and lending rates in the model. (Study Session 12 LOS 51.d)

80. **C** The Standards of Practice have very little to do with investment constraints. (Study Session 12, LOS 49.d)

81. **A** A risk-averse investor prefers less risk to more risk. The lower the correlation, the greater the risk reduction. Thus, a risk-averse investor would most prefer the portfolio with the lowest correlation coefficient and least prefer the one with the highest. Of the choices given, W and Y's correlation coefficient of +0.6 is the highest. (Study Session 12, LOS 50.e)

82. **B** The CAPM concludes that expected returns are a positive (linear) function of systematic risk. (Study Session 12, LOS 51.c)

83. **B** The SML and CML both intersect the vertical axis at the risk-free rate. The SML describes the risk/return tradeoff for individual securities or portfolios, whereas the CML describes the risk/return tradeoff of various combinations of the market portfolio and a riskless asset. (Study Session 12, LOS 51.b, d)

84. **C** Studies have demonstrated that approximately 90% of the variation in a single portfolio's returns can be explained by its target asset allocations. It is very difficult to generate abnormal portfolio returns by market timing and security selection within asset classes. (Study Session 12, LOS 49.e)

85. **B** A price-weighted index will put the most weight on Stock X, which had the worst performance. A price-weighted index will have a beginning value of $(160 + 80 + 60) / 3 = 100$ and an ending value of $(136 + 100 + 66) / 3 = 100.67$, for an increase of 0.67%. The percent change for a value-weighted index is $(13,600 + 10,000 + 66,000) / (16,000 + 8,000 + 60,000) - 1 = 6.7\%$. The percent change for an unweighted index using the geometric mean is $[(1 - 0.15)(1 + 0.25)(1 + 0.1)]^{1/3} - 1 = 5.3\%$. (Study Session 13, LOS 53.a)

86. **A** A portfolio with equal numbers of shares of each stock in the price-weighted index will match the performance of the index assuming there are no stock splits, stock dividends, or changes in the makeup of the index. The return on the index does not include cash dividend payments. Since the reinvested dividends will add to the number of shares of those stocks that pay dividends, Gomez's portfolio return will exceed that of the index. (Study Session 13, LOS 53.a)

87. **C** The top-down, 3-step process goes from the economy to the industry to the firm, in that order. (Study Session 14, LOS 56.a)

88. **A** An investor cannot achieve positive abnormal returns on average by using technical analysis if prices fully reflect all available security market (price and volume) information. The weak form of the EMH assumes prices reflect this information, and the semistrong and strong forms assume prices reflect additional (non-market) information as well. (Study Session 13, LOS 54.a)

89. **A**   First solve for D_5: $D_5 = (D_1)(1 + g)^n = \$1(1.05)^4 = \$1.216$

$$P_4 = \frac{D_5}{(k-g)} = \frac{\$1.216}{(0.15-0.05)} = \$12.16$$

or

$$P_0 = \frac{1}{0.15-0.05} = 10$$

$$P_4 = 10(1.05)^4 = \$12.16$$

(Study Session 14, LOS 56.c)

90. **B**   Mispricings of small-company stocks can persist because the small size of the positions that can be established limits the ability to execute sufficiently profitable arbitrage trades. Restrictions on short sales prevent *overvalued* securities from being exploited by arbitrage traders. Even if a strategy results in positive abnormal returns, it will not necessarily be profitable if the overall market is unfavorable. For example, if the return on the market is −10%, a strategy that generates a positive abnormal return of 5% (relative to the market) will still have a return of −5%. (Study Session 13, LOS 55.d)

91. **C** $P/E = \dfrac{\text{dividend payout ratio}}{k-g}$

$g = ROE \times \text{retention rate}$

Increases in k reduce P/E. Increases in g or the dividend payout ratio increase P/E. (Study Session 14, LOS 56.d)

92. **C**   Underlying earnings should be used in the calculation. These exclude transitory, nonrecurring components of earnings. Also, the most recent earnings information should be used in the calculation. Therefore we get:

$$\text{trailing P/E} = \frac{\$27.50}{\$1.10} = 25$$

(Study Session 14, LOS 59.b)

93. **A**   The risk premium will be a function of business risk, financial risk, liquidity risk, exchange-rate risk, and country (political risk). Stocks do not have default risk. (Study Session 14, LOS 56.e)

94. **A**   A stop buy order is an order to buy a security if the price increases to the specified stop price. This type of order is often used to limit losses on a short position. A limit buy order specifies a maximum price and is executed if the market price is less than or equal to that price. (Study Session 13, LOS 52.e)

95. **B** This is a supernormal growth stock valuation problem.

Step 1: Find the dividends in the supernormal growth period.

$D_1 = 1.00(1.20) = \$1.20$; $D_2 = 1.2(1.2) = \$1.44$; $D_3 = 1.44(1.15) = \$1.656$

Step 2: Use the constant growth model to find the price at the end of period 2.

$$P_2 = \frac{D_3}{k-g} = \frac{1.656}{0.10-0.06} = \$41.40$$

Step 3: Discount all of the cash flows back to time zero.

$$P_0 = \frac{D_1}{(1+k)} + \frac{D_2}{(1+k)^2} + \frac{P_2}{(1+k)^2} = \frac{1.20}{1.10} + \frac{1.44}{(1.10)^2} + \frac{41.40}{(1.10)^2} = \$36.50$$

(Study Session 14, LOS 56.c)

96. **C** Semistrong-form market efficiency implies that fundamental analysis of publicly available information will not generate abnormal returns on average. Portfolio managers should help quantify a client's risk tolerances and return needs, offer portfolio policies and strategies to meet these needs, and construct a portfolio by allocating funds to appropriate asset classes. Portfolio managers can also create value by diversifying their clients' portfolios globally to reduce risk, monitoring and evaluating changing capital market conditions, monitoring their clients' needs and circumstances, and rebalancing their clients' portfolios when necessary. (Study Session 13, LOS 54.c)

97. **C** The OAS is a measure of the yield spread over Treasury spot rates *without* the option. (Study Session 15, LOS 60.e, 63.e and Study Session 16, LOS 65.g)

98. **A** Option-free bonds have positive convexity and the effect of (positive) convexity is to increase the magnitude of the price increase when yields fall and to decrease the magnitude of the price decrease when yields rise. (Study Session 16, LOS 66.g)

99. **A** Municipal bonds are traded in the over-the-counter market supported by municipal bond dealers across the country. (Study Session 15, LOS 62.d, g)

100. **B** The bond is sold at a premium. As time passes, the bond's price will move toward par. Thus, the price will fall.

N = 10; FV = 1,000; PMT = 100; I = 8; CPT → PV = $1,134

N = 9; FV = 1,000; PMT = 100; I = 8; CPT → PV = $1,125

(Study Session 16, LOS 64.d)

101. **B** Semiannual compound rate is $\frac{0.065}{2} = 0.0325$. Ending value must be $888.94(1.0325)^{14} = \$1,391.02$ in order to realize a 6.5% (bond-equivalent) yield over the bond's life.

$1,391.02
−1,000.00 face value at maturity
391.02
−315.00 total coupons (14 × 22.50)
76.02 reinvestment income required

(Study Session 16, LOS 65.c)

102. **B** The two investments combine to form a 10-year, $1,000 face value, 8.0% semiannual coupon bond that would sell at par because the YTM (expressed as a BEY) equals the coupon rate. Thus the combined value is $1,000. The zero-coupon bond is worth $\dfrac{1,000}{1.04^{20}} = \$456.39$, and the annuity payments are worth $543.61 (N = 10 × 2 = 20,

PMT = 40, I/Y = 8/2 = 4, FV = 0, PV = –543.61).

(Study Session 16, LOS 64.c)

103. **C** $\Delta P/P = -D_{effective}\Delta i$

$\Delta P/P = -7.6(+0.0075) = -0.057$, or -5.7%

(Study Session 16, LOS 66.d)

104. **C** The nominal yield (another term for the coupon yield) is less than the yield to maturity for a discount bond. (Study Session 16, LOS 65.b)

105. **C** The key term here is *coupon bond*. While an investor in a fixed-coupon bond can usually eliminate interest rate risk by holding a bond until maturity, the same is not true for reinvestment risk. The receipt of periodic coupon payments exposes the investor to reinvestment risk. A noncallable bond reduces reinvestment risk by reducing the risk of repayment. Thus, an investor most concerned with reinvestment risk would prefer a noncallable bond to a callable bond. Since lower coupon bonds have lower reinvestment risk, this same investor would prefer a lower coupon bond to a higher coupon bond. (Study Session 15, LOS 61.i)

106. **B** A special purpose vehicle is a legal entity to which the assets used as collateral in an ABS issue are sold. This transaction separates the assets backing the ABS from the other assets of the company that creates the SPV. (Study Session 15, LOS 62.i)

107. **B** $_2f_1 = \left[\dfrac{(1+z_3)^{1+2}}{(1+z_1)^1}\right]^{1/2} - 1 = \left[\dfrac{(1+12)^3}{(1.10)}\right]^{1/2} - 1 = 13.01\%$

Note: $\dfrac{(3\times12)-(1\times10)}{2} = 13$ (Study Session 16, LOS 65.h)

108. **C** A flat term structure could be explained according to the liquidity preference theory as a case where investors expect short-term rates to decline slightly, coupled with a maturity premium that exactly offsets the downward pressure contained in investor expectations. The pure expectations theory makes no specific mention of the fact that an upward-sloping term structure is a consequence of investors expecting short-term rates to remain unchanged for a period of time followed by investors expecting short-term rates to rise for a period of time. All this theory says is that an upward-sloping term structure can be explained by investors believing that future short-term rates will rise. Finally, the liquidity preference theory attempts to explain the term structure according to two factors. These are expectations about future interest rates and a maturity premium to compensate for interest rate risk. If the term structure is declining, this could be explained simply by investor expectations of declining future short-term rates coupled with a maturity premium that is not large enough to offset the downward pressure on interest rates due to investor expectations. (Study Session 15, LOS 63.c)

109. **B** Both statements are incorrect. As yields rise, the value of the embedded put option in a putable bond increases and (beyond a critical point) reduces the decline in the value of the bond compared with a similar option-free bond. As yields fall, the value of the embedded put option decreases, and (beyond a critical point) the putable bond behaves much the same as a similar option-free bond since the embedded put option has little or no value. (Study Session 16, LOS 66.b)

110. **B** To calculate a Treasury bond's arbitrage-free value, each cash flow is discounted using the Treasury spot rate that is specific to the maturity of the cash flow. (Study Session 16, LOS 64.f)

111. **B** The holder of a long position in an FRA receives cash if the reference rate is greater than the rate specified in the contract on the expiration date, or pays cash if the reference rate is less than the contract rate. Combining a long interest rate call with a short interest rate put results in the same payoff pattern. A long interest rate call option has a positive value (receives cash) if the reference rate is greater than the strike rate at expiration. The holder of a short interest rate put option must pay cash if the reference rate is less than the strike rate at expiration. (Study Session 17, LOS 70.d)

112. **A** The variability of prices in general is significantly larger than the variability of (uncertainty about) dividend yields, and hence managing price risk is of primary importance, while the uncertainty about dividend yields is of secondary importance. The remaining statements are correct. (Study Session 17, LOS 68.d)

113. **C** This is an out-of-the-money covered call. The net cost is $37 (40 − 3) and the maximum payoff on the position is the exercise price, $42. Thus, the maximum profit is $5. (Study Session 17, LOS 72.b)

114. **B** The buyer of an option (long position) is not obligated to perform any action in the future. The writer of a call option (short position) has an obligation to sell the underlying asset to the option holder if the holder exercises the option. The party taking either side of a swap has entered into a forward commitment. (Study Session 17, LOS 67.b, c)

115. **C** If the margin account balance falls below the maintenance margin level, the account must be brought back up to the initial margin amount. (Study Session 17, LOS 69.d)

116. **C** An American-style call option must be worth at least as much as an otherwise identical European-style call option and has the same minimum value. This fact alone eliminates choice B. Since the American-style call is in the money and therefore must be worth more than the $6 difference between the strike price and the exercise price, you can eliminate response A and select response C without calculating the exact minimum value, which is given by:

$$\max[0, S_t - X / (1 + RFR)^{T-t}] = \max[0, 86 - 80 / (1.03)^{3/12}] = \$6.59$$

(Study Session 17, LOS 70.i)

117. **B** Gains and losses that result from entering into a new, longer-dated futures contract as previous contracts expire or are closed out depend on whether the contract is in contango (futures price greater than spot price) or backwardation (futures price less than spot price). Collateral yield depends on the yield on T-bills posted as collateral (margin). Contract yield is not defined as any particular yield measure. (Study Session 18, LOS 74.b)

118. **A** Mezzanine financing provides capital during the period prior to an initial public offering. (Study Session 18, LOS 73.g)

119. **C** The income approach uses net operating income before financing *and* taxes. (Study Session 18, LOS 73.f)

120. **C** after-tax cash flow = (revenue − expenses − depreciation) (1 − t) + depreciation = (revenue − cost) (1 − t) + depreciation(t)

[$250,000 − (0.04 × $250,000) − $15,000 −($1,000,000 × 0.026)] (1 − 0.35) + (1,000,000 × 0.026)

[($250,000 − $10,000 − $15,000 − $26,000) (0.65)] + $26,000 = $155,350

(Study Session 18, LOS 73.f)

EXAM 3
MORNING SESSION ANSWER KEY

To get valuable feedback on how your score compares to those of other Level 1 candidates, use your Username and Password to gain Online Access at schweser.com and choose the left-hand menu item "Practice Exams Vol. 1."

1. B	31. B	61. C	91. C
2. A	32. C	62. A	92. B
3. A	33. C	63. A	93. A
4. B	34. C	64. B	94. A
5. B	35. B	65. C	95. B
6. A	36. C	66. C	96. C
7. C	37. A	67. C	97. A
8. A	38. B	68. C	98. A
9. B	39. C	69. C	99. C
10. C	40. A	70. B	100. C
11. A	41. C	71. B	101. C
12. C	42. C	72. A	102. A
13. C	43. C	73. A	103. A
14. A	44. B	74. B	104. B
15. C	45. C	75. A	105. C
16. A	46. C	76. C	106. B
17. B	47. C	77. C	107. A
18. B	48. C	78. C	108. C
19. B	49. A	79. C	109. C
20. C	50. B	80. C	110. B
21. A	51. A	81. B	111. B
22. A	52. C	82. C	112. B
23. B	53. B	83. C	113. C
24. C	54. A	84. A	114. A
25. C	55. C	85. C	115. A
26. B	56. A	86. B	116. B
27. B	57. B	87. A	117. C
28. C	58. A	88. A	118. C
29. B	59. B	89. B	119. C
30. C	60. A	90. C	120. A

Exam 3
Morning Session Answers

Answers referencing the Standards of Practice address Study Session 1, LOS 1.b, c and LOS 2.a, b, c, except where noted.

1. **B** Members can accept or reject a disciplinary sanction proposed by the Designated Officer. If the member rejects the sanction, the matter is referred to a hearing by a panel of CFA Institute members. The other statements are accurate. (Study Session 1, LOS 1.a)

2. **A** According to Standard I(B) Independence and Objectivity, members and candidates may accept gifts from clients but must disclose them to their employers. Because Miguel did not disclose the gift to his employer, he has violated Standard I(B). In addition, Standard I(A) Knowledge of the Law states that members and candidates are not to commit any act that they know or should know violates the Code and Standards. Miguel is a CFA charterholder and should know that his actions violate Standard I(B). Thus, by violating Standard I(B), Miguel also has violated Standard I(A).

3. **A** Jones violated Standard I(C) Misrepresentation when he used the work of others without acknowledgment, which is plagiarism. It did not matter that Smith gave Jones the information verbally or that she said he was "welcome to it." Jones used another's work without crediting the source, which constitutes plagiarism. Jones also violated Standard V(A) Diligence and Reasonable Basis because he did not have a reasonable and adequate basis for his recommendation.

4. **B** Watson's excessive drinking is unfortunate but we have no evidence that it has affected his work, professional integrity, judgment, or reputation. His arrest for public intoxication occurred while he was away from work. If he is convicted of a felony or of a crime involving fraud or dishonesty, he would be subject to sanctions.

5. **B** GIPS require a firm to show a GIPS-compliant history for a minimum of five years, or since inception of the firm or the composite if in existence for less than five years. If Reliable has been in business for less than five years, it may still claim compliance with GIPS on a since-inception basis, provided the firm follows all other aspects of compliance. The other choices are requirements for a firm to claim compliance with GIPS. (Study Session 1, LOS 4.a)

6. **A** The recommended procedures for compliance with Standard I(B) Independence and Objectivity include the recommendation that analysts on company visits pay their own air and hotel expenses. This can be considered "best practice."

7. **C** Standard VII(A) Conduct as Members and Candidates in the CFA Program and the Code of Ethics. By writing down information from the Candidate Body of Knowledge and taking it into the exam room, she compromised the integrity of the exam, whether she used the notes or not. Her actions are also in violation of the Code of Ethics by not acting "with integrity, competence, diligence, respect, and in an ethical manner."

8. **A**   The requirement that members and candidates place their clients' interests before their employer's or their own is in Standard III(A) Loyalty, Prudence, and Care. The other choices are included in the CFA Institute Code of Ethics.

9. **B**   Kramer violated Standard V(B) Communication with Clients and Prospective Clients. The problem is with the word "will." Kramer should have used "is estimated to be" to separate fact from opinion. Statistical estimates of future events are subject to change and should not be presented as certainties. She need not give complete details of the statistical model but should indicate its general characteristics and the important factors involved in her projections.

10. **C**   Standard III(B) Fair Dealing requires that all clients be treated fairly. Members and candidates should not discriminate against any client. A family member who is a fee-paying client should not be treated differently from other clients when taking investment action. The firm has acted correctly in simultaneously disseminating the change in recommendation and not giving any clients prenotification so that other clients are not disadvantaged. Following up with phone calls to larger clients is not a violation of the Standard.

11. **A**   According to Standard II(B) Market Manipulation, members and candidates cannot attempt to distort prices or artificially inflate trading volume. Thompson's misleading internet postings violate Standard II(B) since the intent is to manipulate the price of the bond issue. In addition, Thompson did not consider the suitability of the investment for his clients when he chose to recommend Ibex based only on his client's account size rather than investment objectives and constraints. Since some of the clients to which he recommended the investment have low risk tolerances and are unlikely to find a highly risky junk bond issue suitable for their portfolio, Thompson also violated Standard III(C) Suitability.

12. **C**   According to Standard VI(A) Disclosure of Conflicts, Elliott should disclose his beneficial ownership of TECH to his employer and to clients and prospects, because such ownership could interfere with his ability to make unbiased and objective recommendations. Selling his shares or declining to write the report are not required and are more extreme than simply disclosing the potential conflict.

13. **C**   Mendoza has not violated the Standards of Practice or GIPS. Because the presentation was introductory and brief, Mendoza was not required to give any supporting documentation, but he made it available to clients and prospective clients upon request. His claim of GIPS compliance is in the required format. (Study Session 1, LOS 3.c)

14. **A**   According to Standard II(A) Material Nonpublic Information, members and candidates who possess material nonpublic information must not act or cause others to act based on the information. A conference call with several analysts does not constitute public dissemination, and Franklin should urge Level Tech to publicly disseminate the information.

15. **C**   Standard III(C) Suitability requires that members and candidates update client information (the IPS) at least annually. The IPS can be updated more frequently if there are significant changes in the investment strategy or client characteristics.

16. **A**   To comply with Standard III(E) Preservation of Confidentiality, Johnson must not discuss with her charitable foundation anything regarding her client and her client's intentions. It does not matter that her client intends to give money to charities in the near future.

17. **B**   Standard III(A) Loyalty, Prudence, and Care does not require the voting of all proxies. A cost-benefit analysis may support the conclusion that the voting of all proxies is not beneficial to the client in light of the time and effort required. Voting on nonroutine issues that have a material impact is required.

18. **B**   According to Standard I(A) Knowledge of the Law, Gold must comply with the most strict of the laws of Country A, laws of Country B, and the CFA Standards of Practice. In this case, the most strict rules are those in the Standards of Practice. Standard VI(C) Referral Fees requires the disclosure of all referral fees and Standard II(A) Material Nonpublic Information prohibits acting or causing others to act on the basis of material non-public information.

19. **B**   It's best to break this problem into parts to accommodate the change in the interest rate.

   Money in the fund at the end of ten years based on deposits made with initial interest of 5%:

   (1) The total value in the fund at the end of the fifth year is $3,152.50:
   PMT = −1,000; N = 3; I/Y = 5; CPT → FV = $3,152.50. (calculator in END mode)

   (2) The $3,152.50 is now the present value and will then grow at 4% until the end of the tenth year. We get: PV = −3,152.50; N = 5; I/Y = 4; PMT = −1,000; CPT → FV = $9,251.82

   (Study Session 2, LOS 5.e)

20. **C**   With more than one compounding period per year, $FV_N = PV\left(1 + \dfrac{r_s}{m}\right)^{mn}$

   $PV = \$5,000$; $r_s = 6\%$; $m = 12$; $\dfrac{r_s}{m} = \dfrac{6\%}{12} = 0.5\%$; $n = 3$; $m \times n = 12 \times 3 = 36$.

   To compute FV_3, enter PV = −5,000; I = 0.5; PMT = 0; and N = 36 to get $5,983.40.
   (Study Session 2, LOS 5.d)

21. **A**   A t-distribution with sufficiently high degrees of freedom is approximately normal and a normal distribution has thinner tails compared to a t-distribution. The less the degrees of freedom, the fatter the tails. (Study Session 3, LOS 10.i)

22. **A** $R_1 = -10/100 = -10\%$; $R_2 = +9/90 = +10\%$

   $$\text{geometric mean} = \sqrt{(0.9)(1.1)} - 1 = -0.005 \text{ or } -0.5\%$$

   An alternative way to get the geometric mean is:

   $$\left(\frac{\text{ending value}}{\text{beginning value}}\right)^{\frac{1}{n}} - 1 = \text{geometric mean return}$$

   $$\sqrt{\frac{99}{100}} - 1 = -0.005 \text{ or } -0.5\%$$

   (Study Session 2, LOS 7.e)

23. **B** $R_L = \dfrac{2.0 + 151 - 150}{150} = 0.02$

Choose Portfolio X because it has the larger safety-first ratio, $(0.10 - 0.02)/0.14 = 0.57$.

Note: $SFRatio(B) = \dfrac{0.12 - 0.02}{0.20} = 0.50$

(Study Session 3, LOS 9.l)

24. **C** To find the money-weighted rate of return, equate the present value of inflows to the present value of outflows and find the discount rate that makes them equal.

t = 0:	Buy 500 shares @ $22		=	−$11,000
t = 1:	$0.42 × 500 shares		=	+$210
	Buy 500 shares @ $24.75		=	−$12,375
	Net cash flow		=	−$12,165
t = 2:	$0.42 × 1,000 shares		=	+$420
	Buy 600 shares @ $31.25		=	−$18,750
	Net cash flow		=	−$18,330
t = 3:	Sell 1,000 shares @ $35.50		=	+$35,500
	Sell 600 shares @ $36.00		=	+$21,600
	Net cash flow		=	+$57,000

Find the IRR with CFs as follows:
$CF_0 = -11,000; CF_1 = -12,165; CF_2 = -18,330; CF_3 = 57,100.$
The final result is IRR = 18.49%. (Study Session 2, LOS 6.c)

25. **C** The up-move factor equals one plus the percentage increase when the variable goes up, and the down-move factor is equal to one divided by the up-move factor. (Study Session 3, LOS 9.g)

26. **B** No calculations are really necessary here since the MMY involves no compounding and a 360-day year, the BEY requires compounding the quarterly HPR to a semiannual rate and doubling that rate, and the EAY requires compounding for the entire year based on a 365-day year. A numerical example of these calculations based on a 90-day holding period yield of 1.3% is: the money market yield is 1.3% × 360 / 90 = 5.20%, the bond equivalent yield is $2 \times [1.013^{182.5\,/\,90} - 1] = 0.0531 = 5.31\%$, which is two times the effective semiannual rate of return, and the effective annual yield is $1.013^{\,365\,/\,90} - 1 = 0.0538 = 5.38\%$. Calculating the semiannual effective yield using 180 days instead of 182.5 does not change the order. (Study Session 2, LOS 6.d)

27. **B** P(good economy and bear market) = 0.60 × 0.20 = 0.12. The other statements are true. The P(normal market) = (0.60 × 0.30) + (0.40 × 0.30) = 0.30. Given that the economy is poor, the probability of a normal or bull market = 0.30 + 0.20 = 0.50. (Study Session 2, LOS 8.f)

28. **C** Expected value = (0.4)(10%) + (0.4)(12.5%) + (0.2)(30%) = 15%

Variance = $(0.4)(10 - 15)^2 + (0.4)(12.5 - 15)^2 + (0.2)(30 - 15)^2 = 57.5$

Standard deviation = $\sqrt{57.5} = 7.58\%$

(Study Session 2, LOS 8.m)

29. **B**   We can view this problem as the number of ways to choose three analysts from five analysts when the order they are chosen matters. The formula for the number of permutations is:

$$\frac{n!}{(n-r)!} = \frac{5!}{2!} = 5 \times 4 \times 3 = 60$$

On the TI financial calculator: 5 2nd nPr 3 = 60.

(Study Session 2, LOS 8.o)

30. **C**   Choice A is financial risk; choice B is default risk. (Study Session 3, LOS 9.l)

31. **B**   Rejecting the null hypothesis when it is true is a Type I error. The probability of a Type I error is the significance level of the test and one minus the significance level is the confidence level. The power of a test is one minus the probability of a Type II error, which cannot be calculated from the information given. (Study Session 3, LOS 11.b)

32. **C** H_A: X ≠ 0 indicates a two-tailed test, while H_A: X < 0 or H_A: X > 0 indicates a one-tailed test. (Study Session 3, LOS 11.a, c)

33. **C**   Managers act as agents for owners. When managers make decisions that benefit themselves rather than owners, the problem is referred to as a principal-agent problem. (Study Session 4, LOS 16.d)

34. **C**   If the quantity supplied at a given price is greater than the quantity demanded, then that price is greater than the equilibrium price. A price ceiling on electricity set above the equilibrium price will have no effect because the quantity supplied equals the quantity demanded at a price less than this legal maximum. A minimum wage causes a loss of efficiency (quantity of labor supplied is greater than the quantity demanded) when it is set above the equilibrium wage for unskilled workers. Increased search time is an example of an inefficiency that results from a rent ceiling below the equilibrium rent level. (Study Session 4, LOS 15.a)

35. **B**   People who are unable to work due to disability are not included as part of the labor force and, therefore, are not considered unemployed. Others who are not included in the labor force are household workers, students, discouraged workers, and retirees. (Study Session 5, LOS 22.c)

36. **C**   Price elasticity = (percentage change in quantity) / (percentage change in price).

Use average value in calculating the percentage change in quantity and price.
(−20 / 50)/(5 / 27.50) = −0.4 / 0.1818 = −2.20. (Study Session 4, LOS 13.a)

37. **A**   Demand curves are not observable so a monopolist must search for the profit maximizing price. Because demand information is not perfect, a monopolist is a price searcher. The other statements are false. Although a monopolist can earn positive economic profits in the long run, they are not guaranteed profit. If average total costs exceed price, the monopolist will lose money. A monopolist maximizes *profit* where marginal revenue equals marginal cost. (Study Session 5, LOS 19.a, b)

38. **B**   In an oligopolistic industry, the decisions of a firm often influence the demand, price and profit of rivals. Thus, the welfare of each seller is *dependent* on the policies followed by major rivals. (Study Session 5, LOS 19.a, 20.a)

39. **C** From an initial equilibrium, an increase in real money balances will leave households and businesses with more money than they wish to hold, so they will purchase interest-bearing securities, driving their prices up and yields down until a new equilibrium short-term rate is established. (Study Session 6, LOS 24.g, h)

40. **A** An increase in expected future incomes will cause consumers to increase current expenditures (reduce current savings) in anticipation of the higher future incomes. An increase in the money supply will tend to decrease interest rates which will lead to increased consumer spending on durable goods and increased investment by businesses. Both effects increase aggregate demand. (Study Session 5, LOS 23.b)

41. **C** The components of M1 are generally non-interest-bearing and include currency other than that held by banks, checking deposits, and travelers' checks. M2 includes all the components of M1 plus short-term interest bearing deposits (time deposits, savings deposits, and money market mutual fund deposits). (Study Session 6, LOS 24.b)

42. **C** The effect of an increased wage on the amount of labor an individual will supply will depend on the relative strength of the income and substitution effects. The substitution effect leads to an increase in labor supplied as less leisure is consumed because its opportunity cost is increased. The income effect leads to less labor supplied as the wage increase and resulting higher income leads to greater consumption of leisure (less hours of labor supplied). For example, with a wage increase to $1,000 per hour, some workers will choose to reduce the number of hours they work, rather than increase them. (Study Session 5, LOS 21.c)

43. **C** At the efficient, equilibrium price and quantity, the sum of consumer surplus and producer surplus is at its maximum, regardless of which is larger. External costs from production and use of a common resource typically result in output that exceeds the efficient quantity. (Study Session 4, LOS 14.d)

44. **B** If demand is inelastic, the percentage change in quantity demanded is smaller than the percentage change in price; quantity demanded is relatively unresponsive to price changes. A price increase increases total expenditures on a good. (Study Session 4, LOS 13.a, b)

45. **C** These are examples of items that are typically treated as extraordinary under U.S. GAAP. There is no provision for accounting for an item as extraordinary under IFRS. Accounting errors are corrected with prior-period adjustments, which are made by restating results for any prior periods that are presented in the current financial statements. Discontinued operations are not classified as unusual or infrequent items and are reported (net of taxes) after net income from continuing operations but before net income. (Study Session 8, LOS 32.f)

46. **C** Borrowing funds to purchase capital equipment will result in an increase in assets (equipment) and in liabilities (debt). The accrual of the salaries that are owed, but not paid, as of month-end will increase expenses and increase liabilities (accrued salary expense). Therefore, these two transactions taken together will result in the greatest increase in liabilities. (Study Session 7, LOS 30.c)

47. **C** Interest and dividends received and interest paid are considered *operating* cash flows under U.S. GAAP, but dividends paid are considered financing cash flows. (Study Session 8, LOS 34.a, c)

48. **C** The easiest way to calculate CFO here is total cash flow − cash flow from investing − cash flow from financing = $13,000 + 5,000 + 4,250 = $22,250. Alternatively, CFO = $50,000 − 3,250 − 17,000 − 7,000 − 500 = $22,250. (Study Session 8, LOS 34.e)

49. **A** Cash conversion cycle (CCC) = days of sales outstanding + days of inventory on hand − number of days of payables. Days of sales outstanding = 365 / receivables turnover = 365 / 11 = 33.18; 365 / 12 = 30.42. This means the CCC decreases by 2.76 days. (Study Session 8, LOS 35.d)

50. **B** Besides the annual SEC filings, an analyst should examine a company's quarterly or semiannual filings. These interim filings typically update the major financial statements and footnotes, but are not necessarily audited. Annual reports to shareholders and press releases are written by management and are often viewed as public relations or sales materials. (Study Session 7, LOS 29.e)

51. **A** Basic EPS *does not* consider potential dilution from convertible bonds.
Original shares = 2,000,000(12) = 24,000,000
+ Stock dividend = 200,000(12) = 2,400,000
+ New shares = 100,000(3) = 300,000

$$\frac{sum}{12} = \frac{26,700,000}{12} = 2,225,000$$

Alternatively, 2 million (1.1) + (¼) (100,000) = 2.225 million. (Study Session 8, LOS 32.g)

52. **C** The gain (loss) on disposal is the amount by which the selling price exceeds (is less than) book value. Book value = original price − accumulated depreciation. Thus, gain or loss = selling price − (original price − accumulated depreciation), or selling price − original cost + accumulated depreciation. (Study Session 8, LOS 32.a)

53. **B** In the absence of taxes, there is no difference in cash flow between LIFO and FIFO. In addition, using LIFO would result in lower working capital (inventory is lower). Using LIFO would result in lower net income because of a *lower* gross margin (cost of goods sold is higher). (Study Session 9, LOS 36.e, f)

54. **A** Screening for high dividend yield stocks will likely include a disproportionately high number of financial services firms as such firms typically have higher dividend payouts. A screen to identify firms with low P/E ratios will likely exclude growth firms from the sample as high expected earnings growth leads to high P/Es. (Study Session 10, LOS 42.d)

55. **C** Operating cash flow that is less than net income (ratio less than one) or declining over time may indicate low quality earnings from aggressive accounting or accounting irregularities. A ratio that is consistently above one, but highly variable, is not necessarily indicative of accounting irregularities. (Study Session 10, LOS 40.e)

56. **A** Intangible assets purchased from another party are capitalized on the buyer's balance sheet if the economic benefit is expected to be realized over more than one period, but are not amortized in all cases. (Study Session 9, LOS 37.c)

57. **B** Companies typically do not disclose data about estimated salvage values, except when estimates are changed. (Study Session 9, LOS 37.e)

58. **A** The impairment test compares the carrying value of the asset to the *undiscounted* expected future cash flows. Discounted expected future cash flows are used to measure the amount of impairment, here 500,000 − 380,000 = 120,000. The other statements are true. The impairment will be reported as an unusual or infrequent item in income from continuing operations. Writing down an asset decreases future depreciation expense and thus increases net income and leverage ratios. Assets are reduced, increasing turnover ratios. (Study Session 9, LOS 37.i)

59. **B** Straight line depreciation is (100,000 + 10,000 + 5,000 − 25,000) / 6 = 15,000 each year. Double-declining balance depreciation in the second year is: 115,000 (2/3)(1/3) = 25,556. The difference is $10,556. Remember that salvage value is not part of the declining balance calculation. (Study Session 8, LOS 32.d, and Study Session 9, LOS 37.d)

60. **A** A decrease in the accounts receivable amount on the balance sheet indicates that cash collections exceed revenues (sales). This increases operating cash flow because receivables are being collected. An increase in the accounts payable amount on the balance sheet indicates that purchases from suppliers exceed cash payments. This increases operating cash flow because the cash was not used to pay the suppliers. (Study Session 8, LOS 34.e)

61. **C** Interest expense is market YTM times the proceeds, regardless of whether the bonds are issued at a discount or premium. (Study Session 9, LOS 39.a)

62. **A** Working capital equals current assets minus current liabilities and is lower under a finance lease because the current portion of the finance lease increases current liabilities. Total asset turnover is lower because total assets are higher under a finance lease. Companies with finance leases report higher debt-to-equity ratios because liabilities increase and equity is unchanged at lease inception and lower in the early years of the lease. Return on equity is lower with a finance lease because the numerator, net income, is decreased proportionally more than the denominator, equity, from the greater expense of a finance lease in its early years. Over the life of the lease, the expenses are equal. (Study Session 9, LOS 39.g)

63. **A** Warranty expense should be recorded when the inventory item covered by the warranty is sold. A deferred tax asset is created when warranty expenses are accrued on the financial statements but are not deductible on the tax returns until the warranty claims are paid. The full amount of the obligation, $100,000, is recorded as an expense, with a deferred tax asset of $30,000. Note that a deferred tax asset results when taxable income is more than pretax income and the difference is likely to reverse (warranty will be paid) in future years. (Study Session 9, LOS 38.d)

64. **B** Diluted EPS = [NI − preferred dividends + convertible interest (1 − t)] / [weighted average shares + convertible debt shares].

    100(1,000)(6%)(1 − 0.4) = $3,600; convertible debt shares = 50(100) = 5,000

    $$\frac{\$15,000 - \$10,000 + \$3,600}{2,000 + 5,000} = \$1.23$$

    (Study Session 8, LOS 32.g)

65. **C** Noncurrent assets are those that will not be used up during the next year or during the firm's operating cycle. Firm investment is typically in assets that are longer term in nature. (Study Session 8, LOS 33.d)

©2009 Kaplan, Inc.

66. **C**   The initial liability is the amount received from the creditor, not the par value of the bond.

    N = 8; I/Y = 11/2 = 5.5; PMT = 500,000; FV = 10,000,000; CPT → PV = $9,683,272.

    The interest expense is the effective interest rate (the market rate at the time of issue) times the balance sheet liability. $9,683,272 × 0.055 = $532,580.

    The value of the liability will change over time and is a function of the initial liability, the interest expense and the actual cash payments. In this case, it increases by the difference between the interest expense and the actual cash payment: $532,580 − $500,000 = $32,580 + $9,683,272 = $9,715,852. *Tip:* Knowing that the liability will increase is enough to select choice C without performing this last calculation. Entering N = 7 and solving for PV also produces $9,715,852. (Study Session 9, LOS 39.a)

67. **C**   On a horizontal common-size balance sheet, the divisor is the first-year values so they are all standardized to 1.0 by construction. Trends in the values of these items as well as the relative growth in these items are readily apparent. A vertical common-size balance sheet expresses all balance sheet accounts as a percentage of total assets and does not standardize the initial year. (Study Session 8, LOS 35.a)

68. **C**   Covenants protect bondholders from actions the firm may take that would decrease credit quality and reduce the value of the bondholders' claims to firm assets and earnings. Examples of covenants include restrictions on dividend payments and stock repurchases; mergers and acquisitions; sale, leaseback, and disposal of certain assets; issuance of new debt; and repayment patterns (e.g., sinking fund agreements and priority of claims). Repurchases of bonds in the market do not negatively affect the interests of bondholders. (Study Session 9, LOS 39.b)

69. **C**   The weighted average collection period has lengthened by 2.3 days, from 61.6 days at the end of the first quarter to 63.9 days at the end of the fourth quarter. In addition, receivables with 31 or more days outstanding have increased as a percentage of total receivables. Both of these metrics indicate that collections have slowed for Williams. The collection period data do not provide sufficient information to determine whether sales have increased or decreased. (Study Session 11, LOS 46.f)

70. **B**   It is not uncommon for individuals to be members of the boards of directors of more than one firm. This is acceptable as long as they maintain independence and act in the interests of the firms' shareholders. A strong corporate code of ethics should discourage the company from awarding consulting contracts or finder's fees to board members or relatives of board members. (Study Session 11, LOS 48.e)

71. **B**   Introducing a new product or entering a new market involves sales and expense projections that can be highly uncertain. Expanding capacity or replacing old machinery involve less uncertainty and analysis. (Study Session 11, LOS 44.a)

72. **A**   The appropriate method for estimating the cost of equity for a firm in a developing market is to add a country risk premium (CRP) to the market risk premium, so the revised CAPM equation becomes: $k_{ce} = R_F + \beta[E(R_{MKT}) - R_F + CRP]$. The CRP is the sovereign yield spread (between yields on the country's government bonds and a developed country's government bonds) adjusted for the volatility of the developing country's equity market. An alternative approach is to add the CRP (not the sovereign yield spread) to the cost of equity as calculated from the CAPM. (Study Session 11, LOS 45.j)

73. **A** Factoring refers to the sale of receivables without recourse; that is, the risk that the firm's customers will not pay, or will not pay in a timely manner, is borne by the factor, who purchases the receivables. Thus, the amount the factor will pay per dollar of receivables is lower (higher discount or interest rate) if the credit quality of the firm's credit customers is lower. (Study Session 11, LOS 46.g)

74. **B** For a corporation, a percentage of dividend income on the preferred and common stock of other corporations is exempt from U.S. federal income tax. Although interest paid on corporate bonds is tax-deductible, interest income from corporate bonds does not receive favorable tax treatment. (Study Session 11, LOS 46.d)

75. **A** The correct treatment of flotation costs according to the CFA Curriculum is to include their cost in the initial cash outflow of the project. Since flotation costs are included in the initial outlay, they decrease the NPV by an amount that is unaffected by the discount rate, and the discount rate and cost of capital are not adjusted for flotation costs. (Study Session 11, LOS 45.l)

76. **C** The internal rate of return is the rate of discount at which the NPV of a project is zero. On an NPV profile, this is the point where the profile intersects the horizontal axis. (Study Session 11, LOS 44.e)

77. **C** An increase in the tax rate will reduce Thompson's after-tax cost of debt (other things equal) and therefore reduce its WACC. With a relatively lower cost of debt the firm will likely change its capital structure to include more debt and less equity (i.e., to increase its financial leverage). (Study Session 11, LOS 45.b)

78. **C** The audit committee is responsible for evaluating the financial information that the company provides to shareholders. This committee should be able to approve or reject the company's proposed non-audit engagements with its external auditing firm. The audit committee, not management, should control the audit budget, and there should be no restrictions on communication between the committee and the company's internal auditors. (Study Session 11, LOS 48.f)

79. **C** An IPS requires an investor to consider and articulate his objectives and constraints. It also provides an objective standard by which the portfolio's performance will be judged by specifying a benchmark portfolio. Guidance for Standard III(C), Suitability requires members to prepare IPS when beginning advisory relationships with clients. Asset allocation is determined after strategy is developed and capital market conditions are assessed. (Study Session 12, LOS 49.a)

80. **C** In the absence of a riskless asset or zero-beta portfolio, the optimal portfolio for an investor is the point of tangency between the efficient frontier and the highest possible indifference curve for the investor since there is no capital market line. (Study Session 12, LOS 50.f, g)

81. **B** The standardized covariance is the covariance divided by the market variance or the correlation of the stock multiplied by (the stock standard deviation divided by the market standard deviation), which is the formula for beta, which is used in the SML, not the CML. The other statements are true. The CML may kink if the borrowing and lending rates are not equal. Here, the rates are equal at the risk-free rate. (Study Session 12, LOS 51.b, d)

82. **C** Using the CAPM, the required rate of return for each stock is:

$E(R_X) = 4\% + 1.0(10\% - 4\%) = 10.0\%$.

10.0% − 10.0% = 0.0% properly valued.

$E(R_Y) = 4\% + 1.6(10\% - 4\%) = 13.6\%$.

16.0% − 13.6% = 2.4% undervalued.

$E(R_Z) = 4\% + 2.0(10\% - 4\%) = 16.0\%$.

16.0% − 16.0% = 0.0% properly valued.

(Study Session 12, LOS 51.e)

83. **C** Capital market theory assumes there are no taxes or transactions costs. It also assumes shares of assets are infinitely divisible and all investors have homogeneous (not heterogeneous) beliefs about the probability distributions of future rates of return. (Study Session 12, LOS 51.a)

84. **A** Based on the CAPM, the portfolio should earn: E(R) = 0.05 + 1.5(0.10) = 20%. On a risk-adjusted basis, this portfolio lies on the security market line (SML) and thus is earning a risk-adjusted rate of return equivalent to that of the market portfolio. (Study Session 12, LOS 51.e)

85. **C** g = (1 − payout)(ROE) = (1 − 0.40)(16%) = 9.6%

$$k = \frac{\$1.50(1.096)}{\$40} + 0.096 = 13.7\%$$

(Study Session 14, LOS 56.c)

86. **B** The following formula indicates the stock price that will trigger a margin call:

$$\text{long} = \frac{(\text{original price})(1 - \text{initial margin }\%)}{1 - \text{maintenance margin}} = \frac{(\$50)(1 - 0.50)}{1 - 0.25} = \$33.33$$

Professor's Note: An intuitive way to solve minimum margin problems for equity accounts is based on the fact that while the margin amount changes with stock price changes after purchase, the loan amount does not. Stock price is $50, loan is $25, when the margin is 25% the loan must be 75% (of share price). $25 / 0.75 = $33.33. (Study Session 13, LOS 52.g)

87. **A** Internal efficiency refers to low transactions costs in a securities market. External efficiency means prices change rapidly to reflect new information without predictable bias and rates of return are, on average, proportional to risk. (Study Session 13, LOS 52.a)

88. **A**   Price-weighted index $= \dfrac{4+10}{2} = 7$. A price-weighted index is not affected by a split. The divisor is adjusted to account for the price change.

Value-weighted index $= 100 \times \dfrac{\$4(50) + \$5(20)}{\$2(50) + \$10(10)} = 150$

(Study Session 13, LOS 53.a)

89. **B**   Required return = 5% + 1.1(8%) = 13.8%

Sustainable growth = 18%(1 − 0.4) = 10.8%

$\dfrac{P_0}{E_1} = \dfrac{0.40}{0.138 - 0.108} = 13.33$.

(Study Session 14, LOS 58.b)

90. **C**   1-year HPR $= \dfrac{P_{ending} - P_{beginning} + dividend}{P_{beginning}}$.

Here, we are given the beginning and ending price, but need to calculate D_1. $D_1 = D_0(1 + g)$, where g = ROE(retention rate).

g = 0.75(0.333) = 0.25. Then, D_1 = 4.00(0.25)(1 + 0.25) = $1.25.

Then, the HPR $= \dfrac{\$25 - \$20 + \$1.25}{\$20} = \dfrac{\$6.25}{\$20} = 31.25\%$.

(Study Session 14, LOS 56.c, g)

91. **C**   P/E ratio $= \dfrac{\text{dividend payout ratio}}{k_e - g}$

- Dividend payout = 1 − retention = 1 − 0.40 = 0.60.
- $g = ROE(\text{retention rate}) = 0.15(0.40) = 0.06$.
- P/E ratio $= \dfrac{0.60}{0.13 - 0.06} = 8.57$.

Impact of variables:

Increase in dividend payout/reduction in earnings retention. In this case, an increase in the dividend payout will likely decrease the P/E ratio. Since the dividend payout + retention rate = 1, any increase in the dividend payout decreases the retention rate. A decrease in earnings retention will likely lower the P/E ratio. The logic is as follows: because earnings retention impacts both the numerator (dividend payout) and denominator (g) of the P/E ratio, the impact of a change in earnings retention depends upon the relationship of k_e and ROE. If the company is earning a higher rate on new projects than the rate required by the market (ROE > k_e), investors will likely prefer that the company retain more earnings. Since an increase in the dividend payout would decrease earnings retention, the P/E ratio would fall, as investors will value the company lower if it retains a lower age of earnings. (To check this quantitatively, substitute a lower retention rate and carry the calculations through. In this case, the P/E ratio will decline below 8.57.)

With just the retention rate as a variable in the P/E formula we have: $\dfrac{1-R}{0.13-0.15R}$

Increase in the risk-free rate. This is the reverse of the logic for an increase in the expected inflation rate.

- If the risk-free rate increases, the nominal risk-free rate will increase.
- k_e will increase.
- The spread between k_e and g, or the P/E denominator, will increase.
- P/E ratio will decrease.

(Study Session 14, LOS 56.d, f)

92. **B** Dividend payout = 1 – earnings retention rate = 1 – 0.4 = 0.6

$R_S = R_f + \beta(R_M - R_f) = 0.06 + 1.2(0.11 - 0.06) = 0.12$

g = (retention rate)(ROE) = 0.4(0.12) = 0.048

$P/E = \dfrac{\text{dividend payout ratio}}{k-g} = \dfrac{0.6}{0.12-0.048} = 8.33$

Price = E(P/E) = \$4(8.33) = \$33.32

(Study Session 14, LOS 56.c)

93. **A** According to event studies of the semi-strong form of the EMH, investors do not earn abnormal returns by trading before and after releases of significant company information such as stock splits. This finding supports the EMH. The other choices are documented market anomalies. That is, they argue against the semi-strong form of the EMH, and suggest that investors can earn excess returns by exploiting these anomalies. The January anomaly (from a time-series test of the semi-strong EMH) suggests that investors can earn excess returns by buying stocks in December and selling them in the first week of January, due to tax-induced trading at year-end. Cross-sectional tests of the semi-strong form EMH have shown that low P/E stocks, stocks of firms neglected by analysts, and stocks of firms with high book to value ratios can produce superior returns.
(Study Session 13, LOS 54.b)

94. **A** Behavioral finance studies how market anomalies can arise from psychological traits that affect investor behavior and cause investors to make systematic errors such as exiting profitable positions too soon and holding unprofitable positions too long.
(Study Session 13, LOS 54.d)

95. **B** Since the index is price weighted, the value of the stocks will match the index performance. Total returns includes dividend yield, however, and since dividends are not included in the performance of the index itself, the portfolio will outperform the index by the amount of the dividend yield. (Study Session 13, LOS 53.a, b)

96. **C** Analysts should not attempt to use the price-to-book-value ratio for comparing firms with different levels of use of fixed assets. (Study Session 14, LOS 59.a)

97. **A** Only amortizing securities with a prepayment option are subject to prepayment risk. Event risk is the possibility that some event (e.g., natural disaster, change in regulations, merger, restructuring) reduces the issuer's ability to meet its debt obligations. Liquidity risk can be important even for a bond held to maturity if the portfolio manager needs to mark its holdings to market for performance reporting purposes. Low liquidity for the bond can mean the prevailing price is not an accurate measure of the bond's value. (Study Session 15, LOS 61.i, k, o)

98. **A** Default risk is the possibility that the issuer will fail to meet its obligations under the indenture, for which investors demand a premium above the return on a default-risk-free security, and bond ratings indicate relative default risk. Downgrade risk is the risk that a bond will be reclassified as a riskier security by a credit rating agency. Credit spread risk is the risk that the default risk premium on a bond can increase. (Study Session 15, LOS 61.j)

99. **C** A callable bond is made up of a straight bond and a written call option. An increase in volatility increases the value of the call option and decreases the value of the callable bond. On the other hand, a putable bond is made up of an option-free (or straight) bond and a long put option. An increase in volatility increases the value of the put option and therefore increases the value of the putable bond. (Study Session 15, LOS 61.n)

100. **C** A medium-term note is sold on a "best efforts" basis wherein the underwriter does not guarantee a price for the bonds to the issuer but tries to get the best price possible. Price risk is completely borne by the issuing firm. (Study Session 15, LOS 62.h, i)

101. **C** Because the coupon rate on an inverse floater increases when market interest rates decrease, there is an implicit cap on the coupon rate because market interest rates cannot decline further than zero. The bondholder always receives coupon payments made by the issuer. The opposite would correspond to a negative interest rate. The coupon rate, not the principal, is adjusted inversely with market interest rates. (Study Session 15, LOS 60.b)

102. **A** Portfolio duration is an approximation of the price sensitivity of a portfolio to parallel shifts of the yield curve (yields for all maturities increase or decrease by equal amounts). Duration can be a poor approximation of interest rate risk for non-parallel shifts in the yield curve. (Study Session 15, LOS 61.g)

103. **A** Due to convexity in the adjustment of bond prices for changes in yields, for given changes in the required yield, the percentage price increase is *greater* than the percentage price decrease. (Study Session 16, LOS 66.b)

104. **B** First calculate V– and V+, the bond's value at 7.25% and 8.75% yields to maturity. The bond values are $1,052.70 and $950.69, respectively:

N = 20; I/Y = 7.25 / 2 = 3.625; PMT = 40; FV = 1,000; CPT PV = –1052.70

N = 20; I/Y = 8.75 / 2 = 4.375; PMT = 40; FV = 1,000; CPT PV = –950.69

$$D = \frac{V_- - V_+}{2V_0\left(\Delta y\right)} = \frac{1,052.70 - 950.69}{2\left(1,000\right)\left(0.0075\right)} = 6.8.$$

(Study Session 16, LOS 64.c, 66.d)

105. **C** $_1f_4 = \dfrac{(1.055)^5}{(1.04)^4} - 1 = 0.1172$

Note: 5(5.5) − 4(4) = 11.5%. (Study Session 16, LOS 65.h)

106. **B** Had BBB and AAA yields risen from 5% and 4%, respectively, to 6% and 5%, the absolute yield spread would have remained the same, but the yield ratios would have decreased from 5/4 to 6/5, and the relative yield spread would have decreased from 0.25 to 0.20. This is the reason that relative yield spreads are considered a better indicator of yield spread changes than absolute yield spreads. In an economic expansion, relative corporate yield spreads to Treasuries are likely to decrease. (Study Session 15, LOS 63.e)

107. **A** We know that: $r_{BD} = \dfrac{D}{F}\left(\dfrac{360}{t}\right)$

D = $1,000,000 − $987,845 = $12,155
F = $1,000,000
t = 78 days

Substituting we get: $r_{BD} = \dfrac{\$12,155}{\$1,000,000}\left(\dfrac{360}{78}\right) = 0.0561$

(Study Session 2, LOS 6.d)

108. **C** If mortgage rates decrease, prepayments will accelerate. Prepayments affect the values of interest-only and principal-only strips differently. A principal-only strip will increase in price when prepayments increase because the face value of the security will be received sooner. An interest-only strip will receive a smaller amount of total payments because interest will be paid on a smaller amount of outstanding principal. Thus, the price of an interest-only strip will decrease when prepayments increase. (Study Session 15, LOS 62.e)

109. **C** If preferred stock must be redeemed on a specific date, its future cash flows are as predictable as those of an option-free bond: the (dividend) payments are known, the principal repayment date is known, and the security is not convertible or exchangeable. The principal repayment date is not known with certainty for a callable bond and the coupon payments are not known for a floating-rate security. (Study Session 16, LOS 64.b)

110. **B** A spot rate is the appropriate discount rate for a security that makes a single payment in the future. Treasury bills and Treasury strips promise a single future cash flow and their yields represent spot rates. Treasury inflation protected securities (TIPS) have coupon cash flows, so a 2-year TIPS yield is not a spot rate. (Study Session 15, LOS 62.b, c, 63.d)

111. **B** The net cost of the position is 40 − 3 = $37. If the stock price at expiration is ≥44, the gain on the position is $7. If the stock price were to fall to zero, the investor would lose $37. (Study Session 17, LOS 72.b)

112. **B** The payoff diagram from owning stock and a long put on the stock is similar to that of a long call. (Study Session 17, LOS 72.b)

113. **C** The counterparties do not exchange the notional principal on an interest rate swap. (Study Session 17, LOS 71.a, b)

114. **A** According to put-call parity:

$$c_0 + \frac{X}{(1+r)^T} = p_0 + S_0$$

The left-hand side $= \$4 + \dfrac{\$45}{\sqrt{1.06}} = \$47.71$

The right-hand side $= \$4 + 43 = \$47$

Since the value of the fiduciary call is not equal to the value of the protective put, put-call parity is violated and there is an arbitrage opportunity.

Sell overpriced and buy underpriced. That is, sell the fiduciary call and buy the protective put.

Therefore, sell the call for \$4, sell the Treasury bill for \$43.71 (i.e., borrow at the risk-free rate), buy the put for \$4 and buy the underlying asset for \$43. The arbitrage profit is \$0.71. (Study Session 17, LOS 70.k, l)

115. **A** This is a 1 × 3 FRA since it expires in 30 days and is based on 60-day LIBOR which is a 3-month period from the time of contract initiation to the end of the interest rate period. To hedge the risk of an interest rate increase, the firm takes a long position in an FRA. The payoff to the long is found from multiplying the notional principal by:

$$\left[\frac{(\text{LIBOR}_T - \text{forward contract rate})\left(\dfrac{\text{days in underlying rate}}{360}\right)}{1 + \text{LIBOR}_T\left(\dfrac{\text{days in underlying rate}}{360}\right)} \right]$$

Where LIBOR_T is the underlying rate at expiration of the FRA.

We get: $\$50,000,000 \left[\dfrac{(0.050 - 0.048)\left(\dfrac{60}{360}\right)}{1 + 0.050\left(\dfrac{60}{360}\right)} \right] = \$16,529$

(Study Session 17, LOS 68.g)

116. **B** Money is lost on a short futures position when the price of the underlying rises. With a maintenance margin of $1,312.50 per contract, a margin call will be issued when the margin account balance drops below 4 × $1,312.50 = $5,250. From the table below, we can see that this occurs on day 3. The variation margin is the amount that has to be deposited to bring the margin account balance back up to the initial margin level. The initial margin was 4 × $1,750 = $7,000. Therefore the variation margin is = $7,000 − $4,800 = $2,200.

Day	Closing Futures Price ($)	Gain (loss) ($)	Margin Account Balance ($)	Variation Margin ($)
1	345.50	1,800	8,800	
2	348.75	(1,300)	7,500	
3	355.50	(2,700)	4,800	2,200
4	356.25	(300)	6,700	

(Study Session 17, LOS 69.c, d)

Professor's Note: On futures margins problems, start by calculating the per-contract change in margin for a 1-unit change in the futures price. Here, a $1 change in the price of gold is $100 per contract. To reach minimum margin we need a change of 1,750 − 1,312.50 = 437.50, so a price change of 437.50 / 100 = $4.375 does it. Since we're short, an increase of 5.50 results in a 5.5(100)(4) = $2,200 decrease in the margin balance.

117. **C** Because a hedge fund database only includes the more stable funds that have survived, the risk measure of hedge funds as an asset class is biased downward. (Study Session 18, LOS 73.l)

118. **C** The valuation methods for closely held companies include the cost approach, the comparables approach, and the income approach. The comparables approach may include discounts for lack of control and/or lack of marketability or a premium for control, depending on the characteristics of the comparable firm. (Study Session 18, LOS 73.n)

119. **C** A venture capital manager should be prepared to offer both financial and managerial assistance to the venture. Direct investments in venture capital are illiquid and require a long-term investment horizon because the payoff results from bringing a successful venture to market, which may not occur for several years after the initial investment. (Study Session 18, LOS 73.g)

120. **A** Income after expenses = $100,000 − $20,000 − (0.20)($100,000) = $60,000.

$$\text{Market value} = \frac{\text{annual net operating income}}{\text{market capitalization rate}} = \frac{\$60,000}{0.15} = \$400,000.$$

(Study Session 18, LOS 73.f)

Exam 3
Afternoon Session Answer Key

To get valuable feedback on how your score compares to those of other Level 1 candidates, use your Username and Password to gain Online Access at schweser.com and choose the left-hand menu item "Practice Exams Vol. 1."

1. B	31. B	61. A	91. B
2. A	32. A	62. C	92. B
3. C	33. A	63. C	93. C
4. C	34. A	64. C	94. A
5. A	35. B	65. B	95. C
6. A	36. C	66. A	96. A
7. A	37. A	67. C	97. C
8. C	38. A	68. B	98. B
9. A	39. A	69. B	99. C
10. C	40. C	70. A	100. A
11. C	41. B	71. A	101. C
12. A	42. C	72. C	102. C
13. B	43. B	73. B	103. C
14. C	44. A	74. C	104. A
15. C	45. C	75. A	105. C
16. B	46. B	76. B	106. C
17. B	47. A	77. C	107. B
18. A	48. C	78. B	108. B
19. B	49. A	79. A	109. A
20. A	50. C	80. A	110. B
21. C	51. C	81. B	111. B
22. C	52. A	82. B	112. C
23. B	53. C	83. A	113. C
24. B	54. B	84. C	114. A
25. A	55. C	85. B	115. C
26. A	56. A	86. C	116. A
27. B	57. A	87. B	117. A
28. C	58. B	88. A	118. C
29. C	59. B	89. C	119. A
30. B	60. B	90. B	120. B

EXAM 3
AFTERNOON SESSION ANSWERS

Answers referencing the Standards of Practice address Study Session 1, LOS 1.b, c and LOS 2.a, b, c, except where noted.

1. **B** Standard VI(B) Priority of Transactions. Front-running is the purchase or sale of securities in advance of client trades to take advantage of knowledge of client activity and should be completely prohibited, not simply limited. Blackout periods and pre-clearance of employee trades are ways of accomplishing this.

2. **A** Perez violated Standard V(A) Diligence and Reasonable Basis. Perez is responsible for performing diligent and thorough research on the companies he recommends to clients. Overhearing a conversation among analysts who are recommending PharmCo does not constitute a reasonable basis for changing his recommendation and certainly does not suggest independence of thought in his investment recommendation.

3. **C** Under Standard I(C) Misrepresentation, Winkler must identify Thompson as having developed the original model to avoid the prohibition against plagiarism. The only permitted exception is using factual information published by recognized financial and statistical reporting services such as S&P.

4. **C** According to Standard VI(A) Disclosure of Conflicts, Smith should disclose to clients, prospects, and his employer all matters that could reasonably be expected to interfere with his ability to make unbiased and objective recommendations. All actual and potential conflicts of interest need to be disclosed. Clearly the potential exists for Smith to receive a monetary benefit from favorable reports on Braden. Smith may be tempted to issue overly positive recommendations in order to increase the value of his options and maintain a favorable relationship with Braden to ensure his income from the consulting arrangement. These potential influences must be disclosed so that clients, prospects, and his employer can evaluate the objectivity of his recommendations.

5. **A** Standard VII(A) Conduct as Members and Candidates in the CFA Program prohibits cheating on the CFA examination or any other examination. Standard I(D) Misconduct prohibits lying, cheating, stealing, or any dishonest conduct that reflects adversely on a member's professional reputation.

6. **A** Standard IV(B) Additional Compensation Arrangements requires that members and candidates obtain written consent from their employers to enter into the agreement for additional contingent compensation from a client. Harris only received verbal consent. The concern is that such an arrangement might create partiality to Cline's portfolio over those of her other clients.

7. **A** Once a firm has met all the required elements of the GIPS, the firm may only use the statement in answer choice A to indicate compliance. Any deviation in the compliance statement constitutes a violation of GIPS. (Study Session 1, LOS 3.c)

8. **C** Standard V(A) Diligence and Reasonable Basis. Cantor did not have a reasonable and adequate basis for recommending a "Buy." Watson's enthusiasm and claim that everyone knows that the stock will perform well are not Cantor's conclusions. She must perform her own analysis before changing her investment recommendation. She has also violated Standard I(B) Independence and Objectivity since she has not exhibited the independence of analysis and thought that is required by the Standard.

9. **A** The actions are not in violation of the Standards. The use in new employment, of knowledge and experience gained in previous employment, is not prohibited. He recreated the records and did not take records without permission.

10. **C** The first requirement of the Code of Ethics is that members and candidates "act with integrity, competence, diligence, respect, and in an ethical manner with the public, clients, prospective clients, employers, employees, colleagues in the investment profession, and other participants in the global capital markets." Knowing the applicable laws and regulations is required by Standard I(A) Knowledge of the Law. Standard VII(A) Conduct as Members and Candidates in the CFA Program requires members and candidates not to compromise the integrity of CFA Institute.

11. **C** According to Standard IV(A) Loyalty, the interests of a member or candidate's employer are secondary to protecting the interests of the clients. In this circumstance, whistle blowing is justified. As long as his motivation is clearly not for personal gain, he may, according to the Standards, violate employer policies in this case. While he is only required to dissociate from the suspect activity, he is not prohibited from reporting it.

12. **A** The simplest, most conservative, and most effective way to comply with Standard III(E) Preservation of Confidentiality is to avoid disclosing any information received from a client, except to authorized fellow employees who are also working for the client.

13. **B** The marketer's request for daily third-party portfolio analytics for use in client mailings and for print advertising of the firm's investment products does not comply with Regiment's fiduciary duty. Regiment's proposal for the "use of research and investment decision-making services provided by a third party in return for commission business on client trading" is commonly referred to as "soft dollars" and is covered by Standard III(A) Loyalty, Prudence, and Care. Regiment, as an investment adviser who charges a fee, is a fiduciary and as such must adhere to its fiduciary duty in all aspects of investment management. The firm's receipt of soft-dollar services is acceptable, provided the soft dollar services have been disclosed to and provide a benefit for the firm's clients. The use of portfolio information for client mailings and/or advertising, or for other administrative or operational activities, does not benefit the clients who are paying the commissions and should not be paid for with client commissions.

14. **C** Standard VI(C) Referral Fees requires that members and candidates should disclose any referral arrangement in which the member or candidate receives some form of benefit from the referral. Such disclosure will allow the clients and employer to evaluate any impartiality that the referral arrangement may cause.

15. **C** The information received by Jenkins is covered by Standard II(A) Material Nonpublic Information, under which members who possess material nonpublic information related to the value of a security are prohibited from trading, or causing others to trade in, that security. Jenkins received material nonpublic information about the impending closure of the investment bank which was a large subsidiary of the parent company. For purposes of compliance with Standard II(A), Jenkins may attempt to achieve public dissemination of the information, and in the event that this is not possible, inform his compliance officer of the information. However, under no circumstances should Jenkins

share material nonpublic information with other investment personnel for informational purposes or otherwise. Sharing such information may cause others to trade on the information in violation of Standard II(A).

16. **B**   Woods' marketing activities for LAM's new international equity product violate Standard I(C) Misrepresentation by misrepresenting the services LAM could provide and the firm's qualifications in international equity. Members and candidates shall not make or imply any assurances or guarantees regarding the performance of any investment. The marketing presentation created by Woods regarding LAM's international equity product misrepresents the qualifications of the firm and provides assurances of performance in violation of the Standard. Although the new portfolio managers hired by LAM have investment experience in managing international equity, the firm clearly does not have a proven track record, nor overall experience in handling international equity mandates.

17. **B**   According to Standard II(A) Material Nonpublic Information, the use of security analysis combined with nonmaterial nonpublic information to arrive at significant conclusions is allowable under the mosaic theory.

18. **A**   All fee-paying discretionary accounts must be included in composites, but including non-fee-paying accounts is not required. The other statements are requirements for compliance. (Study Session 1, LOS 4.a)

19. **B**   With monthly payments, we need a monthly rate:

6% / 12 = 0.5%. Next, solve for the monthly payment. The calculator keystrokes are:

PV = 200,000; FV = 0; N = 360; I/Y = 0.5; CPT → PMT = –$1,199.10. The balance at any time on an amortizing loan is the present value of the remaining payments. There are 312 payments remaining after the 48th payment is made. The loan balance at this point is: PMT = –1,199.10; FV = 0; N = 312; I/Y = 0.5; CPT → PV = $189,228.90.

Note that only N has to be changed to calculate this new present value; the other inputs are unchanged. (Study Session 2, LOS 5.f)

20. **A**   What is a bond question doing here? CFA Institute examiners can and will insert material from other topics as they see fit. This is just a reminder to be on your guard!

First, find the yield on the note at time of purchase. The appropriate calculator steps are:

PV = –10,440; FV = 10,000; PMT = 600; N = 5; CPT → I/Y = 4.9842%. Next, value the note at a yield of 3.9842% with four years to maturity.

FV = 10,000; PMT = 600; N = 4; I/Y = 3.9842; CPT → PV = $10,731.99.

Finally, calculate the holding period return. The formula is:

$$R_t = \frac{P_t - P_{t-1} + D_t}{P_{t-1}}$$

$$R_t = \frac{\$10,731.99 - \$10,440 + \$600}{\$10,440} = 8.5\%$$

(Study Session 2, LOS 6.c and Study Session 16, LOS 64.c and LOS 65.b)

21. **C** $\dfrac{195}{160} - 1 = 0.21875$, or 21.88%

A longer approach is to calculate the holding period return for each stock for the year, then weight the returns using beginning values.

$$\text{Stock A} = \frac{20 - 10}{10} = 100\%$$

$$\text{Stock B} = \frac{60 + 1 - 50}{50} = 22\%$$

$$\text{Stock C} = \frac{110 + 4 - 100}{100} = 14\%$$

$$\left(\frac{10}{160}\right)(100\%) + \left(\frac{50}{160}\right)(22\%) + \left(\frac{100}{160}\right)(14\%) = 0.06250 + 0.06875 + 0.08750 = 0.21875, \text{ or } 21.88\%$$

(Study Session 2, LOS 7.e)

22. **C** From least to most information, the ordering of measurements scales is nominal, ordinal, interval, and ratio. (Study Session 2, LOS 7.a)

23. **B** $G = [(1.10)(0.85)(1.00)(1.05)]^{0.25} - 1$

$G = (0.98175)^{0.25} - 1 = 0.9954 - 1 = -0.00459 \approx -0.5\%$

Note: Taking a number to the 0.25 power is the same as taking the fourth root of the number. (Study Session 2, LOS 7.e)

24. **B** The mean absolute deviation is the mean of the absolute values of the differences between each number and the mean. Because the mean is $(45 + 20 + 30 + 25) / 4 = 30$, the mean absolute deviation is $\dfrac{10 + 5 + 0 + 15}{4} = 7.5$. (Study Session 2, LOS 7.g)

25. **A** As long as the investor earns at least a 5% return over the next year, the value of her portfolio after deducting the $100,000 down payment will not fall below $950,000. We first calculate the SFRatio for each of the two possible portfolios. We know that:

$$\text{SFRatio} = \frac{[E(R_p) - R_L]}{\sigma_p}$$

$$\text{SFRatio}_1 = \frac{17 - 5}{15} = 0.8$$

$$\text{SFRatio}_2 = \frac{12 - 5}{10} = 0.7$$

$$\text{SFRatio}_3 = \frac{8 - 5}{6} = 0.5$$

The SFR is the number of standard deviations that the minimum return is below the mean (expected) return. The optimal portfolio is the one with the greatest SFR as it has the lowest probability of a return below the minimum. Based on the SFRatio, the investor would prefer Portfolio 1. (Study Session 3, LOS 9.l)

26. **A**   Technical analysis is quite subjective. The other choices are perceived advantages of technical analysis compared to fundamental analysis. (Study Session 3, LOS 12.b)

27. **B**   An unbiased estimator has an expected value equal to the true value of the population parameter. A consistent estimator is more accurate the greater the sample size. An efficient estimator has the sampling distribution that is less than that of any other unbiased estimator. (Study Session 3, LOS 10.g)

28. **C**   According to Chebyshev's inequality, the proportion of the observations within 3 standard deviations of the mean is at least $1 - (1 / 3^2) = 0.89$ or 89%. This holds for any distribution, regardless of the shape. (Study Session 2, LOS 7.h)

29. **C**   Using the addition rule for probabilities, P(analyst or positive) = P(analyst) + P(positive) − P(analyst and positive). P(A or positive) = 130 / 200 + 110 / 200 − (70 / 200) = 0.65 + 0.55 − 0.35 = 0.85. Alternatively, CEOs that predict positive impact = 40, analysts = 130, Prob (CEO positive or analyst) = (40 + 130) / 200 = 85%. (Study Session 2, LOS 8.f)

30. **B**   There are many reasons that a statistically significant result may not be economically significant (meaningful). Besides transactions costs, we must consider the risk of the strategy as well. For example, although the mean abnormal return to the strategy over the 5-year sample period is greater than transactions costs, abnormal returns for various sub-periods may be highly variable. In this case the risk of the strategy return from month to month or quarter to quarter may be too great to make employing the strategy in client accounts economically attractive. (Study Session 3, LOS 11.d)

31. **B**   In simple random sampling, each item in the population has an equal chance of being selected. The analyst's method meets this criterion. (Study Session 3, LOS 10.b)

32. **A**   Nonparametric tests can be used in a variety of instances where the assumptions required for parametric tests cannot be sustained. A runs test can be used to test for the randomness of a sample. Both of the other tests are parametric because they test the value of a parameter of the underlying distribution. (Study Session 3, LOS 11.j)

33. **A**

Average Product	Resource Units	Total Product	Marginal Product	Marginal Revenue Product
25	1	25	25	25 × $20 = $500
22.5	2	45	20	20 × $20 = $400
20	3	60	15	15 × $20 = $300
17.5	4	70	10	10 × $20 = $200

The short-run demand curve for a resource is its marginal revenue product schedule. The price of a resource unit must be less than or equal to the MRP. Since the resource price is $350 per unit, the company will employ 2 units in production because MRP of $400 > resource cost of $350. For a price taker MR = P. (Study Session 5, LOS 21.a)

34. **A**   For a non-renewable resource, the supply curve is perfectly elastic at a price that equals the present value of the expected next-period price, and the quantity supplied depends on the quantity demanded at that price. (Study Session 5, LOS 21.g)

35. **B** (Demand deposits)(reserve requirement) = required reserves

$(400)(0.1) = 40$

Actual reserves (50) − required reserves (40) = excess reserves (10)

The bank can lend $10 million. Note that the banking *system* can increase loans by more than this, but this question concerns a single bank.

(Study Session 6, LOS 24.e)

36. **C** Demand for labor will be less elastic, other things equal, when the production process is less labor intensive. Labor demand is more elastic at low wage rates than at high wage rates, and more elastic in the long run because producers can adjust their mix of labor and capital inputs. (Study Session 5, LOS 21.b)

37. **A** The quantity theory of money hypothesizes that a change in the money supply, at full employment, will cause a proportional change in the price level because velocity and real output will be unaffected. According to the equation of exchange, MV = PY, output of goods and services produced, *Y*, at full employment cannot change, so the price level, *P*, must increase. (Study Session 6, LOS 24.i)

38. **A** The Fed conducts monetary policy by setting a target for the federal funds rate. The Fed uses the rate of change in the core CPI to measure the inflation rate but does not follow a policy of inflation targeting. (Study Session 6, LOS 27.b)

39. **A** Price elasticity of demand = $\dfrac{\%\Delta \text{Quantity}}{\%\Delta \text{Price}}$

The percent changes are generally calculated relative to the midpoint of the change.

$$\%\Delta \text{Quantity} = \left(\frac{6.7 - 7.5}{(7.5 + 6.7)/2} \right) \times 100 = -11.27\%$$

$$\%\Delta \text{Price} = \left| \frac{2.25 - 2.00}{(2.00 + 2.25)/2} \right| \times 100 = 11.76\%$$

Therefore, price elasticity of demand = $\dfrac{-11.27}{11.76} = -0.96$.

(Study Session 4, LOS 13.a)

40. **C** Like all price searchers, monopolists will expand output until marginal revenue equals marginal cost. Monopolists do not charge the highest possible price which would be the price resulting in only one sale. A monopolist seeks to maximize profit, not price.
(Study Session 5, LOS 19.b)

41. **B** Regardless of whether a tax is imposed on suppliers or consumers, the relative burden of the tax to each depends on the relative elasticities of supply and demand. Since demand is relatively less elastic than supply, the burden of the tax will be greater on consumers than on producers. These burdens are equivalent to decreases in producer and consumer surpluses. Total consumer and producer surpluses will be reduced by the amount of the resulting deadweight loss in addition to the total amount of tax collected.
(Study Session 4, LOS 15.c)

42. **C**   A generational imbalance occurs when the present value of government benefits promised to the current generation of workers is not paid for by current taxes and must be paid for by future generations. The generational effect refers to how future generations pay for a generational imbalance through either higher taxes or decreased government spending. Generational accounting involves measuring the taxes owed by and the benefits owed to each generation. (Study Session 6, LOS 26.c)

43. **B**   The supply curve for a firm under perfect competition is its marginal cost curve above average variable cost. As long as price exceeds AVC, the firm will produce up to the quantity where MC = Price, which is also MR in this case. (Study Session 5, LOS 18.c)

44. **A**   Long-run aggregate supply is related to the level of technology and the available quantities of labor and capital. If the prices of productive inputs increase, short-run aggregate supply decreases (the SAS curve shifts to the left), but long-run aggregate supply (potential real GDP) is unaffected. (Study Session 5, LOS 23.a)

45. **C**   The matching principle holds that expenses should be accounted for in the same performance measurement period as the revenue they generate. (Study Session 8, LOS 32.c)

46. **B**   The description of the percentage-of-completion method is accurate. The completed contract method recognizes revenue only when the entire project is complete. The installment method recognizes profit in proportion to cash collected. (Study Session 8, LOS 32.b)

47. **A**   This is the correct treatment of this change. The company must disclose the nature of the error and its effect on net income and restate any prior period results that are presented in the current financial statements. The other choices are incorrect. (Study Session 8, LOS 32.f)

48. **C**   Firms that give employee stock options as part of compensation often buy back stock to offset the dilution from option exercise. Since the cost to the firm of option exercise is more properly a part of compensation expense, the analyst should reclassify the financing cash flow to repurchase shares as operating cash flow. Neither financing payables nor securitizing receivables results in financing outflows. (Study Session 10, LOS 41)

49. **A**

Net income	+100
Adjustment for noncash and nonoperating items:	
Depreciation	+25
Deferred taxes (increase)	+17
Profit from sale of equipment	−5
Adjustment for working capital items:	
Accounts receivable (decrease)	+30
Inventory (increase)	−17
Accounts payable (increase)	+10
Wages payable (decrease)	−5
Cash flow from operations	+$155

Dividends paid are CFF, not CFO.

(Study Session 8, LOS 34.e)

50. **C**   Interest income is considered an operating cash flow under U.S. GAAP. (Study Session 8, LOS 34.a)

51. **C**   Dilution occurs since the exercise price for the warrants ($45) is less than the average market price for the shares ($50). The incremental number of shares outstanding is found from:

$$\left(\frac{\text{market price} - \text{exercise price}}{\text{market price}}\right) \times \text{\# warrants} = \left(\frac{50 - 45}{50}\right) \times 120{,}000 = 12{,}000$$

Number of shares to use in diluted EPS calculation = 500,000 + 12,000 = 512,000. (Study Session 8, LOS 32.g, h)

52. **A**   As an example, start with CA = 2, CL = 1, and Inv = 1.2. We begin with a current ratio of 2 and a quick ratio of 0.8. If the firm increases short-term bank debt (a current liability) by 1 to buy inventory (a current asset) of 1, both the numerator and denominator increase by 1, resulting in $\frac{3}{2} = 1.5$ (new current ratio) and $\frac{3 - 2.2}{2} = 0.4$ (new quick ratio). (Study Session 8, LOS 35.d)

53. **C**   The commitment is an example of an off-balance-sheet liability. Neither the value of the fertilizer nor the liability to pay for the fertilizer would be recognized on the balance sheet. However, Costiuk must disclose the nature and minimum required payments of this transaction in the footnotes to the financial statements. The commitment would likely not be addressed in the MD&A. (Study Session 9, LOS 39.c, i)

54. **B**   U.S. GAAP requires R&D costs to be expensed. IFRS requires research costs to be expensed, but development costs are capitalized. (Study Session 9, LOS 37.c)

55. **C**   LIFO will result in lower net income than FIFO in the current period, during a period of rising prices. The other choices will tend to increase current period earnings. (Study Session 9, LOS 36.e, 37.b, d)

56. **A**   A simple capital structure has only common stock or only common stock and nonconvertible stock. It contains no securities that could ever become or create common stock, even antidilutive ones. Whether warrants are antidilutive depends on the average stock price over the reporting period, not the value at the reporting date. (Study Session 8, LOS 32.h)

57. **A**   Since this company has a simple capital structure, basic and diluted EPS are equal. The numerator equals net income – preferred dividends = 210,000 – (11,000 shares × 0.10 dividend × 100 par) = 210,000 – 110,000 = 100,000. The weighted average shares outstanding = 22,500 – (5,000 shares repurchased × 0.50 midyear) = 22,500 – 2,500 = 20,000. Then, basic EPS = diluted EPS = $\dfrac{100{,}000}{20{,}000}$ = $5 per share.

(Study Session 8, LOS 32.g)

58. **B**   FIFO companies have higher net income and higher taxes. (Study Session 9, LOS 36.c, e)

59. **B**   Under IFRS, inventory values are revalued upward only to the extent they were previously written down. In this case, that is from €25,000 back up to the original value of €28,000. The increase is reported as gain for the period and will increase COGS of units sold during the current period. (Study Session 9, LOS 36.b)

60. **B**   Compared to expensing, capitalizing results initially in higher profitability, increases cash flow from operations, and decreases financing cash flows. Capitalizing reduces ROA in subsequent periods as net income is reduced and assets are increased. (Study Session 9, LOS 37.b)

61. **A** These relationships are reversed in the later years of the asset's life if the firm's capital expenditures decline. (Study Session 9, LOS 37.d)

62. **C** Deferred tax liability refers to balance sheet amounts that are created when tax expense is greater than taxes payable. (Study Session 9, LOS 38.a)

63. **C** EBT / EBIT is the interest burden, the second component in the extended DuPont equation. It shows that more leverage does not always lead to higher ROE. As leverage rises, so does the interest burden. The positive effects of leverage can be offset by the higher interest payments that accompany higher levels of debt. Net income / EBT is called the tax burden and is equal to (1 − tax rate). The higher the tax rate, the lower the ROE level. EBIT / revenue is called the EBIT margin or operating margin. (Study Session 8, LOS 35.f)

64. **C** Issuing debt results in a cash inflow from financing. Payment of debt at maturity has no effect on cash flow from operations but decreases cash flow from financing by the face value of the debt. (Study Session 9 LOS 39.a)

65. **B** The liability method (SFAS 109 of U.S. GAAP) takes a balance sheet approach and adjusts deferred tax assets and liabilities to future tax rates. (Study Session 9, LOS 38.e)

66. **A** Working capital equals current assets minus current liabilities and is higher under an operating lease because the current liabilities are increased by the current portion of the finance lease. Total asset turnover is higher because total assets are lower under an operating lease. The other statements are false. The operating lease has lower expenses in the early years (rental payment only, no depreciation), but over the life of the lease, the expenses are equal. The statement of cash flows is reversed; the entire operating lease payment is deducted from operating cash flow versus only the interest portion of the finance lease. (Study Session 9, LOS 39.g)

67. **C** An asset is considered impaired when its book value is greater than the sum of the estimated undiscounted future cash flows from its use and disposal. (Study Session 9, LOS 37,i)

68. **B** The four general categories are: (1) scale and diversification, (2) operational efficiency, (3) margin stability, and (4) leverage. Larger companies and those with more different product lines and greater geographic diversification are better credit risks. High operating efficiency is indicative of a better credit risk. Stable profit margins indicate a higher probability of repayment and thus, a better credit risk. Firms with greater earnings in relation to their debt level are better credit risks. While the availability of collateral certainly reduces lender risk, it is not one of the general categories used by credit rating agencies to determine *capacity* to repay. Specifically, they would consider (1) several specific accounting ratios and (2) business characteristics. The availability of collateral falls into neither category. (Study Session 10, LOS 42.c)

69. **B** The cost of preferred stock is calculated as the preferred dividend divided by the market price, not the par value. (Study Session 11, LOS 45.g)

70. **A** We know that at a 14% discount rate, the NPV of Project X is zero and the NPV of Project Y is greater than zero. There is no well-defined relationship between the required rate of return and ordinary payback. If Project Y is smaller in size, its NPV may be smaller than that of Project X. (Study Session 11, LOS 44.d, e)

71. **A**   Financing costs should not be included in incremental cash flows. They are reflected in the weighted average cost of capital (WACC). New business at other branches is a positive externality and the $150,000 to sell the property is an opportunity cost. (Study Session 11, LOS 44.b)

72. **C**   To use the pure-play method, an asset beta is calculated by removing the effects of leverage (delevering) from the comparable company's equity beta, then a project beta is estimated by adjusting the asset beta (relevering) based on the capital structure of the company that is evaluating the project. (Study Session 11, LOS 45.i)

73. **B**   An increase in days of receivables outstanding, other things equal, will lengthen both the operating and cash conversion cycles, indicating poorer working capital management. An increase in days of payables outstanding, other things equal, would decrease the cash conversion cycle. A decrease in cash and marketable securities could simply indicate better management of cash (e.g., buying back its common stock or investing excess cash in profitable business opportunities or securities). (Study Session 11, LOS 46.c)

74. **C**   The marginal (or weighted average) cost of capital is the appropriate discount rate for projects that have the same level of risk as the firm's existing projects. For a project with a higher degree of risk, cash flows should be discounted at a rate higher than the firm's WACC. Since this project's IRR is equal to the company's WACC, its NPV must be zero if the cash flows are discounted at the WACC. If the cash flows are discounted at a rate higher than the WACC to account for the project's higher risk, the NPV must be negative. Therefore, the project would reduce the value of the company, so management should reject it. Choice B is incorrect because a company considers its capital raising and budgeting decisions independently. Each investment decision must be made assuming a WACC which includes each of the different sources of capital and is based on the long-run target weights. (Study Session 11, LOS 44.d, 45.a, e)

75. **A**   There are benefits to both an annually elected board and a board with staggered multiple-year terms so neither can be considered a "requirement." An annually elected board provides flexibility to nominate new board members in response to changes in the marketplace. Staggered boards may provide better continuity of board expertise and leadership but are more difficult to replace. (Study Session 11, LOS 48.b)

76. **B** $\text{Capital component breakpoint} = \dfrac{\text{value at which component's cost of capital changes}}{\text{component's weight in WACC}}$

            $\text{Debt breakpoint} = \dfrac{\$200,000}{0.40} = \$500,000$

            (Study Session 11, LOS 45.k)

77. **C**   The yields on investments in short-term securities should be stated as bond equivalent yields (BEYs), and returns on portfolios of these securities should be stated as a weighted average of BEYs. The BEY, which is holding period yield $\times \left(\dfrac{365}{\text{days to maturity}} \right)$, allows fixed-income securities whose payments are not annual to be compared with securities with annual yields. (Study Session 11, LOS 46.e)

78. **B**   On the pro forma balance sheet, total liabilities and equity are less than total assets, holding the amounts of debt and stock outstanding constant. This means projected retained earnings, although positive, are not enough to keep the accounting equation in balance. To resolve this financial deficit (reconcile the pro forma financial statements), the analyst can assume the company issues new debt or stock or reduces its dividend payout ratio. (Study Session 11, LOS 47)

79. **A** $E(R) = 7\% + 0.9(11\% - 7\%) = 10.6\%$. Because the expected return of 10% is less than the required return of 10.6%, the security is overvalued. (Study Session 12, LOS 51.e)

80. **A** The correlation between the two stocks is:

$$\rho_{A,B} = COV_{A,B} / (\sigma_A \times \sigma_B) = 0.001 / (0.05 \times 0.08) = 0.001 / (0.004) = 0.25$$

Note that the formula uses the standard deviations, *not the variances*, of the returns on the two securities. (Study Session 12, LOS 50.d)

81. **B** Even though these two investment decisions (timing and individual security selection) add value to the portfolio, the real foundation of returns comes from the original asset allocation policy decisions (determining allowable asset classes and weighting these classes). Empirical studies have shown that about 90% of the variance in a portfolio's total return comes from the asset allocation policy decision. The other choices describe appropriate actions. The working couple is most likely in the consolidation phase of the investing life cycle, and a long time horizon and moderate risk strategy are appropriate. The college student is just entering the accumulation phase and has a long time horizon, so higher-risk investments are appropriate. (Study Session 12, LOS 49.c)

82. **B** Portfolio 1 does not lie on the efficient frontier because it has a lower return than Portfolio 2 but has equal risk. Portfolio 4 does not lie on the efficient frontier because it has higher risk than Portfolio 3 but has the same return. (Study Session 12, LOS 51.a)

83. **A** Variance is a measure of total risk. (Study Session 12, LOS 51.c)

84. **C** Greenbaum's expected return for the coming year is $(62 / 54) - 1 = 14.8\%$. Its risk premium relative to the risk-free rate is $14.8\% - 8.0\% = 6.8\%$. The market risk premium is $12\% - 8\% = 4\%$. Therefore, the beta of Greenbaum must be $6.8 / 4.0 = 1.7$. (Study Session 12, LOS 51.d)

85. **B** Confirmation bias is the tendency for people to seek out information that supports a decision they have made and to avoid or ignore new information that calls the decision into question. Overconfidence bias refers to the tendency for analysts of growth companies to be too confident in their forecasts of high earnings growth, overestimating the impact of good news while underestimating the impact of bad news. Data mining bias results when many statistical tests of the same data produce a certain number of statistically significant results simply by chance. (Study Session 13, LOS 54.d)

86. **C** The weak form of the EMH implies that an investor cannot earn positive abnormal returns on average using technical analysis (market information), after adjusting for transaction costs and taxes. Evidence has shown that insiders can achieve positive abnormal returns on average, but this relates to the strong form of the EMH. (Study Session 13, LOS 54.a)

87. **B** Price-weighted indexes have a downward bias due to the fact that fast growing companies (e.g., Microsoft in the 1990s) split their shares and have less continuing influence on a price-weighted index. In a market-weighted index, their influence would increase with their great growth in value. Equal weighting (an unweighted index) may be computed using either an arithmetic mean or a geometric mean. The use of the geometric mean will produce lower index values. Market weighting biases the index in favor of stocks of firms with relatively high market values. (Study Session 13, LOS 53.a)

88. **A** The required rate of return on a stock is composed of the real risk-free rate, a premium for the expected inflation rate, and a premium for risk. (Study Session 14, LOS 56.e)

89. **C** *Step 1*: Determine the discount rate. 7.50% − 0.75% = 6.75%.

Step 2: Value the preferred. $V_P = \dfrac{dividend}{k_p} = \dfrac{\$6.00}{0.0675} = \$88.89.$

(Study Session 14, LOS 56.c)

90. **B** Price at which a margin call will occur:

original price × [(1 − initial margin) / (1 − maintenance margin)]

= [\$32.00 × (1 − 0.5)] / (1 − 0.25) = \$16.00 / 0.75 = \$21.33

Hint: Stock price must go down for a margin call on a long position to occur, not up. (Study Session 13, LOS 52.g)

91. **B** ER = RFR + beta(R_M − RFR)

k = E(R) = 0.05 + 1(0.15 − 0.05) = 0.15

Retention (b) = (1 − dividend payout ratio) = 1 − 0.4 = 0.6

g = (ROE)(b) = (0.15)(0.6) = 0.09

$Value = \dfrac{D_1}{k-g} = \dfrac{\$2.50}{0.15-0.09} = \$41.67$

(Study Session 14, LOS 56.c, g)

92. **B** Increasing ROE will increase the growth rate, other things equal, which decreases the spread in the denominator and, thus, increases the price. The other choices will decrease the stock price. (Study Session 14, LOS 56.c)

93. **C** If markets are efficient, investors should not earn consistently superior returns from technical trading rules such as a contrary opinion strategy. A stock price will decrease on a report of an increase in earnings if that increase is less than investors expected based on all the information previously available. An analyst's recommendations could be for stocks with more than market risk, or the analyst's industry may outperform for some period of time. Both could account for outperformance even though markets are efficient. (Study Session 13, LOS 54.c)

94. **A** Both of Rutherford's statements are correct. The required rate of return from a strategy that takes advantage of pricing anomalies should include a premium for strategy risk. Market prices can remain less than perfectly efficient if the transactions costs of the arbitrage trades that would force them closer to efficient prices are greater than the gains that the trades offer. (Study Session 13, LOS 55.b)

95. **C** One disadvantage of the P/BV ratio is that high inflation can cause the book value of a company's assets to be significantly less than their market value. Significant components of book value reflect historical costs, while earnings, sales, and cash flows reflect current prices. (Study Session 14, LOS 59.a)

96. **A** This is essentially a two-stage dividend discount model (DDM) problem. Discounting all future cash flows, we get:

$$P_0 = \frac{1.00}{(1.103)^5} + \frac{1.25}{(1.103)^6} + \frac{(1.25)^2}{(1.103)^7} + \left[\frac{(1.25)^3}{(0.103 - 0.05)(1.103)^7}\right] = \$20.647$$

Note that the constant growth formula can be applied to dividend 8 (1.25^3) because it *will* grow at a constant rate (5%) forever. (Study Session 14, LOS 56.d)

97. **C** The embedded option can be valued by analyzing the difference between the zero-volatility spread and the option-adjusted spread. (Study Session 15, LOS 60.e)

98. **B** Inclusion of a call feature will decrease the duration of a fixed income security. The other choices increase duration. (Study Session 15, LOS 61.c)

99. **C** At the time of purchase, the coupon rate = the market rate, so the bond traded at par. One year later, with interest rates unchanged, the bond would still trade at par, or $1,000. Thus, there would be no capital gain or loss from the sale. (Study Session 15, LOS 61.b)

100. **A** *Liquidity risk* is the likelihood that an investor will be unable to sell the security quickly without offering it at a significantly lower price. *Credit* or *default risk* is the possibility that the issuer will fail to meet its obligations under the indenture such as timely payment of interest and principal. (Study Session 15, LOS 61.a)

101. **C** First find the yield to maturity (YTM) of the first bond and use it in the second bond calculation. The calculator sequence to determine the YTM is: PV = –701.22; FV = 1000; PMT = 80; N = 20; CPT → I/Y = 12.00%. We discount the cash flows of the second bond at 12.00%. The calculator steps are: PV = –701.22; FV = 1,000; N = 5; I/Y = 12; CPT → PMT = $37.12. (Study Session 16, LOS 64.d)

102. **C** Convexity adjustment to %ΔP: convexity measure $\times (\Delta i)^2 \times 100 = (60)(-0.0025)^2(100)$ = 0.0375%. (Study Session 16, LOS 66.g)

103. **C** YTC: N = 10; PV = –895; PMT = 80 / 2 = 40; FV = 1080; CPT → I/Y = 6.035 × 2 = 12.07%. (Study Session 16, LOS 65.b)

104. **A** During economic contractions, the probability of default increases for lower-quality issues and their yields increase. When investors anticipate an economic downturn, they tend to sell low-quality issues and buy high-quality issues, causing credit spreads to widen. (Study Session 15, LOS 63.f)

105. **C** A sinking fund provision is an obligation, not a right, to retire portions of the bond prior to maturity. A nonrefundable bond may be redeemable or callable through means other than refunding. (Study Session 15, LOS 60.a, d)

106. **C** Reinvestment is crucial to bond yield, and interest rate risk is price risk. (Study Session 15, LOS 61.a)

107. **B** Investment grade bonds are BBB and above. This bond is rated BB, which is below BBB. (Study Session 15, LOS 61.j)

108. **B** 10% (1 − x) = 6%, x = 40%. (Study Session 15, LOS 63.i)

109. **A** Effective duration and effective convexity capture the effects from changes in a bond's cash flows when the yield changes. For this reason, they are the appropriate measures of interest rate sensitivity for bonds with embedded options. (Study Session 16, LOS 66.e)

110. **B** Bonds W and Y are most likely callable, and Bonds X and Z are most likely putable. If the option-adjusted spread is less than the zero-volatility spread, the embedded option has a negative value to the bondholder (e.g., a call option), and if the option-adjusted spread is greater than the zero-volatility spread, the embedded option has a positive value to the bondholder (e.g., a put option). Zero-volatility spreads adjust for the fact that nominal spreads (between the yields to maturity of two bonds) are theoretically correct only when the spot yield curve is flat. All of these bonds' zero-volatility spreads are nearly identical to their nominal spreads to Treasuries, which suggests the spot yield curve is, in fact, approximately flat. (Study Session 16, LOS 65.f, g)

111. **B** Baker's net cost of the position is 60 + 4 = $64 per share. At exercise she receives $60 per share. Her net loss on the position is −4(100) = −$400. (Study Session 17, LOS 72.b)

112. **C** Candidate 1 is incorrect. In the futures markets, margin is a performance guarantee. It is money deposited by both the long and the short. There is no loan involved (as opposed to in the equity markets) and thus no interest charges. Candidate 2 is correct. (Study Session 17, LOS 69.c)

113. **C** The put holder will exercise the option at expiration whenever the stock's price is less than the exercise price. (Study Session 17, LOS 70.f)

114. **A** A futures contract must be settled in some way; it cannot be cancelled. (Study Session 17, LOS 69.e)

115. **C** If LIBOR, at the expiration date, is below the rate specified in the FRA, the short receives a payment from the long. FRA contracts are settled in cash. Neither party will borrow from or lend to the other at expiration. (Study Session 17, LOS 68.f)

116. **A** Decreasing volatility of returns on the underlying stock will decrease option values for both puts and calls. An increase in the risk-free rate increases the values of call options on equities and decreases the values of put options on equities. (Study Session 17, LOS 70.n)

117. **A** Diversification is an advantage of ETF relative to traditional equity investments. On the other hand, a low volume ETF may have a large bid-ask spread. (Study Session 18, LOS 73.c)

118. **C** Hedge funds do not typically trade on exchanges. (Study Session 18, LOS 73.i)

119. **A** While commodity futures retain the risk and correlation characteristics of the underlying commodities, the investor does not incur storage costs. Derivatives cannot have higher correlation with spot prices than the commodity itself, as its price is the spot price. Commodity derivatives can have greater price volatility than the physical commodity. (Study Session 18, LOS 73.q)

120. **B** Of the three sources of return for a long commodity futures investment, only the price return can be negative for a market in backwardation. Roll yield is positive because futures prices are less than spot prices when the market is in backwardation, so the investor realizes gains when rolling the position out of expiring contracts and into new contracts. Collateral yield is the interest earned on the T-bills deposited as margin. (Study Session 18, LOS 74.b)

Notes